LIFTING THE COVERS

ALAN MILLS

LIFTING THE COVERS

The Autobiography

headline

Copyright © 2005 Alan Mills

The right of Alan Mills to be identified as the Author of
the Work has been asserted by him in accordance with the
Copyright, Designs and Patents Act 1988.

First published in 2005
by HEADLINE BOOK PUBLISHING

1

Every effort has been made to fulfil requirements with regard
to reproducing copyright material. The author and publisher will be glad
to rectify any omissions at the earliest opportunity.

A CIP catalogue record for this title is available from the British Library

ISBN 0 7553 1229 5

Typeset in Monotype Baskerville by
Palimpsest Book Production Limited, Polmont, Stirlingshire
Printed and bound in Great Britain by
Clays Ltd, St Ives plc

Headline's policy is to use papers that are natural, renewable
and recyclable products and made from wood grown in sustainable forests.
The logging and manufacturing processes are expected to conform to the
environmental regulations of the country of origin.

HEADLINE BOOK PUBLISHING
A division of Hodder Headline
338 Euston Road
London NW1 3BH

www.headline.co.uk
www.hodderheadline.com

To

My wife Jill for her love and support over the last forty-five years: without her I doubt if I would have started and certainly would not have finished this book

Our parents, our children Barry and Penny, Barry's wife Ann and Penny's husband Stuart, and all our grandchildren – Eliza, Jack, Holly and Charlie

Contents

Acknowledgements

Thanks to: Penny for all her help, legal advice and for just being Penny; Barry for all his support and encouragement and for just being Barry; Tim Phillips, Chris Gorringe and the All England Lawn Tennis and Croquet Club; everyone who has worked in my office for the last twenty-three years; Eddie, Jim and all the ground and maintenance staff at the All England; David Wilson and Lorraine Jerram and Headline for all their help; Niall Edworthy for his research and help with the book.

I am also grateful to Angela and John, Shirley and Roger, Mike, Gloria, Mal, Allan, Caroline and all our old friends who have jogged our memories and encouraged us, and to some special people we have met on our travels who we hope have become friends. Lack of space does not permit us to mention you all by name but *you* know, and if nothing else this book gives us the chance to thank you all for contributing so much to our lives and to the story which would not have been written without you.

Chapter One.

A Meeting with Mr McEnroe

The first three days had been quiet. A bit too quiet for my liking. The weather had been glorious, the tournament schedule was running to plan and John McEnroe and the other big shots had been as nice as pie. There had been a handful of skirmishes on the outer courts, but they had been quickly dealt with and nobody had taken too much notice because the offenders were a bit too far down the food chain for the big-game hunters in the media. It was the leading names, the usual suspects, that everybody was looking out for, especially the Americans. There was McEnroe, of course, the undisputed king of on-court histrionics, and then there was the champion himself, Jimmy Connors, to whom bullishness and downright cussedness came as easily as his thunderous ground-strokes. Ivan Lendl, the No. 3 seed, could scowl, sulk and moan as well as any man on the circuit. But there were plenty of other firebrands too among the 128 men in the singles draw with the potential to unleash the havoc that Wimbledon was so keen to avoid and some of the journalists, ravenous for controversy, were so eager to report to their readers.

Among a clutch of lesser-ranked but no less fiery players, who included Hank Pfister, Steve Denton and Fritz Buehning, there was also the former South African Kevin Curren, whom

I would soon have to fine for smashing up my photocopier. All of them had a bit of form, and heaven knows how many new trouble-makers might emerge from obscurity to write themselves on to the back pages, or even front pages, of the nation's newspapers. Experience had also shown that even the most mild-mannered characters could have their moments. Until recently, tennis had been a gentlemanly, relatively sedate sport when the winner would walk off with his arm around his opponent and buy him a drink or two in the bar after-wards. But since the late 1970s, a different kind of animal had come to stalk the court, and once the barriers of good conduct had been broken down, this new breed had begun to stampede into the former bastion of civilised behaviour with a terrifying lack of embarrassment or shame. The clout of the professional tennis player had been growing year on year since the advent of the Open era in 1968. With every nought added to the end of their prize-money cheques came a proportionate rise in the amount of power the players felt was entitled to them. As far as many of them were concerned, some of the chair umpires and line judges were just doddery old amateurs who had left their day jobs for a free Wimbledon ticket and nice day in the sun. In certain cases they were right.

The widely held view, or at least the one expressed in the press, was that the 1983 Championships would be the year that men's tennis went into meltdown, when weak officiating and player anarchy would combine to bring the game to crisis point. But thus far the uprising and collapse of law and order had failed to materialise. The silence was like a conspiracy. As the man charged with putting down any rebellion, mine would be the first head to roll if the barbarians succeeded in breaching Wimbledon's hallowed gates. I had been, to put it mildly, a little nervous as I sat at my desk casting my eye over the bank of television monitors spread around my narrow, claustrophobic, stuffy little first-floor office overlooking the front courts to the church on the hill in the distance.

From the moment I woke up on Thursday morning I felt that today was going to be the day, my first day of reckoning as the referee at Wimbledon. I knew it had to happen some time and I felt a little tension in my stomach and fuzziness in my head as I gulped down the first of my daily 20 or so cups of coffee, kissed my wife Jill goodbye, put on my suit jacket and stepped into the back seat of the Wimbledon courtesy car waiting outside my home.

The journey from Weybridge to Wimbledon up the A3 through the morning rush-hour takes about 40 minutes, and during that time I ran through my mind the possible scenarios that lay ahead. McEnroe was due to play a second-round match against a young Romanian called Florin Segarceanu. As the No. 2 seed and the bookies' favourite this year we expected him to come through the match with room to spare – but that was not necessarily a good thing from my point of view. I knew from my experience as assistant referee over the previous six years that this walking volcano of a man was prone to erupt in the most unlikely circumstances and with the least warning. Often it happened against the weaker opponents, as if he was deliberately trying to work himself up into a froth in order to raise his game. Rarely, if ever, did he start throwing his toys around when he was playing Borg – for the simple reason that he didn't need any more motivation against the great Swede, a player and character he held in almost reverential respect. It was against the lower-ranked players, the ones he could beat in his sleep playing right-handed, that he needed to draw deep from the bottomless pit of his contempt, in order to fire his spirit and carry him to victory.

On many more occasions than I wish to remember I had watched with horror as my predecessor and mentor Fred Hoyles, a kindly gentleman-farmer from Lincolnshire, had experienced the rage of this brilliant but wild young New Yorker. I had been on court at Fred's shoulder when McEnroe, his racket slung like a gun at his side with his hands on his hips, railed against the injustices of the world and spat out his fury in all directions. I suppose, looking back on it now, there was something mildly comic about the sight of the man with his tight shorts and shaggy hairdo raging and wailing. I consider myself a phlegmatic, cool-headed, easygoing man – but I can assure you it's very difficult to feel at peace when you are standing surrounded by 14,000 people with the eyes of tens of millions of others around the world looking on to see how you might tame the most intimidating player ever to set foot on a tennis court. You just had no idea what might happen in the heat of the exchanges. I also knew that those in charge at the All England Club would be watching my performance intently. I was on a one-year contract and was effectively on trial. The reputation of their Championships, the oldest and most august tournament in tennis, to a large extent depended on how the officials, with me as their chief, would cope over the coming fortnight.

'Good day Mr Mills,' the security guard said as I walked through Gate 13 and headed up the concourse to my office near the main entrance of the club. I'll be lucky, I thought, and threw him a smile, doing my best to look as cheerful and relaxed as possible. As the car had wound its way down Church Road from Wimbledon village to the grounds, I had remembered, with a little alarm, that McEnroe was on Court 1. McEnroe hated the old Court 1 with a passion. He loved Centre Court. For him it was the greatest tennis arena on the planet, but Court 1 was one of the worst. He would do anything to avoid playing on it, and I always had the impression that he would rather be banished to Court 17 rather than walk out on Wimbledon's second show court. Court 1 was smaller than Centre Court by about 25 per cent: the spectators were crammed right up against the playing area, generating a highly intimate, pressure-cooker atmosphere. Personally, I always had a tremendous fondness for the old court, but for McEnroe it might just as well have been hell itself. Year on year at the Championships there always seemed to be one match in the early rounds that McEnroe liked to make difficult for himself, the match to rouse his demons for the rest of the tournament. Would this be the one?

I sat down at my desk as my colleagues hurried here and there, fielding phone calls, photocopying documents, searching through filing cabinets and talking to the players, coaches, agents, television people and club members who troop in and out all day long with a stream of requests and queries. We may as well have had a revolving door put in. When I was appointed referee, I went out of my way to stress that my door was always open, especially to the players. I didn't want to come across as a sort of headmaster figure from a bygone era, hidden away in my study. I wanted to foster a closer relationship with the players, to encourage them to give vent to any frustrations or concerns they might have so as to nip any problems in the bud. As a former player I liked to think I could understand their anxieties.

I was by now on about my sixth coffee of the day and

feeling a little more apprehensive than usual when the McEnroe match got underway. Malcolm Huntington was in the chair. A newspaperman from Yorkshire, Malcolm was a very good, solid umpire from the old school, the pre-professional era when officials had day jobs and were paid peanuts for the dubious privilege of sitting on uncomfortable chairs, often in intense heat, and staring at tramlines while being glared at by angry young men. He was as good as any we had in our pool of about 40 chair umpires and I had put him there because I knew he had the strength of character and experience to deal with any trouble that might erupt. He didn't have long to wait.

I heard the crowd whoop, and quickly looked up at the television to see McEnroe take a divot out of the beautifully manicured court. Malcolm rightly handed him a warning.

The volcano was rumbling. It was just a matter of time now before I would make my first appearance on Court 1 as referee, and I could feel the blood pressure rising a little as I returned to my work, drafting a rough order of play for the following day. I had the television turned on in the background in anticipation of problems, and as I scribbled away, I heard the words 'foot-fault'. At the first time of calling I thought little of it, but when it happened again soon afterwards and I heard the crowd starting to stir, I knew there was trouble afoot and immediately got up and reached for my jacket. As I closed the door of my office, I heard that distinctively shrill and urgent voice cry: 'I wanna see the referee!'

'Here we go,' I thought, as I strode as quickly as I could along the back way through the labyrinth of corridors to get to the court. I had played on these courts myself, in front of packed audiences. I had represented my country in the Davis

Cup and I had been on television in front of millions of viewers, but I have to confess that I was as nervous as I ever had been as I hurried my way through the bowels of the All England Club to confront one of the best-known sportsmen in the world at the time. I have never quite forgiven myself for becoming a smoker – a habit I picked up in America – and I have been battling the dreaded weed for about 30 years in total, but at that particular moment a quiet cigarette would have been extremely welcome. That, however, was clearly out of the question. It would have been a photographer's dream to snap me nervously sparking up before heading out for my first encounter with the man the press liked to call Superbrat.

McEnroe was distinctly fed up by the time I arrived, and many in the crowd seemed tickled pink by the spectacle of the man in a fit of serious pique. This, unfortunately, was what many of them had come for, like people gawping at a road accident. McEnroe had asked for the foot-fault official to be replaced and had threatened to walk off court unless his request was granted. He had also said to Malcolm: 'You're doing a wonderful job for someone who doesn't know two plus two.' It was a pretty rum situation. If McEnroe had carried out his threat, he would have walked himself out of the Championships. You cannot leave the court without the umpire's permission and he risked automatic default by doing so. At this stage I had no real idea how to deal with McEnroe, and it was only in my later associations with him that I began to understand that his *modus operandi* was to push a disciplinary situation right to the wire before reining himself in. He was clever like that. He always knew exactly how far he could push it. For the time being, however, I had every reason to take his threat seriously. To lose the former champion and bookies' hot favourite on the fourth day of the Championships would be a disaster from everybody's point of view, not least for the spectators and viewers who had been mesmerised by his particular brand of tennis magic in recent years. It was the worst-case scenario and would cast a pall over the rest of the tournament as well as bring the subject of the players' conduct, the hot issue of the day, to an unpleasant head.

As I walked on court around 10,000 heads turned towards me and a huge cheer went up. I felt a bit of a lump in my throat, my stomach muscles tightened a little and my heart began to beat even faster. It was a boiling hot day and I could feel the sweat under my collar. I headed straight to talk to Malcolm in the chair. My policy in these situations is to try to let the aggrieved player hear what the umpire is saying to me so that he knows exactly what the case against him is. Malcolm looked slightly uncomfortable as he leant down from his high chair and explained the situation.

I turned to McEnroe who said plainly and simply: 'I have never been foot-faulted in my life.' He said it as if that was the beginning and end of the matter, as if the truth of the situation had just spoken for itself. I heard a little voice in my head say 'Well you have been now, my friend.' But I looked around the court and said to him: 'You have a group of the most competent officials you could ask for sitting on this court at the moment. If I were to replace any of them, you might end up with someone even less acceptable to you.'

McEnroe fixed me with that uniquely intense and insolent glare and drawled: 'Do you actually know the meaning of the word "competent"?' Under normal circumstances, I might not feel so disposed to take such a comment on the chin, but these were not normal circumstances and so take it on the chin I did, I had to. The last thing you want to do as a tournament referee is escalate the problem. It is my challenge to remain calm and defuse these situations, to put the fire out, not throw more fuel on the flames. A man's instinct when insulted is to hit back and stand up for himself, but as a referee you have to have a certain amount of humility. I also knew that if he went one step further and told me or any of the officials on court to 'F*** off!' or called us anything stronger, then he would be defaulted. McEnroe knew this too and I said to him quietly but quite firmly: 'Yes, "competent" means they know their job. If they say you have foot-faulted, then you have foot-faulted.' Why, after all, would they make it up, I thought, as McEnroe turned around and headed back to his end of the court.

I knew this wouldn't be the end of the matter. McEnroe didn't like losing arguments, but I also had the strong feeling that this match against an unknown 22-year-old had failed to fire his imagination. It was almost as if he was a little affronted by the obligation to spill some sweat against an opponent of whose existence he was only dimly aware, and simply couldn't wait to get to the later rounds and get stuck into some of his big rivals, like Connors and Lendl. Now they *really* got him fired up. Poor old Segarceanu even had the temerity to take the first set off the great man!

Expecting another eruption at any moment, I had planned to stay near the court, but as I slipped behind the screens at the back end of the court, an idea came to me. I walked around to the media area on the opposite side of the court to the umpire and parked myself very low down with a perfect view right along the baseline from where I could see McEnroe serving. It was the only time in all my dealings with McEnroe down the years that he didn't notice my presence on court. I still find it perplexing today, even a little disturbing, that McEnroe had this very curious sixth sense, almost as if he could smell me. (There was one particular incident which, when I recall it, still sends a slight shiver down my spine but we'll come to that later.)

The match resumed, but it was not long before the line official hollered 'foot-fault' again. The red rag had been waved and, sure enough, the bull scraped his hoof, blew steam from his nostrils and charged towards the umpire. 'I wanna see the referee again!' he exclaimed, as a tremor of edginess swept around the crowd amid mutterings and the odd heckle. McEnroe was facing the corner where he expected me to enter, but I sprang from the dugout and quickly marched across court. I came up behind him and said: 'Hi John, do you want to talk to me?' He spun around, and I think I gave him a bit of a fright. He spluttered something again about never having been foot-faulted in all his years . . . But even as he was saying it I think his quicksilver brain had worked out why had I come from across the court. McEnroe certainly had one of the keenest minds I have come across in a tennis player. I explained to him where I had been sitting and that I had had a perfect view of the foot-fault. 'The decision was completely correct,' I said, which he accepted. One thing I liked about McEnroe, or at least grew to like about him, was that if you could answer his question, he would accept it. In this instance I had answered his question, or addressed his gripe, with an unequivocal answer and, to his credit, he just got on with it.

That was the end of the foot-fault matter but it wasn't, unfortunately, the end of the controversy in this particular match, and I was forced to make a decision that caused me a lot of anguish and ruffled a few feathers in the umpire fraternity. Nor, by any means, was this the only match to be disrupted by player tantrums. Trouble was flaring up like bushfires all around the grounds. It was proving to be a very long, very hot, very stressful day.

In the fourth and final set of his victory over the young Romanian, McEnroe experienced a further flash of anger when he missed a simple volley at the net. His reaction was to take a ball from his pocket and smash it into the net. This is not something you want to encourage, but equally it didn't, in my view, merit the penalty point that the chair umpire Malcolm awarded against him. Players inevitably feel frustration and, within very clear limits enshrined by the rules, they are allowed to express it. If he had crashed the ball into the crowd or at an official, then he could expect to be dealt with severely, but this was a victimless crime, so to speak. He was merely angry with himself. It's not necessarily a bad thing if players can let off a bit of steam every now and then. If their frustration gets bottled up, it could erupt in a far more explosive and uglier fashion later in the match.

Overruling an umpire, especially a very good one like Malcolm Huntington, is the last thing you want to do. You are effectively telling him he hasn't done his job properly. In 99 per cent of cases you go with the umpire, but in this particular instance I thought he had made a mistake and I have always felt strongly that if you want to win the confidence of players you have to show them that you are prepared to pull up an official if they too have erred. If you don't, then players' suspicions that there is some kind of conspiracy of officialdom working against them would begin to carry more weight. As the referee, I have to play straight down the middle and show

11

fairness to all parties. So it was with a heavy heart that I came on court and overruled Malcolm. I knew all the other officials watching the match on television would be groaning their disapproval and I knew that Malcolm would be feeling a little peeved – it's an unrewarding job at the best of times. But in the interests of fairness it had to be done. McEnroe was certainly surprised. He bowed to me as I left the court. It was all getting a bit surreal.

In my first year as assistant referee six years earlier – my very first day in fact – I was summoned to sort out a problem with the umpire during the qualifying tournament that takes place at Roehampton. I was called up to be told that trouble was brewing in one of the matches right across the other side of the extensive grounds. It is quite a hike to get there and when I finally arrived I saw a small chubby-cheeked figure, with an enormous beehive of curly hair and headband, looking a little disgruntled at one end of the court. The young man was called John McEnroe, just another American collegiate player I thought at the time. I approached the chair umpire, quite an elderly gentleman, and enquired as to the nature of the problem. He seemed to have no idea what I was talking about and so I went to the players, who *both* complained that the umpire was probably the worst they had ever come across and had been calling balls in that were over a foot out. Normally, if just one player lodges a complaint, he or she is probably losing the match, or has a bit of history with that particular official. When both players complain, then you can be fairly certain that something is amiss. In those days there were not as many line officials as there are today, and often in junior or qualifying matches the chair umpire would do their work for them. That was the case in this particular match and I decided to stay and see how he was getting on for myself.

As the match resumed, I saw another chair umpire walking past the court who I knew to be extremely experienced and competent, so I beckoned him over and asked him to wait with me for a while. Within a couple of minutes, close to where I was standing, the ball landed smack between the tramlines, a good 12 inches shy of the line, but the umpire did not call it out. Both players turned to me and held out their arms as if to say: 'See what we mean?' I did see very clearly what they meant and immediately made my way over to the chair where the umpire looked down and smiled at me vaguely.

You never, ever want to remove an umpire from the chair. It is extremely humiliating. Imagine you were working in an office and you thought you were doing a fairly reasonable job and your boss sidled over one day and said: 'Well, thanks very much, but you're free to go now. There's a good chap. Good luck with everything.' I was effectively going to fire him because it was highly unlikely he would ever work again. It was a very delicate situation and I tried to make it as pain-less as possible by giving him a chance to make an excuse for the poorness of his performance. 'You're looking a little under the weather today, are you sure you are feeling quite all right?' I asked.

'Feeling absolutely tip-top thanks very much,' came the reply.

That left me a little stumped so I tried a more direct route. 'How did you see that last ball?' I asked.

'Well, it was very clearly inside the line – by at least a foot I'd say.'

I wondered briefly whether it was me going mad and then

I clocked it – the man thought he was umpiring a doubles match!

Now there are mistakes and there are mistakes, and this was certainly one on the higher end of the scale. How can a man not notice that there are only two players on a court? That takes some oversight. In those days when they used to hold the officials' annual cocktail party *before* the start of play on the first Tuesday of the Championships, it was not unknown for the odd umpire to have been seeing double when they took the chair. One official even fell asleep. But on this occasion it had nothing to do with too much champagne and vol-au-vents. The poor fellow was just a little past it, his mind somewhere off in cloud-cuckoo-land.

'I think you should have a bit of a rest and let the other chap have a go. I'd say it's his turn now,' I said, helping him down from his chair.

With the experienced umpire now in charge, I wandered back towards the office with my dreamy friend and tried all the way to give him an opt-out clause by insisting he must be feeling pretty poorly. He didn't take the bait and so his performance was recorded in the report as rank incompetence. I never saw him again, but I hope he got home all right that day.

That was my first encounter with John McEnroe and on that occasion he had every right to feel aggrieved about the quality of officiating. (For the record, McEnroe qualified for the Championships that year and burst to international prominence by reaching the last four where he was beaten by Connors.)

If the foot-fault fracas was the controversy that grabbed all the headlines the following day, there was certainly plenty of competition from McEnroe's fellow firebrands elsewhere on the courts that Black Thursday in 1983. As we totted up the catalogue of code violations and tantrums from around the grounds, I began to wonder how on earth I had allowed myself to get into this refereeing lark. The match between the American Vitas Gerulaitis and Mark Edmondson had also produced some fireworks. With his long blond hair and penchant for the nightlife Gerulaitis was always a colourful character, but he was certainly drawing attention to himself for all the wrong reasons in an ill-tempered clash with his Australian opponent. Edmondson was warned for a verbal obscenity, but his offences were mild by comparison with the behaviour of Gerulaitis who abused line judges, hit a ball at a cameraman and hurled two rackets into the crowd after losing the match.

In over 20 years at Wimbledon I have only had to disqualify one player – Tim Henman of all people – but Hank Pfister, a highly-ranked American player with a feisty temper, came within a whisker of suffering the same fate that day. A new 4-point code violation had just come into operation: 1 – warning; 2 – point penalty; 3 – game penalty; 4 – default. Pfister, the 15th seed, managed to lose a tiebreak as the result of being handed successive penalties for racket abuse, swearing and time-wasting. As I looked in from the corner of the court it came as a great relief to me that he actually managed to complete the match and, even better, he lost in the fifth set to Chilean Ricardo Acuna and thus would take no further part in the tournament. The press, already gorging themselves on a feast of indiscipline, would have had a field-day if a player had to be defaulted for bad conduct. As I watched Pfister receive his third code-violation penalty I could see the headlines being put together: 'Wimbledon In Crisis As Anarchy Reigns'.

Fritz Buehning, another American with something of a short fuse, was doing little to help the cause either, although the main reason for the rumpus in his match was not strictly his fault. We had put an umpire called Dr Mark Cox in the chair for his match against a then little-known Australian called Pat Cash, and I had no reason to suspect that this was going to be a problem for the official or the players involved. But as the match was about to begin, word reached the office that Buehning was refusing to play if Cox was in the chair, on the grounds that the pair had clashed at the Queen's tournament a couple of weeks earlier. This put my nose out of joint, to put it mildly, but it was towards Cox and not Buehning that I felt the greatest annoyance. Whenever we hand the umpires their assignments for a given day, we ask them to come back and inform us if they have had any problems with the players in their matches and, if so, we switch them to other courts. It's a sensible policy and we would soon take it much further by asking all the chair umpires and the players before the start of the tournament to draw up a list of all those they would like to avoid over the tournament. Using the internal phone system I called Dr Cox and, without much warmth in my voice, it has to be said, I asked him why he had neglected to tell me about his recent bust-up with Buehning. He said he didn't think it was important. Terrific!

I was left with no choice but to replace him with another umpire. Cox, needless to say, was not especially impressed by my decision and nor were some of his colleagues. To their mind, I was simply surrendering to player power and under-mining their authority. It was the second time that day that I had been forced to come down on the umpires following my overrule in the McEnroe match. Both scenarios are fairly rare and to have both happen on the same day was an ugly coincidence that I could really have done without, especially given all the other trouble that was breaking out. I was later absolved of blame on both counts, but that didn't stop one or two of the umpires squealing their displeasure in the press.

On Saturday, a report appeared in the *Daily Star* claiming that the umpires were on the verge of rebellion, and accused me of siding with the players and making the officials look like fools. An umpire, who chose not to give his name, was quoted as saying: 'We are absolutely disgusted with the decisions of that man Mills . . . We are looking stupid and all for 27 quid a day!' The piece went on to say that umpires expected me to be their 'guiding light' and their 'Superman'. I felt quite upset by the article, and although the thought crossed my mind that I should turn up to work on Monday to confront these childish umpires, I decided that it would be best to try to maintain a dignified silence and let the matter pass, even though I actually knew who was behind the story. What upset me most about this ugly little spat was that the disgruntled individual did not have the courage and decency to come and talk to me face to face like a grown man. We are, after all, in it together. I was very happy to read in his column in the *Sunday Mirror* that Bjorn Borg backed my decision to overrule the penalty against McEnroe. Furthermore, no one in their right mind would have seriously expected me to allow Cox to stay in the chair once Buehning, who had caused quite a rumpus in his first-round match, had threatened to pull out of his match.

I like to think I have enjoyed a relatively harmonious

relationship with the umpiring fraternity down the years, and life has certainly improved since the early 1980s with the introduction of a more professional system. The governing bodies (ITF, ATP for the men's circuit and WTA on the women's) now have a pool of properly paid, well-trained and qualified officials who work their way up a grading system. The most junior officials are awarded a white badge and they then graduate to bronze, silver and gold. Some chair umpires now get paid a lot of money at Wimbledon, up to £2,000 for the fortnight plus living expenses for accommodation, food and travel. It is their biggest payday of the year and it is interesting that nowadays I rarely hear any rumblings of discontent during the Championships. Nor is it a coincidence that the general improvement in the players' behaviour has gone hand in hand with the improvement in officiating. There are other factors as well, but the players certainly seem to have far more respect for the men and women in the chair than they did back in the late 1970s and early 1980s. Although there were some extremely able officials back then, when some of the players' behaviour was questionable, there were also far too many who were weak. Some of the officials, who lived and worked in the London area, used to go to work in their offices in the morning, grab a sandwich at lunchtime and pop down on the bus for a spot of umpiring in the afternoon. That, in my view, was not perhaps the best way to prepare for working at one of the most prestigious sporting events in the global calendar in which hundreds of thousands of pounds are at stake. Back then officials often received free tickets in lieu of money for their two weeks' work, but some of the less scrupulous among them decided to cash in by selling them on the black market. That practice was brought to an abrupt end when the

Wimbledon authorities, together with the police, trapped the wrongdoers by placing ads in the papers. The wasps were drawn to the honeytrap and thus their association with Wimbledon came to a sticky end.

I still have run-ins with umpires today – it goes with the territory – but not nearly as many as before. At Wimbledon I work closely with the chief of officials who, together with his team of assistants, comes up with a list of recommendations for the various matches on a given day. Sometimes, knowing there is a bit of history between a player and an official, I ask them to make changes. As a matter of course, strong umpires are always assigned to the matches with players who have a history of indiscipline. As I have the final word, it is to me that the unhappy umpires come to register their displeasure. Overall, the umpires are a good bunch, but as in any group of people there are some you like and respect more than others. Before the days of the grading system, when there was nothing but reputation and personal knowledge by which to rank the umpires, it would often get a little fraught from the quarter-final stage onwards when there were only a couple of dozen matches left to play in the five draws. There were some umpires – and there still are some – who used to come to me a little put out because they had not been given an assignment, or because they had not been put on Centre Court or Court 1, and so on.

There was just a small handful of what I would call these prima donnas, and they made me wonder quite what it was that motivated them to become umpires in the first place. Most were just decent people and tennis-lovers who had started by helping out at their local clubs and then found themselves called up to help on the county or regional circuit before progressing to national and international events. It was not so much a calling as a drifting. But there were definitely some who simply loved the power and the glory – if you can call it that – of taking charge of a blue riband match on one of the show courts. You got the feeling that they saw the match as being as much their show as that of the players. I have always been a little suspicious of the ones who like to preen themselves in the chair, or appear to relish the exercise of their power and the confrontations with the players. The truth is of course that nobody goes to a tennis match or turns on the television to watch an umpire hand out a code violation. It is true that many people came to love the spectacle of McEnroe losing his head, but the umpire was never anything more than a stage prop in the drama. You ended up just feeling a little sorry for the few who thought they were more important than they were.

In many ways umpiring and line-officiating are thankless tasks – certainly in the days before they got paid a reasonable amount of money. Generally, they just sit there all day long staring at white lines, and when it's over, nobody says anything to them or comes to thank them. They just get changed out of their uniform and go home. (They also need to have an extremely strong bladder.) If they have a single moment's inattention and make a bad call, all hell can be let loose. Players scream at them, television cameras and commentators highlight their mistake. Then, once again, they get changed and go home. Why?

There was so much pressure on me at Wimbledon in that first year that I could have done without the gossiping among a small group of the officials. A few malcontents can quickly create a sour atmosphere, and this was the last thing we

needed with the eyes of the tennis world looking to Wimbledon
to restore some kind of order, or lay down the law, to the
rebels in the men's game. The build-up to the Championships
had been dominated by discussions about the indiscipline of
the players and there were plenty of calls in the newspapers
urging me to expel 'the louts' at the first sign of trouble to
serve as a warning to other potential trouble-makers. There
were also conspiracy theories doing the rounds at this time
about how referees were under pressure from tournament
organisers and the wider tennis authorities not to expel top
players. There was the constant fear of litigation lingering in
the background, particularly so with the Americans and their
writ-happy lawyers, but people were worried that the absence
of big names would reduce the appeal of the event and television viewing figures. This pressure undoubtedly existed at
smaller tournaments on the circuit, but I can honestly say that
in over two decades at Wimbledon nobody has ever tried to
persuade me to go leniently on the players.

I wasn't under any specific orders from the club chairman
or chief executive about how to act – that's not really the way
Wimbledon goes about its affairs – but one or two comments
were made in passing about the importance of running a tight
ship that year. I was also aware that the club had taken out
a seven-figure insurance policy with Lloyds to cover them in
the event of a player being thrown out.

On the Monday morning, at the start of the Championships, I addressed the 330 officials taking part over the fortnight and then had a separate meeting with the chair umpires,
but contrary to press reports the following day I didn't 'lay
down the law' with a tough speech. There was no song and
dance or rallying cry to come down hard on the players, but

I did stress the importance of appearing to be in complete control if trouble erupted. Any sign of weakness would certainly be jumped upon by a player losing his head. With the new code violation system in place there was no need for Churchillian speeches to the officials. They simply applied it according to the rules. Confrontation would only make matters worse. My message was simple and boring: be firm but fair. Privately, I was steeling myself for a default scenario and I had decided that whenever possible I would head to a court when a player had received the second of the four code violations. It's amazing what effect a man in a suit standing in the corner with his arms crossed and his brow furrowed can have on the behaviour of players.

All my worst fears appeared to have been realised on that hectic, boiling Thursday, and I was a mightily relieved man when play finished, we had issued the following day's order of play and settled down for a drink and a bite to eat, around about 10 p.m. The first drink never touched the sides. Before leaving the office that evening, I was sitting at my desk when Fritz Buehning popped into the office for a chat. Fritz had given us our fair share of headaches that week and was near enough topping our bad boys' league in terms of code violations. But it's curious how so many players who have been breathing fire on court all day can be so contrite and courteous once the adrenalin has subsided and they have cooled down with a shower and something to eat. A lot of the players come into the referees' office at the end of their championship to thank us for our efforts. My colleagues in the downstairs office, who are responsible for the day-to-day administration of the order of play and work their socks off from dawn to dark, are always particularly touched when a player takes the time to thank them for their hard work. Andre Agassi, Steffi Graf and Monica Seles have always been especially thoughtful, but it's surprising how many others make the effort as well.

I have to say that I was a little surprised to see Fritz standing before me after all that had gone on in his two matches, and for a moment I feared that he was coming to give me both barrels about his treatment at the hands of the officials. It had been one of the most intense and stressful days of my working life and all I wanted to was to slump into the back of my courtesy car and be spirited to the comfort of my home as soon as practicably possible. The prospect of an anger-management counselling session with my big American friend was distinctly unappealing at that particular moment. So I was a little taken aback when, with great humility, he thanked me for our help over the previous days and apologised for his behaviour. He seemed a little worried that his feistiness would be held against him at future tournaments. I assured him it wouldn't and said something about everyone being entitled to a bad day or two at the office every now and then. As he was leaving, he put his head back round the door and said: 'I do have just one complaint to make, Alan.' My heart sank. 'Next year can you do something about the toilet paper in the players' area? It's so hard, it's been causing me terrible problems all week.' So that was his problem. I had never made the link between hard toilet paper and player behaviour, but maybe there's something in it. I knew all about bears with sore heads but tennis players with sore behinds was something quite new to me. It was the first time I had smiled all day I think.

I slept that night as if someone had hit me on the head with a club, and it took several strong coffees the following morning to raise the eyelids and get the circulation and heartbeat back up to something like normal speed. I have never had a problem sleeping, even in the times of the greatest stress. I could sleep on a clothesline if I had to, but during the Championships it does take me a couple of hours to unwind as the adrenalin of the day drains away and my mind stops buzzing. I generally get home about midnight and then sit down and talk through the day with Jill. I'm never happier to see Jill than during the Wimbledon fortnight when 16-hour working days combined with only six or so hours of sleep per night pushes my powers of endurance right to the limit. We have made a good mixed doubles team on and off the court for almost 45 years now. By and large, I love my work at the Championships, but I'm certainly in need of some serious rest and relaxation once the covers are pulled on for another year. I might have a nightcap or a final cup of coffee as we talk through the events of the day. On that particular day, there was a good deal of sympathy floating around the club as the members and club officials watched the various incidents flare up and watched me rush from one court to the next.

After the storm of the day before, came the calm on Friday. It was almost as if the tempest had blown itself out, thank heaven, because I'm not too sure how I would have coped with another day like that. To my further relief, McEnroe was on his best behaviour during his third-round straight sets win over Brad Gilbert on Saturday, but I later had to fine him for a verbal obscenity after a woman in the crowd had said something to him during his doubles match. Comments from the crowd are not especially helpful and you have to have a bit of sympathy with the players sometimes. They are like sprung coils out there, straining every fibre, pushing themselves to the limit and concentrating intently on every ball. When someone throws a daft or derogatory comment in their direction, you can at least understand the reasons behind a player's riposte, even if you cannot give your approval to it. If some stranger walked past my desk at a particularly critical moment in my day's work and said 'Get on with it you bloody idiot', I too might be tempted to respond with an expletive. But the rules are clear and it is part of the challenge facing the modern tennis player – and sportsmen in general – to keep their composure even under the most severe pressure or provocation.

On the Monday I also had to fine the champion Jimmy Connors for swearing at Kevin Curren as he crashed to a sensational fourth-round defeat in four sets. Connors was never above giving his opponent the benefit of his feelings towards them – or for that matter anyone else who happened to be bothering him. He was one of the most aggressive and intimidating individuals I have ever come across on a tennis court, and although he rarely threw full-blown tantrums, he was forever muttering dark remarks under his breath – generally just out of earshot of the officials – challenging decisions, giving officials the eyeball and generally prowling around the court. His willpower and grit were second to no one's in the entire history of the game, but my immense respect for him as a player was always tempered by what I saw as the bully in him and by his occasional displays of vulgarity. Like so many of the truly great sportsmen, he came with his own character, without which I suppose he might not have reached the heights that he did. You had to admire him.

Curren fired 33 aces past Connors in that match in an awesome display of power-serving, but the big story of the men's draw that year was a gutsy New Zealander called Chris Lewis, ranked about 90 in the world. After beating the ninth-seeded Texan Steve Denton in the opening round, he swept all the way into the final, beating Curren in a ferociously fought semi-final. He was a tremendous little character Lewis, a real have-a-go hero, and it was one of the great Wimbledon moments to see him get to the final. But his five-set match with Curren was spiced with one highly controversial moment in the final set when the chair umpire overruled a decision in Lewis's favour, which meant Curren lost his serve. Curren went mad, and he had good reason to be incensed, before Lewis went on to edge out the set 8–6 to claim a place in the final against McEnroe.

McEnroe had dropped just one set – in that second-round match against the young Romanian Segarceanu – on his way to the final, and was now outright favourite to regain the title he had lost to Connors in the longest ever Wimbledon final the year before. He was not, however, all sweetness and smiles as he bulldozed his way through the bottom half of the draw. Perhaps he had been using too much of the Wimbledon toilet paper, but whatever the reason for his ill-humour during his quarter-final match with fellow American Sandy Mayer, it threatened to get extremely ugly on several occasions. At one point, McEnroe picked up a ball and smashed it across the net at his opponent, prompting Mayer to tell the umpire that he would take matters into his own hands if he failed to take action. Now that would have been a first at Wimbledon: two men rolling around on Centre Court throwing punches and gouging each other's eyes out. Once again, however, McEnroe reined himself in just at the point that it looked as if the situation was on the verge of spinning out of control, and then humiliated his opponent 6–0 in the final set. There has been no more impressive sight in tennis than a fully focused, controlled McEnroe putting someone in his place.

The second Friday was billed by the press as 'Dynamite Day'. It was 'The Howl v. The Scowl' as McEnroe came up against his nemesis, Ivan Lendl. The Czech was by no means a natural grass-court player and made little effort to hide his contempt for the surface, and to a lesser extent for Wimbledon, in the early years of his career. Grass is for golfers and cows he liked to say. He was not the most popular figure with the Wimbledon crowds back then and his standing with the British public was not exactly enhanced by his comments in the build-up to the tournament. 'With no offence to Britain,' he said, 'if I had to pick a major tournament to win it would be the US Open. It's well organised with better conditions for the players.' He might also have added that the courts didn't have that really annoying green stuff on it. The year before he declined even to come to Wimbledon, complaining about the attitude of the club and what he saw as the limited amount of time made available to him for practising.

In time, Lendl would win over the Wimbledon crowd as he burst every blood-vessel in his body in an effort to land the one significant title missing from his career portfolio. He was soon to become a US citizen, but opinion about him over there was also divided at that time. *Time* magazine described him as 'a chilly, self-centred, condescending, mean-spirited, arrogant man with a nice forehand'. Quite a put-down that, but his friends insisted he was just shy and misunderstood. He also had a very dry sense of humour, and once famously described Andre Agassi as 'a forehand and a haircut'. He had grown up in Ostrava, a place known as 'the Black City of Europe' owing to its multitude of smokestacks, and they said that the only reason he never smashed his tennis racket as a junior was because it was the only one he had. His background perhaps explains the ferocity of his determination and his almost incredible preparation. Just as it was for so many young players growing up behind the Iron Curtain, tennis was Lendl's passport out of there and to a better life in the West.

There is no doubt that Lendl revolutionised men's tennis. His fitness levels were incredible and he would be running as hard at the end of the fifth set as he had been at the beginning of the first. He dramatically raised the bar of athleticism in the game and forced the rest of the men's circuit to follow his example. In 1981 he had won 15 out of 24 tournaments, collecting two million dollars in prize money alone along the way, and by the time he returned to Wimbledon in 1983 he was the world No. 1. Ivan and I had our moments down the years, but I always liked him and respected him even more so.

McEnroe, meanwhile, had so much natural talent that he didn't need to take Lendl's extreme measures in order to stay at the top of his game. Lendl, to his credit, was always the first to admit that he had been born with just a fraction of McEnroe's gifts and made no secret of the fact that it was only his downright bloody-mindedness and manic drive that allowed him even to grace the same court as the elegant, volatile New Yorker. There was little love lost between the two on court, and as far as I'm aware they weren't exactly bosom pals off it either. In most respects, they could not have been more different to each other as players or characters. McEnroe was the artist, Lendl the artisan: the rapier or épée to Lendl's broadsword. McEnroe gave spectacular vent to his frustrations; Lendl generally bottled them up and brooded. McEnroe could play every shot in the book and cut his opponents to pieces with sublime skill; Lendl would bludgeon and harry them to defeat. McEnroe rushed the net; Lendl preferred to sit back behind the baseline . . . They made for an absorbing contrast of styles and personalities, and their rivalry was always fascinating to behold. Some have argued that their rivalry was the greatest in the history of tennis and it is diffi-cult to disagree when you consider the intensity and drama of some of their encounters when both men were close to the peak of their game.

On his day, McEnroe was virtually unbeatable on grass, but Lendl was the world No. 1 and, like his opponent, had lost just one set on his way to the last four. Lendl had also beaten McEnroe seven times in their last nine meetings, although the left-hander had triumphed in their two most recent encounters. In the event, however, it was a non-contest. McEnroe simply dismantled his opponent with a display of irresistible artistry as he rushed to a straight-set win. And not once did McEnroe blow his top and have me called out, to my great relief. I had had enough anger-management, coun-selling and fire-fighting in that fortnight to last me for an entire year. Mercifully, he was in total control of the game and his emotions throughout. By the end of it, you had to feel a little sorry for Lendl who, as ever, ran himself into the ground but was never in contention. McEnroe was ruthless.

It was a similar story in the women's draw that year as Martina Navratilova strolled to her fourth Wimbledon title, beating the pigtailed 18-year-old Andrea Jaeger 6–0, 6–3 with embarrassing ease. But Jaeger, a child prodigy who was 'burnt out' by the time she reached her 21st birthday, need not have felt ashamed to have lost so quickly and heavily. Martina was a phenomenon, and it would be another five years before she experienced defeat at Wimbledon. That year, far from losing a set, she dropped just 25 games in her seven matches, and only once did an opponent take more than three games off her in a set. Her domination of the women's game during this period was absolute. Like her fellow Czech Lendl in the men's, Martina was revolutionising the women's game, perhaps in an even more dramatic fashion. Like Lendl she too had to suffer an enormous amount of criticism from the press and public before she finally won over the grudging respect of both.

She could be quite a demanding customer, mainly because she was so meticulous in her pre-match preparations. But she could also be extremely accommodating. One year on finals day there had been a backlog of matches and the semi-finals of the mixed doubles still had to be played. The final was scheduled to be played after the men's singles final, and I was hoping the mixed doubles semis would finish earlier, so that the winners could rest up before taking to the court again. As it turned out, the matches finished at almost exactly the same time. Under normal circumstances, players are understandably reluctant to play back-to-back matches, but I thought I would ask Martina how she felt about the idea. My colleague Jean Sexton, assistant referee for many years and a great friend, hurried down to the locker-room to put my suggestion to her. After a moment's thought, she said: 'If you can get a plate of boiled potatoes to me I will be ready in 30 minutes.' With that, Jean sped off to the kitchens and was told she would have to boil them herself. Jean produced the potatoes and Martina was as good as her word and went straight out to play the final. But it was that very focus and attention to detail which helped make her the greatest women's player of all time. I don't like making comparisons between players, but you would have to say that Martina's record is second to none, and all the more staggering because she was playing in a highly competitive era, and still is.

The men's final on the Sunday was also a procession, as McEnroe dismissed the challenge of the rank outsider Lewis 6–2, 6–2, 6–2. It was a consummate display of tennis and one's heart went out to the young New Zealander as he ran around the court with his distinctive bandana wrapped around his head, doing his best to limit the damage McEnroe was inflicting from the other side of the court. Lewis was as surprised as anyone to be in the final and he looked even more shell-shocked when he wandered to the net to congratulate McEnroe after one of the shortest men's finals in the modern era.

At the end of each final I always come on court for the awards ceremony and I make a point of getting to the loser as soon as possible to try and pick him up a little and congratulate him for getting there in the first place. It is always an emotionally charged event and I have seen several players overwhelmed by the occasion down the years. Lewis was clearly upset that no matter how he had battled, he simply lacked the power to compete with McEnroe in that mood. I tried to tell him that there was not a tennis player on the planet who would have fared much better that day, and by the time he got back to the locker-room he seemed to be his normal self again. How many other people, after all, had reached the final of the world's oldest and probably most prestigious tennis championships? In a hundred years' time, his grandchildren would be able to tell their own family about the heroics of their ancestor way back in 1983. In the following year's final, McEnroe destroyed his old rival Jimmy Connors with even greater brutality, and one of the first things he said afterwards was: 'Well, I hope that makes Chris Lewis feel a little better.'

I am always given a pat on the back at the awards ceremony and many people seem to think that I must have a mantelpiece full of medals of my own. The truth is I don't actually receive any kind of medal or memento, which is just as it should be, but I have had an awful lot of royal handshakes, mainly from the Duke and Duchess of Kent. It must have been very difficult for them to know what to say each time I was summoned to be greeted by them and, by and large, the script of our brief conversations barely changed down the years. The Duke said, 'Well done, it seems to have all gone very smoothly this year', while the Duchess, who presented the trophies in the women's singles, always said, 'You haven't had too many difficulties this year, have you?' She has always been very charming and kind, but as I shook her hand and smiled, invariably I thought: 'If only you had been sitting where I was for the last two weeks.' There is no reason on earth why she should have had the faintest idea what had been going on behind the scenes over the fortnight, but by the end of it, when I have been having little sleep each night, I'm often reminded how little people know about what actually happens in my office. Even the members and leading officials at the club have precious little idea about what my job involves. I suspect that they, like most members of the public, imagine that I just sit around all day yawning and twiddling my thumbs, waiting for it to rain or for someone to lose their temper before I stroll out on to court to order the covers on or have a word in the ear of a player. If only that were the case I could keep going for another couple of decades!

In all my years at Wimbledon I have lost my temper just once, and I was as surprised by my McEnroe-style outburst as the poor man whose throat I jumped down. I don't think I actually said: 'You cannot be serious!', but in all the other respects I think I did a very good impression of my fiery friend from New York. It must have been at some time during the mid-eighties when we had recently installed a new computer system in the office to help us put out the order of play. In those days, computers were nothing like as sophisticated or reliable as they are today and the new programme had been experiencing considerable teething problems.

Getting the following day's order of play out as quickly as possible is an urgent priority for us. It is essential that everybody, not least the newspapers and television companies, knows what is planned for the next day. It can be horrendously complicated, and it was especially so back in the 1980s when so many more players also entered the doubles events. To make matters even more difficult and fraught we are inundated with requests from players, coaches, television companies – even members of the club, infuriatingly – to have matches played at particular times. Sometimes it's like trying to solve a mathematical puzzle fit for Einstein, as I sit there staring at a blur of hundreds of different names and struggle to find the right time and the right court for the right player. The equation goes something like this: A can play singles in the morning and men's doubles in the evening, but his playing partner B is down to play mixed doubles that same day and is also due to play singles in the afternoon, but his playing partner C is still involved in the women's singles and her match also has to be finished that day too but her women's doubles match has been delayed due to the rain, etc., etc. . . . .

We were having one of those evenings, and as the computer experts were struggling to resolve the problem, I was growing more and more frustrated by the knowledge that, using a pencil and paper as we used to, we could have had the order of play out much earlier and could now be finishing and heading home. As it was, it was going to be hours before we finally drove through the gates that night. I was becoming so angry that I thought it best to get out of my cramped little office and cool down outside. I was walking along one of the corridors when the Championships' director Richard Grier ambled around the corner and said, breezily but perfectly innocently: 'Good heavens Alan, what on earth are you still doing here? You don't normally work late do you?' It was, if you will, an overhead smash right in the face. The poor chap must have thought I had a swarm of bees in my trousers the way I went at him, and he looked quite stunned as he shuffled off down the corridor.

I have to say that I too was a little shaken by my own ferocity. Not once in my playing career did I even get close to having a tantrum. I think once I may have said to an umpire, 'Are you quite sure about that?' after a particular decision had gone against me. I even used to receive letters commending me on my composure and good conduct on court, and was told that my habit of just grinning when calls went against me used to infuriate my opponents. I had been a member at Wimbledon for about 20 years and can say with some confidence that not once had I even raised my voice in anger. Imagine then the surprise of the Championships director when I suddenly turned into the Incredible Hulk with rabies. The following day Richard came into my office to see me and I apologised for the way I had reacted. He said he hadn't been able to sleep that night and had tossed and turned wondering quite what it was that had made me so furious. I said there was no excuse for the way I had spoken, but tried to explain to him that so few people, if any, in the Wimbledon hierarchy had any notion of the pressures we experience in the office. He was very understanding and ever since the incident he has been a great ally, always fighting our corner when the need has arisen.

My first year as referee had been an experience, to say the least, and I was thankful that the final weekend passed off without thunder and lightning in the heavens or down on court. After so much drama in the earlier rounds, I suppose the finals were a bit of an anti-climax. The one-sidedness of the two singles deciders was repeated in the doubles, where McEnroe and Peter Fleming crushed the Gullikson twins, while Martina and Pam Shriver were also straight-sets winners over Rosie Casals and Wendy Turnbull.

It had been a particularly dreadful year for the Brits, and the gloom was only partially lifted by the triumph of John Lloyd, partnered by the Australian Wendy Turnbull, in the mixed doubles. Only two British men had survived the first round, Stuart Bale and Andrew Jarrett, and neither of them made it into the third round. In the women's, only three reached the second round, and although Virginia Wade reached the quarter-finals, the overall performance of the British was lamentable. Unfortunately, it is a pattern that has continued to this day, and Henman's success in recent years has been no more than a fig-leaf covering up our embarrassment as a tennis nation. In 1983 Virginia Wade became the first woman committee member at the club – a long overdue development, to my mind. Wimbledon has always been a very male-orientated domain, and it still is to a large extent, but at least that has all begun to change, albeit quite slowly.

It was slightly disconcerting for Virginia and me that year in our new roles at the All England Club because we were both kitted out with microphones and followed around by a cameraman wherever we went. I think Wimbledon was making some kind of in-house video, and the production team were keen to record our every movement and utterance. The disturbing thing was that I had no idea when the tapes were rolling, so when I was hurrying to and from one incident to the next on those particularly fraught days, I felt especially self-conscious and pressurised. I was on trial with the club as it was, and knew that I would only be offered a new, possibly longer, contract if I acquitted myself competently over the fortnight. I also felt the hot breath of the media pack on the back of my neck for the whole two weeks after all the talk about clamping down on player indiscipline. If it had all gone pear-shaped, I would probably have been looking for a new job by the end of the summer. No matter how easygoing and phlegmatic I tried to be, it was difficult to get away from the feeling that my every move was being scrutinised and it was with some relief on Sunday evening that I watched the crowds flow out of the gates while Jim Thorn and his ground staff pulled the covers over the court for the last time that year.

After thanking my staff for all their efforts and throwing back the sweetest-tasting gin and tonic a barman can muster, all I wanted to do was to get home, have a hot bath and sleep for a week. Unfortunately, that was not to be the case and it would be another seven days before I could finally put my feet up. First of all there was the annual champions' dinner up in the West End when several hundred people connected with the Championships put on their evening wear and descend on the Savoy Hotel. It used to be that the men's champion would dance with the ladies' champion but that tradition, like a number of others at Wimbledon, has been discontinued. (The tradition of curtseying and bowing to the Royal Box is the latest to have been brought to an end, at the insistence of the club President, the Duke of Kent, who felt it was out of keeping with modern life.) As the celebrations get underway about one hour after the final ball is struck, the evening is always in full swing by the time I have closed down the office and stepped out of the courtesy car at the back of the hotel down by the Embankment. It can be quite good fun, especially for the junior champions and their families as they get to rub shoulders with some famous names and get a taste of the high life that might await them later in their careers. Many of them go off and continue their celebrations in other bars and clubs, but by then I tend to be snoring in the back of the car as Jill and I are driven back down the A3 to Weybridge.

I was virtually sleepwalking when I arrived for the dinner at the end of the 1983 Championships, but I was touched to receive so many slaps on the back from the other Wimbledon members and officials. They seemed to be genuine, too, and not just the empty words people often utter just to be polite or break the ice.

We arrived back home in the small hours, but the lie-in that my body and soul craved had to wait. Perhaps foolishly, with hindsight, I had agreed to act as the referee at the Scottish Championships at Craiglockhart in Edinburgh, which in those days began on the Monday after Wimbledon. So I hauled my weary body out of bed and stumbled into the car before Jill drove me up the road to Heathrow. (One of the reasons why we have never moved from our house in Weybridge, which we have lived in for over 40 years, is its proximity not just to Wimbledon but also to Heathrow and Gatwick. Wimbledon is just one of many tournaments where I work, and I spend roughly about two-thirds of the year abroad. Air travel and hotels are a permanent feature of our life, so it has been a happy coincidence that we chose to live near Britain's two biggest airports all those years ago.)

My flight that day was scheduled to leave around noon, and after Jill dropped me at the departures area I wandered bleary-eyed to the check-in desk, collected my boarding card and then slid into one of the seats right outside the gate from which my plane to Edinburgh was due to leave. I woke up with a start three or four hours later to discover that my flight, and plenty of later ones, had been and gone since I had first sat down. It struck me as extraordinary that none of the airline staff a few yards away from me thought it might be a good idea to wake me up and ask me what flight I was booked on. (You don't, after all, hang around in airport departure lounges except to depart somewhere! As passengers came and went on various flights you'd have thought someone would have had the initiative to give me a nudge.) Suffice it to say, I wasn't overly impressed by the guile and wherewithal of the nation's airline staff when I finally emerged from my slumber.

I felt a mild sense of panic sweep over me, knowing full well (in those pre-mobile phone days) that the organisers of the Scottish Championships would be in something of a flap about my absence. They had sent someone to the airport to collect me and when I had failed to arrive on my scheduled flight . . . and then the one after that . . . and the one after that, they had become increasingly concerned for my welfare. They called Jill at home and she too became slightly alarmed and told them that she herself had dropped me at the airport. A number of possibilities were turning through her head – I might have fallen asleep because I had been so tired, or I might even have been taken ill – and she sat there nervously waiting for the dreaded knock on the door. I got to a telephone as quickly as possible and called Jill and the organisers to explain what had happened and then booked myself on to the next available flight.

I finally arrived in Edinburgh, one of my favourite cities, at around seven o'clock that evening, and I fully expected that as play would surely be about to draw to a close I would be taken directly to my hotel where I could fall straight into bed and get a good 12 hours' sleep and feel nice and refreshed before starting work the following morning. But to my dismay I was told that we were heading straight to Craiglockhart, where play was scheduled to continue for another three hours or so. Three hours and then the order of play to put together! I had forgotten about the midnight sun Scotland experiences during the summer, and as I watched it set that evening over the Pentland Hills, beautiful as it was, I decided that this would be the last time I would referee a tournament the week after Wimbledon. I was a zombie.

Chapter Two

Sleepwalking in Torquay

When my playing career was drawing to a close in the mid-sixties, the future looked somewhat uncertain for me. For the better part of 15 years I had travelled Britain, Europe and the rest of the world, enjoying a wonderful life as an amateur tennis player. I considered myself remarkably lucky – not least because I took up tennis in the first place almost by mistake. At school I was keen on all sports and played cricket and football for the 1st XI, but I did not begin playing the game that was to become such an important part in my life until I was 13, when I went down to the local tennis club to watch some friends play. When I arrived there were only three of them on court and as there was a spare racket it was suggested that I join them until the fourth member of the group showed up. I had never held a racket before – let alone played on a court – and I very much enjoyed the experience, which went on for longer than anticipated, as the fourth player never arrived to take my place. While I was playing, one of the club members was watching and suggested to my parents that perhaps I should have a few lessons. I jumped at the chance and began entering tournaments, apparently showing some promise.

I ended up winning a local event, which impressed my headmaster, and although they did not have any tennis facilities at my school, he marked out a court in the playground, bought a net and told some of the staff to hit with me during the lunch hour! I continued to improve, and it was suggested that perhaps I should try to take up the game seriously. My parents had no money to spare, but they were incredibly supportive and said that if this was really what I wanted to do, they would do all they could to help – to the degree that they took out a second mortgage to allow me to play tournaments all over the country. With such a lot of support behind me I didn't want to let anyone down and worked as hard as I could at my game, eventually ending up being ranked in the British top ten during 1957–66. I competed at Wimbledon for 17 years, reaching the last 16 of the singles twice, and was a semi-finalist in the doubles in 1965.

Throughout my career I visited many of the world's great cities and towns, meeting a host of extraordinary characters and making some great friends, while all the time earning a reasonable living first with Cussons and then as a sales promotion rep with Dunlop. I could not have hoped for a better life as a young man. And into the bargain I met my wife Jill. It was in 1954 during a tournament at Shirley Park, near Croydon, in one of the first events of the year and I was playing mixed doubles with Pauline Titchener (now Cox) against Jill and a New Zealander named Barry Sumner. In those days you still smiled on court and I was often told that I did not look as though I was taking things seriously enough, although I suspect my beaming face did tend to irritate opponents, so it had its advantages. As we changed ends during the match I was smiling away at Jill which I know now she thought quite odd – and assumed it was because I

was winning. When we finished we had a drink together –
again as you did in those days – started chatting and met
again at a tournament some weeks later in Surbiton. The
rest, as they say, is history. Jill was a good tennis player herself
(she represented England, played Wimbledon for 16 years
and we partnered each other in mixed doubles) and an
exceptional table tennis player (again representing England).
We married in 1960 and our lives dovetailed nicely as we
often travelled together on the circuit. In those days, international travel was nothing like as easy as it has become
today and when you flew out of Britain you tended to stay
abroad for several weeks at a time before returning home.
As a result many players spent long periods away from their
loved ones, but it was our good fortune that we were able
to be together and share so many wonderful experiences in
exotic locations.

One trip to India particularly sticks in the memory – especially as the day before we left we were told that we would
be parents in seven months. Fortunately, the doctor's advice
was to go and carry on as normal, and I am glad we did, as
we were treated incredibly well throughout the whole trip. On
our first night in Calcutta we stayed with a charming couple
who took us out to a cocktail party, a wedding reception and
then on to dinner. The next morning we headed off to a club
to practise and there were servants to help me get dressed and
undressed in the changing rooms, which I found rather embarrassing as I was not used to being waited on. The club also
provided ball-boys – even for practice. We moved from there
to Alahabad (where we shared our bedroom with some very
friendly lizards) and then on to Jaipur, where we were able to
see emeralds being sorted and cut, and then on to Delhi,

which of course was fascinating. Tennis-wise the trip was a success, and Barry to this day still relishes the story of his role in being the ladies' singles and doubles champion of various parts of India.

I played against Ramanathan Krishnan in the final of the All India Championships in Delhi, and he and his doubles partner Naresh Kumar have remained friends of ours ever since. They helped us purchase a carpet while we were there, and we picked it up months later from London Docks, where we had no problem at all clearing customs. One look at Jill's very pregnant stomach and the officials checked us though as fast as they could. Just as well I guess – Barry was born the next day. We still see Naresh and Sunita, his lovely wife, at Wimbledon each year, and Ramanathan's son played at the Championships while I was referee and is now captain of the Indian Davis Cup team.

Wonderful days indeed, but as we reached the end of our 'serious' playing careers, things began to change as we were forced to start thinking about the rest of our lives, raising a family and getting a steady job on civvy street. By late August 1964 our son Barry was gurgling away in his cot (he would be joined by Penny three years later) and there is nothing like the arrival of little ones into your life to focus your mind on the future.

I had not given a great deal of thought about what I might to do with the rest of my working life – I had after all just turned 30 – but it quickly dawned on me that, comfortable as my job at Dunlop was, I did not want to spend the rest of my life as a travelling salesman or a London commuter. Once you have had a taste of foreign travel and the itin-

erant life, it is difficult then to swap it for the more seden-
tary and sedate life of an office desk and the 17.32 out of
Waterloo. Furthermore, I would miss the thrill and the adrenalin rush of competition, the outdoor life with the sun on
my back and the camaraderie of the circuit. In short, the
comedown was too painful to contemplate, and I began to
look for a more interesting line of work, related to tennis if
possible. But the only way to earn money *and* remain involved
in tennis was to turn professional, and so in 1966 that was
exactly what I did.

It will all seem very strange to younger readers, but aban-
doning the amateur code for the professional was a move
fraught with controversy. It was an issue that dominated a lot
of the major sports at that time and provoked fierce opinions
on both sides of the argument. It seems incredible now to
think that I was actually thrown out of the All England Club
the moment I announced that I was becoming a professional,
and little could I have imagined that a couple of decades later
I would be back as a high-profile official.

There were, and still are, only about 360 full members of
the All England Club, and so I felt a tremendous sense of
pride when I was invited into the most exclusive and prestigious tennis club on the planet. There are a number of
honorary and temporary members, but the waiting list for full
membership is so long that most applicants can expect to die
before their own claim reaches the top of the secretary's in-
tray. The joke at the club is that the quickest way to become
a member of the club is to win Wimbledon. However, in those
days the club often invited good and promising players to
become members. Needless to say, I jumped at the chance,
but my joy at becoming a member at so young an age quickly

turned to despair, mixed with anger, when I received a curt letter, shortly after the announcement in the press that I was to turn professional, informing me that I was no longer a member of the club. Happily, about a year later the club invited me back as an honorary member, which carried the same status as being a full member except that I had no right to vote. It was only years later, once professionalism had been accepted as a fact of life, that I finally regained full membership status.

When I turned pro in 1966 I was offered a job as the resident professional at a resort hotel called Treasure Cay in the Bahamas. The well-known American player Gardnar Mulloy helped get me the job and a friend of his generously offered us her beachside villa for the six-month stint. When we arrived the hotel threw a magnificent party to launch the official 'opening' of the tennis centre and there were a number of great tennis figures there, including Don Budge, Vic Seixas and Ham Richardson, as well as the clothes designer Oleg Cassini to add some glitz and glamour to the occasion. It was a brief but wonderful period of our life, most of it spent on the long, deserted expanse of white sands outside the front door of our beautiful house. We settled in very quickly, and Barry had a wonderful time as everyone made a great fuss of him. We made some good friends and were able to borrow one of the very few cars on the island once a week to go to the shops, 15 miles away, in the only town, Marsh Harbour. To get there we had to drive down an unmade road that needed the Bahamian equivalent of a snowplough to clear it of rocks.

In the brochure I had been shown before accepting the job, much was made of an 18-hole golf course at the hotel, water skiing, wild boar-hunting and a tennis shop. In fact the golf course was nine holes, the water skiing depended on a young boat-owner with a girlfriend on another island who seemed only to be available if he had had a row with her, the tennis shop was a table and umbrella between two courts and the wild boar very sensibly never made an appearance.

The tennis coaching was far from intense, but when a plane landed on the island carrying visitors from overseas, many of them coming with a view to buying land, we were obliged to get anyone at the hotel who could hold a racket out on to the courts. This included the cooks, cleaners, waiters and office staff. Palm trees were wheeled into the foyer, the fountains were switched on, and for a few happy hours the complex was miraculously transformed into a hive of happy activity. As soon as the visitors had left, out went the palm trees, off went the fountains and everyone returned to their duties.

During our time in the Bahamas, a group of very keen American tennis players flew over a few times, in a private plane. One of them offered me a job at an indoor tennis club in Toledo, Ohio. Our stay at Treasure Cay was fun and very different, and we would love the opportunity to go back there as we hear that it is now a superb resort, but at the time it was only for six months, so we decided that Toledo would indeed by my next assignment. We packed our bags, put them on the last company plane off the island, and the three of us went home happily to await the arrival of our daughter Penny.

We might not have made it back to Treasure Cay yet, but I did return to that neck of the woods – Florida in fact – some 20 years after our departure from the Bahamas to referee what has become one of the largest and most popular tournaments outside of the Grand Slams, and I am delighted to say I have been back every year. The event is now well established at Key Biscayne but getting there certainly wasn't smooth sailing for the organisers. The tournament, for many years sponsored by Liptons, was the brainchild of Butch and Cliff Buchholz, both former Wimbledon players, who wanted, in essence, to create a fifth Grand Slam. The original location was Delray Beach and then Boca Raton before it settled at Key Biscayne, much to the aggravation of many of the local residents. Their resistance to the tournament becoming a permanent feature meant that for a long time everything was run out of Portakabins and temporary facilities. From what I gather, there were endless meetings with various councils before agreement was eventually reached and permission was granted – on the condition that extra palm trees were planted in order that nothing would show from the road – to build a permanent, and as it has turned out, very attractive stadium which doubles as a USTA training facility when the tournament is not on. Butch and Cliff's many years of hard work have certainly paid off.

The job in Toledo which I'd been offered was for a six-month stint over the winter and I did it for two years. On my returns from the States back to England over that period I coached at Millfield, the sports-orientated public school in Somerset. While the winters in Ohio were colder than anything I had ever experienced, with snow often piled up three feet high outside our door, my workload was exhausting. I worked six days a week, from the crack of dawn until late into the evening, and did more coaching in my first week there than I had done in the entire six months in the Bahamas. When I finally got home I would invariably fall asleep in front of the television.

My association with Millfield lasted only another year, until 1969. I liked the school and the people there, but as I was unwilling to move the family to the West Country, it meant I only had a day and a half at home each week. The children were still very young and I wanted to be around to see them grow up.

What I needed, I realised, was a steady job, in tennis and close to home. What better job than the role of professional just up the road from home at our local club, St George's, in Weybridge? St George's was regarded as quite an exclusive club in those days and my long association with it began after I won the annual open tournament there in the early seventies. After collecting my trophy, the secretary called me aside and said: 'So you want to become a member of the best tennis club in the world?' I replied that, as a member of the All England Club, I understood that I already was. 'That's terribly funny, but they don't actually count, as far as we are concerned,' he replied, before quickly changing the subject to the weather and the recent rise in interest rates.

Shortly afterwards I was invited, out of the blue, by a committee member to apply for the job as the club's tennis professional, and I remember my interview with a mixture of embarrassment and amusement. One of the committee members conducting the interview spent much of the time trying to get me to give free coaching lessons to his children, which made me feel rather uncomfortable to say the least. Despite this slightly disconcerting discussion, I was given the job, and our links with the club lasted the better part of three decades. For a long time it seemed to be the perfect arrangement, partly because it was close to home and partly because we made a lot of extremely good friends. I certainly never grew rich from my work there and coached at local schools to supplement my income. They were happy times, and even when I became referee at Wimbledon we came to a contractual arrangement that allowed me 16 weeks off in the year to referee the Championships and other tournaments. It was all very amicable and we had come to feel almost part of the furniture there, when for reasons we are still not quite able to fathom, it all went a little sour, even downright ugly by the end.

For 20 years or so, my contracts with the club had run for between three and five years but at some point in the mid-nineties, we were told that from then on it would be renewed on an annual basis. No one explained this sudden change of policy. I was informed by letter and I felt something was amiss. You sometimes never know what kind of political shenanigans are going on behind the scenes in a tennis club, or any other institution for that matter.

The atmosphere suddenly became very frosty, and when the club started to query the coaching fees I was charging members for lessons, we knew for certain that something was afoot. No one had raised questions about my fees in all the time I had been there, and I certainly hadn't received any complaints from anyone. St George's always used to like to compare itself to some of the great private clubs, like Queen's and the Hurlingham in west London, and it seemed a little curious that the functionaries there should now choose to measure our fees with those being charged at the little local clubs in Surrey, while at the same time congratulating themselves on being so exclusive and grand.

It seemed to me that the club was trying to force us out. The air became thick with plots and intrigue, and our friends wanted to push for an extraordinary general meeting in order to have the issue brought out into the open. However, those behind the dispute chose not to air the matter frankly and reasonably, which was a great pity. Such an atmosphere of subterfuge was hardly required – this was after all a job at a suburban tennis club we were talking about, not a plot to overthrow the government.

By then I realised that I had little interest in remaining involved with the club, but my contract had a few months to run and so I was obliged to see it out. On its expiry, the relationship was effectively over, but surprisingly we were made honorary members and about a year later I was offered a three-year consultancy role, which I accepted as there had been a change of officials by that time. When that contract expired I never heard anything again. Nowadays the only correspondence we receive from the club comes in the form of circulars and letters for Penny and Barry, informing them of all the junior events, which is a bit odd as they are now nearer 40 than 15.

On the one or two occasions that I have returned there, I have been taken aback by how much it has changed, both physically and atmospherically. It was an entirely different place to the one I remembered, and it does sadden me that the memory of so many happy years there were so inexplicably ruined by the events of the final months.

I held a number of other coaching posts in my early career as a professional. For a short period in the early seventies I was the national coach of Wales, but that came to an end when the country's Sports Council decided that the coaches of all the national teams had to live in Wales. We had tried to buy a cottage, but the surveyor's report intimated that if the deathwatch beetles stopped holding hands it could fall down!

I was also the professional at the All England Club, for many years, but the thought of becoming a referee had never crossed my mind until the moment I agreed to become one. I was minding my own business and then a few moments later I had agreed to a new career. Terrifying really when I think about it! However, it proved to be the best decision of my working life, and was all the more surprising for it being made virtually in my sleep.

It was the autumn of 1976 and Jill and I had gone to Torquay to play in a tournament at the Palace Hotel where we had spent our honeymoon 16 years earlier. It is a beautiful hotel, set in about 25 acres of landscaped grounds looking out towards the sea. It was virtually the last tournament of the British season – and it was always tremendous fun. We went every year we could, and lots of our tennis friends were always there. There were also a few foreign players who used to stay on for the end of the British season before their round-the-world air ticket expired and they headed home. British tennis may already have been in decline, but the Lawn Tennis Association (LTA) has always put on a very good tournament and looked after the foreign players extremely well.

Torquay was more of a party than a serious tennis event, and a slightly mad party at that, particularly that year. There was always a big entry, but as there were only two indoor courts, matches would often continue late into the evening. In 1976 the roof had leaked, which meant there was only one court and the organisers had no option but to play around the clock for the first few days to clear the backlog of matches. (Players were a lot more tolerant back in those days. When I ran Wimbledon's qualifying tournament it rained so persistently one year that we were in grave danger of being unable to complete the event before Wimbledon proper began. Drastic measures were needed, so I called in all the players and suggested we played their remaining matches on a wooden court laid over the swimming pool at Roehampton. It was not perhaps the ideal way to qualify for the world's premier grass-court tournament, but there was no other option. All but one of the players agreed, but I don't know how that would go down today.)

The court problems in Torquay led to the bizarre scenario of reception calling up to the players' in the middle of the night: 'Good morning Mr Mills, it's now 3.30 a.m. and you and Mrs Mills are on court in half an hour.' We changed out of our pyjamas, put on tennis clothes, drifted downstairs like ghosts and slumped into one of the deep armchairs there waiting to be called on to court. I was staring blankly into space, still half asleep, holding my racket across my chest when Fred Hoyles, who was overseeing the Torquay tournament, wandered over and sat down. Fred was a very conscientious referee, and I wasn't surprised to see him still up making sure all the matches got underway at the right time. Lesser men would have retired for the evening.

'Would you be interested in doing some refereeing next year?' he asked me, completely out the blue. I had never done any serious refereeing in my life, save for a handful of junior tournaments at St George's. In my day as a serious player, most referees seemed to be retired army and RAF officers, all military efficiency and strict discipline. They didn't do it for the money, that's for sure, because there wasn't any – though they might have got a bottle of whisky at the end of the tournament if they were lucky. I had had a couple of years in the RAF doing my national service in the late 1950s, but after a month or so of square-bashing I spent the rest of the time playing tennis. It was great and I loved it, but when I finally passed out, I could hardly consider myself a military man. I boarded an aeroplane only twice the whole time I was in the RAF, and on both occasions it was to be taken to a tennis tournament. It was lucky a war didn't break out because all I would have been good for was smashing a few tennis balls in the general direction of the enemy.

In those days the referee didn't seem to do much more than produce the order of play, and there was no real problem with player discipline – it was an amateur sport with none of the additional pressures that money brings and all the players were strictly answerable to the LTA. Such was the authority of the LTA then that on one occasion I was in the British Davis Cup Team that was going to play in the French Open on the way home from Austria. Jill was an individual entry in the tournament, and we had arranged to meet at the hotel in Paris. John Barrett was our captain, and probably doesn't remember this event, but when we arrived he had to phone the LTA to see if it would be all right for me to share a room with Jill. (We were married at the time.) However, the answer that came back was a definite no, which placed John in a dilemma. He couldn't ask Jill to leave, as she was playing in the tournament. The alternative would have been to move the whole team to another hotel, which would have been very difficult as rooms in Paris at that time of year were hard to come by. Can you imagine explaining to the concierge in a French hotel, in very poor French, that yes we were married but no we couldn't share a room. The French have always suspected the English are crazy – this would have confirmed it! A compromise was reached, and I ended up sharing with John on the second floor, with Jill in a single room on the sixth.

Against this background, the role of the referee seemed, in short, quite a boring job to me. But the game was changing rapidly and becoming bigger, richer, more intensive and more professional by the year. I looked at Fred. He wasn't a former services officer. He was a farmer. He had taken over at Wimbledon from Captain Mike Gibson, who blotted his copybook somewhat by making some unflattering comments about Wimbledon's grass surface while he was at the US Open. 'Why not?' I thought, and so I agreed there and then to join his team for the following Wimbledon. We shook hands on it and I walked away bleary-eyed to play my match.

The following June I reported for my first day's paid work at Wimbledon; not that the pay was anything special. In fact the year before I had been paid more money by Slazenger for a far less demanding and less prestigious job calling the matches at the qualifying tournament in Roehampton. Down the years it has dawned on me that many people think I must be very rich, probably because I appear on television and have become the public face of the All England Club during the fortnight. This, sadly, is not a very accurate impression. What is certainly true, however, is that the kudos of my position at Wimbledon has opened a lot of doors at tournaments elsewhere around the world and I have certainly found work because of my association.

When I began my career as an assistant referee in that Silver Jubilee year, which also happened to be the centenary of the men's singles event, I had no qualifications to speak of. There weren't any to acquire back then. I had only a rough idea of what my assignment would involve, although I knew that I would never be sent out on my own to Centre Court or Court 1, which were the exclusive domain of the senior referee. I had a few attributes in my favour which might come in handy. I had never particularly excelled academically because sport was my great passion and I was just 16 years old when I left Waterloo Grammar School, near Liverpool, to take up an apprenticeship as an electrical engineer in Southport – a post which allowed me to concentrate on playing on the British tennis circuit. I did, however, have a pretty reasonable mathematical brain, and this is probably the quality you need more than any other as the referee of big tournaments where the permutations of matches can be mind-boggling. I was also blessed with a fair amount of common sense and an unflappable nature, which would stand me in good stead to deal with the turbulence that would soon engulf the men's circuit. But I think the main reason why Fred asked me to join his team was because I was a former player who had reached a decent standard. Fred himself was not an especially accomplished player, as far as I know, and, sensing that the players were starting to become more quarrelsome, he wanted to have someone around him who they felt could better understand their frustrations.

One of the first things he told me when he sat down and ran through my tasks that year was that he wanted me at his side, or 'in his back pocket', as he put it, when he was called out to deal with an unhappy player. On each occasion that we headed out to a court, we would talk about the problem along the way and he would ask me what I thought the player was feeling. For Fred, to be forewarned was to be forearmed, and I thought his decision to get an ex-player on board was extremely sensible. I think I was the first referee in over a hundred years or so of the Championships who had played the game to a reasonably high level. I never won a major tournament, but I had reached the last 16 of the singles at Wimbledon, as well as the semi-finals there and at the French Open in the doubles events. I had captained England in the home internationals and represented Britain in the Davis Cup. Most of the players know that, so when I talk to them, I like to think they respect what I say because they know that I too have experienced their frustrations. When McEnroe ranted at Fred he was probably thinking something like, 'You're just a gentleman-farmer from Lincolnshire – what would you know about the pressures of Grand Slam tennis?'

In 1981 I was in Fred's 'back pocket' when McEnroe exploded on Centre Court in a match against his fellow American Tom Gullikson. It was one of John's most infamous outbursts during which he screamed, 'You're the pits of the world!' to the umpire Ted James. By the time his tirade had finished I could barely even remember what the cause of it had been, but several thoughts struck me as it was unfolding. Firstly, McEnroe's arguing went on for so long that Gullikson, who was a lovely, mild-mannered character, had gone completely cold. While McEnroe was working himself up into a fury which would help fire his game, Gullikson, who had been holding his own up to that point, was going flat as the adrenalin ebbed away. He just stood around kicking his heels and once it was all over it became obvious that any rhythm and momentum he had managed to build up was no longer there. McEnroe had taken it away from him. This, I felt, was palpably unfair, and though I doubt – unlike some people – that McEnroe engineered such scenarios in order to put off his opponent, I resolved there and then that, faced with a similar situation again I would make sure it was dealt with as quickly as possible so that the opponent would not suffer.

I have always thought that tennis in that difficult period – and the career of John McEnroe – might have been entirely different if Gullikson had been a less reasonable man and just walked off court and disqualified himself. He could have approached the chair and said: 'Look, I'm cold, I'm bored, my legs have stiffened up, my adrenalin has gone and I am simply no longer in the right frame of mind to continue,' and with that just packed his bags and disappeared back into the dressing-room. It would have been a defining moment. The press and the players, who were getting more and more critical of McEnroe's antics, would certainly have thrown their support behind Gullikson. McEnroe, who was never a bad man, just a wild one, would probably have felt ashamed that he had been responsible for ending a fellow professional's tournament in that way. Gullikson would effectively have gone on strike, and the tennis world could have united and said, 'Enough is enough.'

John gave Fred a terrible going over that afternoon and it

must have been a very galling experience for him. It was bad enough just listening to it. I know Fred was quite shaken by the incident, but what he did when he was walking off court spoke volumes for his courage. As he headed towards the corner, McEnroe swore at him. Fred could have just carried on walking because he and I were probably the only ones who heard what he had said. But, to his credit, Fred turned on his heel and told the chair umpire to issue another code violation. I've always regarded that as a very brave thing to do because who knows how McEnroe in that type of mood might have reacted.

That incident effectively prompted Fred to end his career as the Championships' Referee. McEnroe was fined the maximum $10,000. In those days you had to serve a fine on a player rather as you have to serve a subpoena on someone in law – you actually had to hand it to them. In this instance, the rule gave rise to the ludicrously comic scene of Fred chasing McEnroe through the crowds waving his fine above his head as he went, before finally catching up with him at the gates and handing it to him under the no doubt grateful eyes of the world's press photographers.

McEnroe went on to win his first of three Wimbledon titles, beating Borg in four sets. However, the club was so appalled by his behaviour that they decided to withhold the honorary membership which was traditionally bestowed on the champions of the two singles tournaments. When McEnroe returned to the club for the following year's Championships, he found his club member's tie hanging up in his locker. Nothing was said – very Wimbledon that!

I found myself embroiled in the McEnroe membership fracas when we were packing up the office at the end of the fortnight and preparing to head off to the champions' dinner at the Savoy. The phone rang. It was John McEnroe Snr, a tough-talking New York lawyer who you would often see in the crowd wearing a floppy white sunhat. Like his son earlier in the tournament Mr McEnroe was not in the best of moods, I quickly gathered. He informed me that John Jnr would not be attending the dinner in view of what had happened between John and the Wimbledon authorities during the tournament. In my view this was going to be very poor PR for all involved and would bring relations between the two parties to a new low. Still, I was hardly in a position to order his appearance at the Savoy. It was a free world and it was his decision.

I passed on the news to Wimbledon's chief executive Chris Gorringe, but no sooner had I replaced the receiver than the phone rang again. It was McEnroe Snr, this time informing me that his son would be coming after all and would be bringing a party of about ten friends and family. 'Fine,' I said. 'I will let them know. That's great news.' Why he was calling me I have no idea, but I presume the referee's office was the only Wimbledon number the McEnroe family had.

It turned out that this was not be the last of our conversations over the next hour or so, and he soon called again to say, in fact, no, John wouldn't be coming to the dinner but that he *might*, if the urge took him, come along and make the traditional speech by the champion. If he did come, however, I was told, he would not be wearing formal evening wear, but would appear in his tracksuit. I was perfectly polite to Mr McEnroe throughout our game of telephone tennis, and I continued to pass on the various developments in John's dining, travel and clothing arrangements that evening. As the farce continued and I relayed the messages to the appropriate officials I began to feel as if I were taking part in a *Carry On film*.

McEnroe didn't come in the end, and the following day I was slightly bemused and a little angry to read a story in the papers quoting McEnroe Snr as saying that the man he had spoken to at Wimbledon had been extremely rude to him. I can barely remember being rude to anyone in my life and it certainly wouldn't have been very 'politic' of me to have given him the brush-off. I hadn't even tried to put pressure on his son to attend. I rang the club immediately on seeing the story and assured them that I had been perfectly civil. The then chairman, Air Chief Marshal Sir Brian Burnett, leapt to my defence and issued a statement insisting that he had every confidence that I had not been rude and that there had obviously been some kind of misunderstanding.

Fred was so appalled by his on-court experiences with McEnroe that year that he told the All England Club that he would not be returning the following summer. The club was very sympathetic and succeeded in persuading him to stay on for the 1982 Championships. It would otherwise have looked like a victory for unruly player power over the forces of law and order.

I liked Fred very much. He was a great character to work for, and every springtime he sent us a bag of bulbs from his fields in Lincolnshire where he lived with his sisters. I always had the impression that he felt a little lonely when he came down to Wimbledon each year. In all, he would be there for about six weeks, and it became clear soon after starting work in his office that he enjoyed both my company and that of his other assistant, Tony Gathercole, during that period. In the weeks before the tournament began, Tony and I would often be there until long past ten o'clock at night, going over list after list of entries. Fred was fastidious in his attention to detail and always thoroughly prepared.

We were generally the last people to leave the grounds each evening, and we often had to run the gauntlet of the security team's pack of Alsatians before escaping through the gates. It could be quite hairy sometimes as you tiptoed through the dark, only to turn a corner and find a growling guard dog straining at the leash. It got to the point where we would not dare step out of the office without first calling security to let them know we were coming out and to ask them to call off their dogs. The only animals you find on the grounds these days are foxes, which have proved a considerable nuisance to the ground staff down the years. You often see them wandering around without a care in the world, sometimes even in broad daylight. The groundsmen hate the foxes because when they urinate on their beautifully nurtured courts they leave yellow patches, which look awful. Now the two main show courts have electric fences around them. Pigeons have also been a problem, but each year they bring in Harry the Harris Hawk (who also works at the Houses of Parliament) to frighten them away.

Although we were keen to get home, Tony and I were happy to stay on with Fred because he was a good man and a friend and we felt a little sorry for him being holed up in his flat for those six weeks (Fred used to paper the flat with the giant sheets of paper detailing the draws in Wimbledon's five main competitions, adding new layers at the end of each Championships).

Fred made it clear to the All England Club that he wanted to retire, but he didn't tell any of us in the office and it came as a bolt from the blue when he telephoned me shortly after the 1982 Championships to let me know he had stepped down. He wanted to make sure that I didn't read about it in the papers and be caught unawares as the media began their speculation about who might succeed him. I knew that I would be in the running for the job, but there was absolutely no question that I would be the automatic choice. Three weeks went by in which I had no contact with the club at all while the papers mulled over a host of different candidates, including a handful of overseas people. I was beginning to grow a little apprehensive, but didn't want to appear too eager by calling the club to find out when they might make a decision. I was refereeing a junior tournament in Woking when the chief executive Chris Gorringe (whom I had got to know pretty well as a fellow member of St George's) telephoned to offer me the job. I didn't need him to give me the hard sell and I said that, subject to details about my salary package and job conditions, I would be delighted to accept. I was given a one-year contract, which thereafter became a three-year contract until I reached the official Wimbledon retirement age of 65 in 2000, after which it reverted to an annual basis. Fred came down to Wimbledon during my first year in charge, but he only popped in once, clearly not wanting to step on my toes or make me feel under any more pressure. As he watched me hurry from court to court to deal with the various incidents that erupted that year, I felt sure he wouldn't have regretted his decision to step aside. Tony Gathercole became my right-hand man and stayed until his retirement at the end of the 2002 Championships.

Chapter Three

Men Behaving Badly

At the start of the 1984 Championships – my second as referee – the issue of player indiscipline, far from subsiding, once again dominated the build-up to the tournament. It was the talk of tennis throughout this period and despite the introduction of the four-point penalty system, players were still happily blowing their tops and haranguing match officials from Montreal to Munich. John McEnroe, the odds-on favourite to land the title for a second year running, was playing the best tennis of his life and had won 48 out of 49 matches heading into the fortnight. A week earlier at Queen's he had called umpire Roger Smith 'a moron', reminding us (if we needed to be reminded) that we as officials could expect just as much of a challenge as his opponents. There was mild amusement amongst tennis officials when it was announced before the start of the tournament that McEnroe had been elected to the players' union committee to represent them on a range of matters, including, of all things, their conduct on court.

The headline writers in the papers were becoming ever more ingenious as they endeavoured to come up with fresh ways of describing the man they all loved to hate. 'Superbrat' was now 'Mac The Mouth' or 'McEnrowdy', but despite the stigmatising of him, you had the feeling the journalists were relishing his return. He was, after all, an easy story. Journalists just sat back and waited for him to lose his cool, and bingo! The story was written for them and off they went to the press bar for a few pints to bemoan the collapse of good manners and sportsmanship in the modern game. There was no looking under stones and hovering in the shadows for a good story when J.P. McEnroe was about.

In the run-up to the Championships, Mr McEnroe Snr had expressed his concern that Wimbledon, as well as the press, were going to crucify his son if he stepped out of line. Buzzer Hadingham, the new chairman of the club, publicly insisted that there would be no witch-hunt, saying Wimbledon didn't want to act like schoolmasters in their treatment of the players, but he did take the unusual step of saying: 'My head is on the block and if we fail to act on serious breaches of code of conduct I will be headless.' Wimbledon also took out another huge indemnity with Lloyds Insurance to guard against being sued for loss of earnings by a disqualified player.

The 1984 Championships also presented an opportunity for commentators to make a sentimental retreat into the golden past as the club prepared to celebrate two special milestones in Wimbledon history. A parade had been planned to commemorate the 100th anniversary of the first ladies' singles tournament, with 17 out of 20 surviving champions present, including Kitty Godfree, the oldest living winner. In addition, a statue of Fred Perry was unveiled by the Duke of Kent to celebrate the fact that it was 50 years since Fred, the last British man to win Wimbledon, won the first of his three consecutive titles. Completing this feast of nostalgia, Bunny Austin, a Wimbledon runner-up, was readmitted to the All England Club 40 years after being blackballed for going to the United States during the Second World War and joining an organisation called the Moral Movement, a religious crusade opposed to the hostilities. Back then, and for many years after, the All England Club hierarchy was dominated by military men and there was strong feeling at the club that Bunny should have fought the Nazis as a British soldier. During the war Wimbledon was suspended and nearly all the staff were called up for active duty. The grounds themselves even contributed to the war effort with one of the car parks being turned into a vegetable garden and the front concourse used by the London Welsh and London Irish regiments as a parade ground. The military connection with the Championships continues to this day, although it is not as strong as it was in the immediate post-war years. In 1945 Lt-Col. Duncan Macaulay, who had worked at the Championships since 1922, first as an umpire and then as assistant referee, was appointed Wimbledon secretary, and he recruited service personnel who took voluntary leave to act as stewards. As the Championships have grown so have the number of service stewards, and they are now an integral part of the fortnight and still take voluntary leave to attend.

While on the subject of stewards, it is worth mentioning the honorary stewards who also perform such an important function at Wimbledon, controlling and helping the crowds. The role of honorary stewards began in 1927 when the secretary of the All England, worried about the size of the crowd that was attending the Championships, asked officials from the Rugby Football Union at Twickenham for advice and subsequently enlisted the help of six of their stewards. By

1948 this number had risen to around 30, and the decision was taken to establish an association, which held its inaugural meeting in July 1950. The AGM of 1951 reported that there were 33 active members, and this number has continued to grow.

Tennis, of course, had changed beyond all recognition since the playing days of Kitty, Bunny and many of the other past champions who attended that day, and you wondered what they thought had become of the game they used to grace with such style and elegance. When they opened their papers in the build-up to the tournament and saw countless pictures of Carling Bassett, 'sexiest players on the circuit' features, column after column about the millions of dollars being earned in prize money, and all set against a dark background of player anarchy, they could only have been staggered by the changes in the game and society at large that had taken place since they used to play tennis for no other reason than the sheer fun of it.

I met Fred Perry several times in my playing career, and my wife Jill worked for his clothes company when she wasn't travelling on the tennis and table tennis circuit. At that time everybody in British tennis was wearing Fred Perry or Teddy Tinling clothing. The first time I met Fred must have been in the early 1950s when I was a young teenager just starting to make a name for myself in junior tournaments in my native Lancashire. He and Dan Maskell, the player and commentator who was then the LTA's national coach, went around the country holding clinics for young players and generally promoting the game. I was completely star-struck as I practised with Fred, and I recall being amazed at how hard he hit the ball. They say that when he was a youngster,

Fred didn't stand out as a potentially great player of the future. He had a fabulous forehand, but he was forever hitting the top of the net and was encouraged by coaches to hit the ball more gently to make sure it got over. It was only once he became a senior player, and was that much taller, that his powerful ground-strokes improved and he became such a major force in the game.

Fred was a very humorous and confident person. He had a busy mind and was always on the move – a bit of an action man. Nowadays of course he has become a legend, and every year a British man fails to win Wimbledon his mythical status grows still further. By the time the 100th anniversary of his last Wimbledon title comes around let's hope that someone has reclaimed the trophy. In their quest to do so they could do worse than remember Don Budge's comment on Fred: 'He was the only Englishman bloody-minded enough not to want to lose.' Fred, like Dan Maskell, came from what I suppose you would call an 'ordinary' background. Tennis in Britain has always been regarded as an elitist sport, played only by the middle and upper classes, and that was certainly true when the game came into existence in the latter half of the nineteenth century. But it is not the case that all the great characters of the twentieth century were born with silver spoons in their mouths. Far from it!

When I was growing up in Formby after the war, tennis was seen as a 'cissy' sport. 'Come over here and play with a hard ball, you big girl's blouse,' the cricketers used to shout at me, as I practised on the courts next to their ground. But in my experience of life on the circuit, most of the players appeared to have come from relatively humble origins – not quite from 'the ghetto', but the majority of them certainly could not be described as rich or privileged. For my part, I was born in a two-up, two-down in Stretford, Manchester, and grew up in a semi-detached three bedroom house in Formby. My father was a railway controller, my mother a railway clerk until she gave up work to look after my brother Brian and me. We were never short of food or clothes, but there certainly wasn't any money left over for luxuries at the end of the month. I remember one year during the war when my father's office in Liverpool was bombed by the Luftwaffe and our Christmas presents were destroyed in the raid. I found out years later that my mother, lacking the money to replace them, had pawned her favourite ring to make sure we didn't go without presents.

Fred Perry was born in Stockport, and as the son of a Labour MP had no time for the snobbish traditions of British tennis. Dan Maskell grew up in the poorer part of Fulham; so he too was not exactly welcomed into the establishment with open arms. Dan became the professional at the Queen's Club in west Kensington, a stone's throw from where he grew up, but he was distinctly 'below stairs'. In addition to his duties coaching the club's members, he also had to string their rackets and fulfil other manual and menial tasks. He was emphatically not allowed to enter the members' bar. Good heavens no! A professional in the bar – it was quite unthinkable!

Dan and Fred, and most of the players of my generation, had to fight to get to where they were, and it wasn't until the professional era began in 1968 that the class barriers started to come down. It was the same in cricket at that time. The gentlemen and the players, even in the sixties, used to enter the field of play by separate gates and eat their meals at different tables.

For me, one story in particular highlights the aloofness and arrogance of the tennis establishment in those days. Angela Mortimer (later Barrett after her marriage to John) had won the French Open singles title in 1955 and the press threw a party to celebrate. The next day she was asked whether she had enjoyed the party. 'What party?' she replied. It turned out that Angela was never even invited and spent the whole evening sitting in her modest hotel bedroom reading a book!

It is not comparable to what happened to Angela after winning a Grand Slam tournament but I too learnt very early the LTA attitude. I must have been about 15 and was travelling to an LTA training camp somewhere on the South Coast. Before boarding the train in London, I was standing on the platform right next to the chairman of the LTA. I had all my kit with me, as well as a heavy suitcase with my other belongings. It could not have been more obvious that I was heading to the same destination as him, but he completely ignored me before getting into a first-class carriage. (I was in third class.)

When we arrived at the other end I was struggling down the platform with all my bags, and without so much as a 'Hello, young laddie, see you at the camp', he breezed straight past me and climbed into a taxi while I bumbled off in search of the bus stop. There was nothing extraordinary about this incident then. It was par for the course.

When I played for the RAF, it was a similar story. Once we went to Gibraltar to play an annual fixture against the station there. The officers in our team were put up in the mess, but we were lodged in the barracks next to the kitchens and woken up at about 4 a.m. the following morning by the cooks banging their pots and pans as they went about their duties. We complained and the next night we were put up in a nearby hotel. It was, I suppose, an early demonstration of player power!

Even in the early 1970s when I was working as the coach at St George's Hill Club in Weybridge, there remained a considerable amount of suspicion amongst the members towards professionals. A friend of ours tells a story about the time she had been having a coaching session with my predecessor and invited him into the bar for a drink, believing no one would really mind in these modern times. But he had barely set foot inside the inner sanctum of the club when he was asked to leave and finish his drink outside in the hallway. It was as if he were a leper or had a personal hygiene problem.

By 1984 tennis had changed beyond all recognition. Today it is the players who are rich and pampered, not the people who run the game. If you board an aeroplane on the way to an international tournament, it is the players you will find stretching their legs out in first class, while the rest cram into the economy seats. When I was on the circuit – it was all amateur back then of course – we used to hitch rides just to get to tournaments and we often did some umpiring to earn a meal-ticket and save some money. You may have got the odd backhander from the organisers, but in my case it was rarely more than a few pounds. I think £20 was the most I ever received, though some of the really big names we knew were receiving considerably larger amounts to appear in tournaments. They called this practice 'shamateurism' and it was not long before the tennis authorities were forced to accept modern reality and usher in the professional era.

One of my contemporaries, the Welshman Mike Davies, one of our best-ever Davis Cup players, once slept under a hedge travelling to a tournament because he couldn't afford even to stay in a cheap bed and breakfast. Today, players have a whole team around them: one to arrange their sponsorship and promotion deals and manage their share portfolios; one to give them psychological counselling; one to work on their biomechanics; one to rub their feet, and so on. I'm not saying the game was any better or worse back then, but simply pointing out the enormous changes that have swept through it in the Open era. The only thing I would say is that the players today seem to have far less fun than we did. We all travelled around together, went out in the evenings together, and those of us with cars would try to give lifts to others. Some of our best friends are people we knew from our playing days. Today, the players rarely socialise with each other. They finish their match, have a massage with their physical trainer and disappear back to their hotels. You won't very often find them in the bar enjoying a couple of beers after the match.

However, there is one tournament, in Monte Carlo, where that feeling of camaraderie and fun does still exist – even if it is on a lesser scale than when Jill and I were playing. The tournament, at which I have refereed for many years, going back to the 1980s, is in the Masters series and is staged in one of the most beautiful clubs in the world, built on a hill overlooking the bay.

Years ago, dating back to the 1920s, every spring

tournaments were run in various towns along the coast of the South of France, and when Jill and I were newly married we played in these for a few years. We were put up at various hotels that gave a few rooms for the use of the tournament, and the tournaments gave us about 10 francs for an evening meal. On one trip we stayed at a hotel on the apex of two roads, with a railway line down one side. Added to this there were roadworks with arc lights and pneumatic drills going all night. The floor of the room was reminiscent of a golf club cloakroom that had been walked on by many spiked shoes. Bare feet were out of the question, as was sleep. A lady called Mrs Butler gave afternoon tea to the competitors of one particular tournament, and as we were thanking her daughter and telling her about the hotel, she started to laugh and suggested we came to stay with her for a couple of nights' proper sleep. Very gratefully we accepted. This left our room free, so Roger Taylor (then one of our promising young players) who was sharing a tent with a very tall Australian player, Barry Geraghty, moved into our hotel room. Grim as it was, it was still one up from their tent.

The culmination of these small tournaments was at the Monte Carlo Country Club. For some of the players it was their first tournament in Europe, and it always had a strong entry. The lady who had rescued us that year was Gloria Butler, and her father had built the club. He had seen Suzanne Lenglen practising on a court over a garage somewhere and decided she should have something much better. His main interest at that time was to have a doubles championship, with the partners being from the same country, as he knew that the Davis Cup could turn on the doubles result. This he called the Butler Cup, and it was a great success. When the Second

World War broke out, however, the tournament ceased and Mrs Butler and Gloria went back to the United States, where Gloria played her tennis.

They returned after the war to find the club in such a terrible state that the Casino wanted to tear it down and build apartments. Mrs Butler and Gloria tried to persuade them not to, and eventually promised to pay half the costs of getting the tournament started again. They succeeded, and it is worth remembering that this wonderful and popular tournament would not exist but for those two strong-minded ladies, their love for the game and their incredible generosity.

I played with Bobby Wilson one year and actually managed to win the Butler Cup by benefiting from a stroke of good fortune in the quarter-finals. We were up against a Spanish pair who held a match point in the fourth set. Bobby played an acute-angled volley, and as one of our opponents rushed for the ball he tripped and clattered into the umpire's chair, cutting his head. There were no trainers in those days, so he had to be carried off, and we went through into the semi-finals where we beat Merlo and Pietrangeli and then Jovanovic and Pilic in the final.

One of the highlights of the tournament was the incredible cabaret that Gloria organised – a tradition that still exists to this day. An Australian player, Alan Kendall, nephew of Jack Crawford, always played in the tournament. Alan's, 'day job' was as a TV producer and he helped to organise the sketches and musical numbers. The Casino loaned a lot of the costumes and others were made – no expense was spared. It was a very splendid affair. Even Barelli, the famous conductor, gave his services for the show, as did the famous ballerina Rosella Hightower, who had a ballet school in

Cannes, and offered to send someone to help train the players.

Everyone was very fond of Gloria, and entered into the spirit of the event. Jenny and Lew Hoad, Ken Fletcher, Virginia Wade and John Newcombe all took part. Fred Stolle mimed as Shirley Temple, Roger Taylor took on the part of Marlene Dietrich and Nicola Pietrangeli performed in many difference guises. Going back further, Gardnar Mulloy, Hugh Stewart and Art (Tappy) Larsson all contributed. One year even Althea Gibson sang. I should add that Jill and I only ever helped behind the scenes! As I said, this cabaret continues to this day with Jonas Bjorkman, Todd Woodbridge, Gustavo Kuerten, Max Mirnyi and many other leading players starring. With all the pressures that come with tennis today I suspect the Monte Carlo entertainment is a welcome throwback for many of the players to a time when there was without doubt more fun on the circuit. I don't think, however, that it has quite the same budget as it used to.

The same can't be said, however, for the prize money that is in the game today. In 1984 the winner of the men's singles title at Wimbledon received £100,000 and the winner of the women's £90,000. If you were a second-round loser in the men's, you received a cheque for £2,200 –£200 more than Rod Laver was handed for winning the first Championships in the professional era back in 1968 and three times more than Billy Jean King received for winning the women's. The sums involved today are mind-boggling. In 2004 Roger Federer won £602,500 for landing the title, as Wimbledon paid out a total of almost £10 million in prize money. The organisers of the US Open, who always wait until Wimbledon have announced their prize money for the year so that they can trump it, are the first tournament to award seven-figure sums (albeit in US dollars) to the winners of their singles competitions.

To Fred Perry and Kitty Godfree and all the other champions who returned to the club that year, modern tennis must have seemed a very strange world indeed. One thing they could not bemoan, however, was the quality of the tennis, and once again it was McEnroe and Navratilova producing the magic, as well as some spectacular showdowns in the post-match press conferences. McEnroe was on reasonably good behaviour that year and I cannot recall even once having to go on court to confront him. By the start of the second week, the press were even talking about 'the conversion of St John' and I suspect that his good behaviour had everything to do with his superb form at the time.

The defence of his title had not started all that promisingly, however, and before he had even hit a ball in anger, he had the Wimbledon hierarchy muttering 'Good Lord!' into their gin and tonics. As he headed out from behind the screen on to Centre Court for his first-round match against Paul McNamee, under the gaze of his great fan Princess Diana as well as the Duke and Duchess of Kent, my eyes nearly popped out of their sockets when I saw that the champion was sporting a pair of blue shorts. Blue shorts, or any item of coloured clothing for that matter, tend to have roughly the same effect on the All England club as a streaker might have at a vicar's tea party. Wimbledon simply does not do coloured clothing.

Personally, I would be very upset the day they ever get rid of the white-clothing rule. It's part of Wimbledon's unique appeal. Not everybody would agree with me, least of all the giant clothes manufacturers who have been hammering on Wimbledon's gates for years to change the rule so that they can use the Championships to promote their latest ranges. (They simply cannot market white.) I don't like the idea of traditions being sacrificed for commercial interests and I also think there is something aesthetically pleasing about the white of the clothes against the green of the grass and the surrounding walls. Most people, including the majority of the players, still support the rule which was recently modified from 'predominantly white' to 'almost entirely white' because the big manufacturers argued that 'predominantly' meant 51 per cent and thus allowed their players to wear either coloured shorts or a shirt. The rule is one of my biggest headaches as the manufacturers are always trying to stretch it to the limit and we have to be constantly vigilant throughout the Championships.

McEnroe, I think, was just trying it on on this particular occasion, and when the Master of Ceremonies, who leads the players out from the locker-room, ran after him to point out his error, he smiled and quickly ran back off to change. It could have been a genuine mistake on McEnroe's part, as the players are allowed to wear what they want on the practice courts when they loosen up before a match. But I doubt it – I think it was just a good-natured tease.

The one match in which we were expecting some serious trouble was McEnroe's fourth-round clash with fellow American Bill Scanlon, a tough-talking, intimidating Texan. The bad blood between the two players had increased at the US Open the year before when Scanlon had beaten his younger opponent in a stormy encounter. Before their meeting at Wimbledon, neither player exactly went out of

their way to put an end to the hostilities. McEnroe reportedly said: 'Bill Scanlon is someone who is like a friend on
the outside, but stabs you in the back.' According to the
papers, Scanlon said: 'Let's just say we haven't been out to
dinner since we have been in London.' We decided to put
Georgina Clark in the chair – she was a mother of five with
plenty of experience of dealing with childish behaviour and
she once gave McEnroe an impressive dressing-down for
swearing at the Queen's tournament. We were all a little
nervous when the match got underway, but in the event it
was an embarrassingly one-sided affair as the champion blew
Scanlon off court with a 6–3, 6–3, 6–1 victory. The press
were clearly disappointed that the match failed to live up to
its sensational billing, and one journalist commented that it
was 'a bit like having a ticket for the Rolling Stones and
finding Val Doonican topping the bill'.

Pat Cash, the youngest Wimbledon semi-finalist since
McEnroe in 1977, talked a good game before their meeting,
saying that the last time he had played the American (in a
doubles match) he had served 'like a little girl'. I don't know
whether the comment fired up McEnroe even more, but Cash
probably regretted the slight after the New Yorker made him
look like the little girl's rag-doll by the end of the semi-final
with another magisterial three-set victory.

McEnroe dropped just one set on his way to landing his
third title, and his destruction of Jimmy Connors in the final
(6–1, 6–1, 6–2) was truly breathtaking to behold. My heart
on this occasion went out to Connors after he was pulverised
by his great rival and fellow American. Ten years earlier,
Connors himself had given the old-timer Ken Rosewall an
equally severe mauling in one of the least popular results in

Wimbledon history. The tennis gods had now taken their revenge. Poor Ken was runner-up at Wimbledon four times, but never got his hands on the famous trophy. He reached his first final as a youngster back in 1954, losing to the veteran Czech Jaroslav Drobny, but everyone said 'Don't worry Ken, it'll be your turn soon.' Sadly, it was never to be, and his demolition by the bullish young Connors at the end of his career was a sad spectacle.

At the end of the McEnroe–Connors match, I headed straight to the loser, who was slumped in his chair with a towel over his head, mortified by his humiliation. I spent what felt like an eternity trying to offer him some consoling words, but there was nothing but silence coming from beneath the towel. This proud street-fighter of a player was as devastated as I have seen anyone at the end of a tennis match. McEnroe's performance was the greatest individual display of tennis I have ever witnessed, and after finally giving up my efforts to lift Connors from his gloom I approached McEnroe to congratulate him. I said: 'John, that was as fine a display of tennis as I have ever seen. It was wonderful. I counted that you made just four unforced errors in the entire match.' McEnroe fixed me with an intent stare, and cocking his head to one side, replied: 'Four? I made it two unforced errors and two bad bounces.'

It was a truly awesome performance, and no matter what you thought of the man and his occasionally wild behaviour you had to concede that he was one of the finest players ever to pick up a racket. I would still hold that Australia's Rod Laver was the best all-round player in the history of the game because he is the only player to have twice won all four Grand Slam tournaments in the same year. But McEnroe, who never won the Australian Open or the French – throwing it away spectacularly against Lendl in the final a month earlier – is certainly up there amongst the very greatest. The late Arthur Ashe, the former Wimbledon champion and US Davis Cup captain, put it rather well: 'McEnroe doesn't bludgeon you, he doesn't use the sabre or foil or even the rapier – he just pulls a delicate little stiletto from his sock and you don't feel much, but pretty soon there's a helluva lot of blood on your side of the court.'

Martina Navratilova was equally dominant in the women's tournament, and once again she did not drop a set on the way to yet another title. Martina had won 211 out of 216 matches over a 2½-year period heading into the Championships and, outstanding though her tennis undoubtedly was, her clear superiority was in danger of making women's tennis a bit boring. Not even the great Chris Evert, the losing finalist that year, was able to put up a decent fight against Martina in her prime. It cannot be good for any sport if you are almost 100 per cent sure who the winner will be at the end of it all. Sport thrives on uncertainty, upsets and underdogs overcoming the odds, but when Martina was at her peak, and a very high and long peak it was too, the rest might just as well have not bothered turning up. Disturbingly for her rivals, if you could call them that, Martina always seemed to have plenty left in reserve while her opponents were killing themselves just to avoid being whitewashed. There was, however, a very bright ray of hope on the horizon. Her name was Steffi Graf, and though she only reached the last 16, where she was beaten by Britain's Jo Durie, you could tell she was going to be something a bit special. She oozed talent and hit the ball so hard.

Martina's biggest struggle that year – and in many others besides – was with the press, who had developed an ugly obsession with her private life. I always felt very angry when I attended press conferences during which newshounds bombarded Martina and the other the top players with personal questions. It is a peculiarly British phenomenon, and you rarely come across it elsewhere in the world, unless the interviewee happens to be someone like Anna Kournikova or Maria Sharapova. It was particularly bad that year and the papers were full of sensationalist nonsense about Martina. She was deeply upset by the intensity and relentlessness of the press intrusion, and it is a testament to her composure and powers of concentration that she did not let it put her off her game. I often wonder what it must be like to wake up in the morning, pull back your curtains and see dozens of photographers crawling around in bushes and climbing up trees. It must be dreadful. I had nothing but the greatest sympathy for her when she lost her cool at one meeting with journalists and threatened silence for the rest of the tournament.

McEnroe was experiencing similar problems, and at one particularly tense question-and-answer session I feared that a fight might break out. Earlier in the week he had refused to do interviews if there were television cameras present, complaining that the production teams edited their films in such a way as to make him look stupid. Like Martina, he became increasingly fed up with the questions about his private life and he too threatened to cut off all contact with the media. At the start of one press conference he said he would only cooperate if he was asked about tennis matters and that as soon as someone asked him something personal he would simply get up and walk out. About a minute or so into the conference, some blockhead sparked an uproar when he ignored McEnroe's request for respect and raised a question about his love life. McEnroe got to his feet, a sneer half-way up his cheek, and for a moment it looked as if he was about to leap into the throng and give this man a good thrashing. In the event, he didn't need to because the other reporters jumped on the man and, after a bit of a dust-up, shoved him unceremoniously out into the corridor. I have to say it was an excellent moment, not least because it showed that the tennis boys in the press weren't going to put up with the newshounds causing trouble on their patch. After all, it is not in their interests to have poor relations with the leading players, and I think McEnroe was quite impressed to see them put their house in order in such an emphatic way. It also showed McEnroe that, like him, most people in the room just wanted to talk about tennis.

I thought Wimbledon's reaction to the press issue that year was admirable: it threw its authority right behind the players. When the harassment of Navratilova and McEnroe reached a critical point, the club issued a statement saying it was 'seriously disturbed' by the instrusions and threatened to ban some reporters if they persisted in their mudraking. The club also said players would be fully entitled to walk out of a press conference if they felt unhappy about the line of questioning. At the end of the men's final, the press were up in arms because Connors, still burning with shame, just packed his bags and fled the grounds as fast as he could without giving the customary conference. Again, the club stuck up for the player, saying that losers should have the right to choose if they want to face the press or not. That became official Wimbledon policy for a long time, but now all the players are contractually obliged to appear, win or lose, and they get heavily fined if they fail to show. (Lleyton Hewitt has recently been involved in a bitter legal battle with the ATP authorities after they fined him for non-appearance.)

The media is certainly a different kind of beast now than in my days as a player. Then just a handful of reporters followed the circuit and you would have the odd word with them in the corridor or wherever you might bump into them around the tournament. They were chiefly interested in what you did on the court rather than what you had to say afterwards, and they certainly would not have had the temerity to ask you about your romantic life. The relationship between the two groups was extremely good and many of the reporters became good friends. The vast majority of today's tennis correspondents are a pretty decent bunch – and there are some extremely good writers among them – but their relationship with the players is still suffering to some extent from the breakdown in trust caused by their less scrupulous colleagues on the news pages who have no long-term interest in building up strong ties with the men and women on the circuit.

To some extent you could argue that the intrusion goes with the territory, that it's just part and parcel of the glamour of a being a celebrity tennis players. Perhaps it is just a small hardship for a multi-millionaire to bear, but most of the players didn't set out in their careers with the aim of becoming celebrities, they set out to become great tennis players.

By and large I have enjoyed a fairly amicable relationship

with the press down the years, but there was one incident where I managed to upset the entire British tennis pack at a stroke. In recent years there have been just two possible stories for the beleaguered British tennis journalist: Tim Henman or Greg Rusedski. There is of course also that hardy annual, 'the demise of British tennis' story, but their staple weekly diet, the bread and butter of their work, is provided by the country's only two world-class players. You have to wonder what the journalists will do for a living, outside of the Wimbledon fortnight, when the pair finally decide to call it a day. There is simply no one about to break through to the top ranks who would justify the expense of sending a reporter around the world to cover them. That said, with the emergence of Andrew Murray, who won the 2004 US Open junior title, and Miles Kasiri, who reached the final of the Wimbledon junior event in the same year, there is hope on the horizon for both the press and the public. These two have a great future, I think, if they continue to build on their recent results.

In 2001 Henman was knocked out of the Rome Masters early in the competition and decided to head straight to Hamburg to prepare for the tournament there the following week. One of the biggest logistical problems as referee is trying to find top players willing to play early on the first day of a tournament. Most of the players only arrive at a tournament a day or so before it starts – the finalists of the event just finished often don't make it until the new event is already underway – and they like to delay their opening match as long as possible to give themselves the maximum amount of time to rest and prepare themselves for the week ahead. You would be amazed by the number of players who call me up over the weekend before a tournament, including the Championships, to report that they are suffering from a non-specific niggling injury and would be *so* grateful if I could put their first-round match on as late as possible. Greg Rusedski and I often joke about the times he would like a late start. It is a bit of a problem because the event organisers and the television companies understandably want to start the tournament with a big bang to drum up public interest.

Knowing that Tim had enjoyed virtually a whole week off, I asked him if he would be happy to play the first match in Hamburg at 12 noon on the Monday. He agreed readily, and I thought that this would go down superbly with the British press because it gave them plenty of time to write their stories and make their deadlines. But what I didn't know was that on the Sunday evening the entire British tennis press corps were still in Rome after attending a big post-tournament party. When they discovered that Tim was due on court at noon on Monday several of them telephoned me and went absolutely bananas: 'How could you do that to us, you knew we weren't coming till tomorrow . . .' One of them told me that I would have to change the order of play because there was no way they could get to Hamburg on time. Images of tails wagging dogs sprang to mind, but I held my peace and reminded the callers that there was simply no chance of revising the schedule. Once the order of play has been issued, that's it. It is irrevocable.

In the end the journalists were forced to hitch a lift on a private plane which a television company had hired. Although it arrived very early on Monday morning it was unable to land at Hamburg, owing to some poor weather,

I haven't changed a bit! Me, aged 10.

JOHN WARBURTON

Jill displaying a fine forehand and an interesting line in sportswear.

A. R. MILLS.

The young hopeful, thrilled to be featured on an official Wimbledon postcard.

MICHAEL COLE

Poised to strike, eyes firmly on the ball. I hope both members of the crowd were appreciating my style.

The happiest day of my life.

The Davis Cup team at Vienna airport. L-R Fred Perry, George Worthington, Mike Sangster, John Barrett, me, Billy Knight and Tony Pickard.

Jill, me and Barry with Ham Richardson and his wife on our first weekend at Treasure Cay in the Bahamas. We had a wonderful six months there.

'Womble' and I work on the order of play.

1987 brought another new team member – Penny, me and a lot of famous names.

I've been privileged throughout my time as Wimbledon referee to witness and take part in some truly memorable moments.

TOPFOTO.CO.UK

I don't think John is very happy with the umpire's decision. Ken Farrar and I try to sort things out. John certainly gave me a few anxious moments, but I respected him and we became friends.

1988: A young Steffi Graf wins her first title and ends Martina's six-year reign.

GETTY IMAGES

GETTY IMAGES

EMPICS

1995: What a year. Almost unbelievably Tim became the first player to be disqualified after smashing a ball in frustration and accidentally hitting this ball-girl . . . and then there was Jeff Tarango, about to default himself by walking off court.

MIRRORPIX

1996: Cliff and his backing group brought some cheer to a rain-soaked Centre Court.

1998: Tears of joy this time for Jana, after being runner-up twice previously.

Below Nelson Mandela, without doubt top of the list of amazing people I have been lucky enough to meet.

Below right Henman Hill: The excitement that Tim has generated has been wonderful for the Championships and his Wimbledon record is quite exceptional.

EMPICS

EMPICS

2004: Centre Court in the twenty-first century – amidst all the excitement, Maria tries to call her mother to share the moment with her.

PA

Outside the Palace, Barry, Jill and Penny share my proud moment.

and was forced to divert to Hanover, over 100 miles away. From there the journalists had to race down the autobahn to get to Hamburg on time, and when they finally jogged bleary-eyed into the press centre I have to confess that I have seen a happier-looking group of people in a dentist's waiting-room. These were distinctly unhappy campers and the awful thing was that I thought I had been doing them a great favour.

I also found myself under the cosh from the press at Wimbledon in 1984 following a highly controversial incident involving Ivan Lendl. The world No. 1, who had just won the French Open, had descended into one of his darker moods long before he even set foot on court for his quarter-final match against fellow Czech Tomas Smid. With Connors and McEnroe also playing in the last eight I had put Lendl's match on Court 2, and he was singularly unhappy about it. The top players always make a fuss if I don't put them on one of the show courts as they feel it is a slight, but there is never anything personal about it. They are not being victimised. It's just a matter of logistics and trying to rotate them as best as I can under the constraints of the schedule. All the top players have had to play on the outside courts at some point, but every time I pencil one of them in for a match on Court 2, or any of the other outer courts, I sit back and wait for the phone to ring or for the rap of knuckles on my door.

Lendl actually won his match with great ease, but his conduct on court was pretty abominable, and at one point he smashed a ball and hit Smid in the back. The biggest controversy came after a lineswoman made a call against Lendl who promptly went berserk. He called her 'blind and deaf', had me brought out to court and demanded that the chair umpire Les Maddock be replaced. It was certainly not Ivan's finest hour at Wimbledon, but I am powerless to act in these situations because the nub of the controversy was a point of fact, not a point of law. I *could* have replaced the chair umpire or lineswoman, but that would have been a gross overreaction and I never considered it for a moment. At his press conference after the match, Lendl tore into the Wimbledon administration, accusing it of favouritism and moaning that McEnroe had not had to play on Court 2 for two years and that Connors had not once been exiled to the outside courts in this year's Championships. Connors, who liked to rile Lendl apparently by calling him a 'chicken', a 'quitter' and a 'commie', spiced up his upcoming semi-final against him with the tart remark: 'Tell him from me that if he ever wins the tournament then he will have earned the right to complain about what court he plays on.' Ouch!

I knew that it would cause a commotion, but after careful consideration of the umpire's report setting out all the extenuating circumstances, I decided that the warning that Lendl had been given during the match was sufficient punishment and I wouldn't fine him. I thought that on balance that was the fairest response, but once some of the press had called for Lendl to be kicked out of the tournament, I suppose it was only inevitable that they would then turn on me because it would have looked to the outside world as if they had overreacted. Some very unflattering headlines appeared in the newspapers and one journalist wrote of my decision to await the umpire's report – a standard procedure in these matters – that it was the equivalent of a 'judge asking the clerk of court's permission to sentence a man for murder'. I felt that that too was something of an overreaction.

The incident led to a glut of stories about the role of referees, umpires and supervisors in modern tennis. It had been a fairly quiet Wimbledon in terms of player tantrums and you had the feeling that the press, especially the tabloid journalists, were itching to stir up some kind of controversy to keep them busy and their readers interested. Unnamed officials were quoted in the papers saying that nowadays they were terrified not so much of the players but of upsetting the organisers. A referee who disqualifies a player from a tournament was unlikely to be invited back, or might struggle to find work elsewhere, the theory went. Captain Mike Gibson, Fred Hoyles' predecessor at Wimbledon, was quoted as saying that the time he had disqualified Ilie Nastase at Bournemouth in 1975 was 'the beginning of the end' for him. Another umpire, anonymous of course (and I wonder whether he actually existed), was reported to have said that leaving the matter to the referees themselves to sort out was the equivalent of a corrupt police force mounting an investigation into its own activities. The implication behind these stories was that I had been under pressure from higher authorities not to expel players and that we were putting weak umpires in charge of tough matches, effectively giving the green light to the troublemakers to do as they pleased. The Lendl incident was presented as proof of this theory.

I knew that my decision not to fine Lendl would ruffle a few feathers, but I have to confess that I was quite taken aback by the vehemence of the criticism that followed and by the almost laughable murkiness of the conspiracy theories. If only my life was that exciting! The truth was far more prosaic.

After receiving the umpire's report, I simply felt that it would have been unfair to punish him further. I do not base my decisions on press reports.

Whenever there is a controversial incident at Wimbledon, the local postmen must groan at the prospect of hauling the sacks of correspondence into our office in the days that follow. In 1984 it was no different and predictably the Lendl incident led to a flood of angry letters from the public. Our postman's lumbago was not helped by a story in one of the national newspapers – it might even have been a letter to *The Times* – in which the headteachers of the local schools supplying our team of ball-boys and ball-girls complained about the disgusting behaviour of the modern tennis player. The players, they said, were setting an appalling example not just to their pupils but to children in general. The teachers were especially upset about the modern practice of spitting on court and I have to say I was in complete agreement with them. I find it disgusting, but most of the players seem to do it these days, even the impeccably mannered Tim Henman. (Our postbag becomes especially heavy whenever the camera catches Tim in the act of clearing his airways.)

Most people object just to the *sight* of spitting, and we have received a number of letters calling for Wimbledon to give the players on-court spittoons. One letter I received recently said: 'Dear Mr Mills, Why don't you give these bloody animals handkerchiefs? Yours disgusted, etc.' But there is a real health issue involved too because the ball-boys and ball-girls have to put their hands on the ground where the players might have spat and they must pick up balls that may have rolled through the phlegm. Unfortunately, there is nothing in the rules about spitting, so the best we have been able to do is to appeal to conscience of the players by putting up signs in the locker-room.

I am no longer amazed at or put out by the amount of letters of complaint I receive during the Wimbledon fortnight, but it did take me some time to work out why most of it seemed to come directly to me and not to the club's higher authorities. I seem to appear on television more frequently than some of the other members of the committee. A great deal of the letters are from fans of Greg Rusedski who complain that I show favouritism to Tim Henman and always give him a nice draw and the best courts, and that Greg is always in the tougher half of the draw, and so on. Others concern themselves with the alleged bias of the umpires – particularly in relation to overrules – but there is also plenty of what you might call 'eccentric' correspondence. Last year I received one such letter which went like this:

'Dear Mr Mills, Why is it that every time I turn on my television, all I get is tennis, tennis, tennis and more tennis. I hate tennis. I demand that you refund me part of my television licence. Yours, I.M. Loonie, etc.'

Most correspondents get a standard reply, but many are answered personally. Probably the biggest pile of mail we received came in 2003 after Rusedski turned the air blue in his match against Andy Roddick. The match was always going to be about the big serves, and the American had won the first two sets on tiebreaks, but Rusedski was leading 5–2 in the third. Roddick was serving, when a man in the crowd called 'out' to one of his shots. Greg hesitated for a moment but carried on with the rally, which Roddick duly won. When the umpire then applied the rules of the game quite correctly and refused to replay the point, Greg let his feelings become all to clear. It was a strange point for Greg to get so upset about as it was on Roddick's service game and he had his own serve next at 5–3, but the whole incident clearly upset him and he went on to lose the set 5–7, and the match. When we are forced to fine a player, we now have a fairly scientific system in place. The supervisors and assistant referees look at the levels of fines for similar offences on the circuit that year and then we set the punishment accordingly. Rusedski was fined £1,500 because that, so to speak, was the going rate. To have fined him any more or less would have been inconsistent and unfair. That, however, was not how many members of the public saw it and we were swamped with complaints saying we were too lenient.

The tone of these letters generally hovers somewhere between politely indignant to outraged and appalled, via frosty and 'I'm a bit jolly cross actually'. Only once have I received a letter that worried me. It was from a man in Kent, who complained that I did not put Goran Ivanisevic on Centre Court enough. This is pretty standard stuff and I gave it little thought until a second letter arrived threatening to do me some damage unless I obliged the correspondent by seeing that Goran was the given the court he deserved. The stupid thing was that the letter was signed and gave an address at the top, as if he was writing to complain about his water bill. I handed the letter over to the police, but when they got back to me later in the day, they said he was just a harmless nutcase and that I should not take his threat seriously. I should add, in case I give the wrong impression, that we do also get plenty of favourable correspondence as well.

The main demands of my job as a referee at Wimbledon and elsewhere have changed constantly down the years, but for a number of reasons I would say that I have found them easier to cope with year on year. This is partly because I am more experienced and I am less likely to be thrown by a situation. It is also because the quality of officiating has improved dramatically, while the computerisation of the order of play has long since become a help rather than a hindrance. In 2000 we moved out of our cramped little office in Wimbledon into magnificent new premises, at the back of the Centre Court overlooking the back courts and the new Court 1. It has felt like the equivalent of swapping a bedsit for a luxury pent-house, and we can now get on with the challenges of the fort-night in relative comfort. If only the wretched rain could be equally accommodating, then the conditions of my job would be just about perfect.

The most significant development in recent years, from my point of view, has been a general improvement in the behaviour of the players. Fuses are still blown and tantrums thrown, but nothing like on the scale of the eighties. (That said, the most traumatic and spectacular player blow-out we have had at Wimbledon actually occurred in 1995, but I'll hold fire on that for the time being.) But it is important to remember that the majority of the top players even back in the eighties were generally fairly well-behaved, and the Swedes, especially Stefan Edberg and Mats Wilander, wouldn't even have caused a stir in a debating chamber. But the pattern established and example set by the likes of McEnroe, Connors and Lendl – men who could start a fight in an empty room – had effectively torn up tennis's book of etiquette and given the green light to the younger players emerging in the game to start throwing their rackets around when the mood took them. In any competitive match, a player will experience an often overwhelming sense of frustration, especially if he is losing. Whereas once it was considered the height of bad form to misbehave on court, players now seemed happy to let rip, feeling vindicated by the precedents established by the great players of the day.

At the end of 1984 I experienced one of the most trying episodes in my entire career, and by the time I flew back to England James Scott Connors wasn't in my good books. It was the weekend before Christmas and the eyes of the tennis world were trained on the Scandinavium Stadium in Gothenburg for the Davis Cup final between Sweden and the United States, the two undisputed superpowers of tennis at the time. One of the criticisms often levelled at Connors was that he never played Davis Cup because he was too interested in his own career to commit himself to the national cause. Statistics show that his appearances for the national team were very limited (he played just three years in a career spanning 20).

By 1984 Connors was 32, and he knew that the best of his career was already behind him – his battering by McEnroe in the Wimbledon final that year was proof of that. He had won just about everything in the game: five US Open titles, two Wimbledon and one Australian. He had been world No. 1 from 1974 to 1978 and he won a record 109 titles in total by the end of his career, amassing nearly $10 million in prize money alone by the time he finally called it a day. Apart from the French Open, the only other honour missing from his collection was a Davis Cup winner's medal. The American public and media put great pressure on him to play because they wanted to see what they called the 'dream team' of Connors and McEnroe in the singles, with McEnroe and Fleming in the doubles. McEnroe was a terrific supporter of the Davis Cup and always gave his all for the national team. He later became Davis Cup captain himself and remains fiercely critical of 'unpatriotic' players who do not drop all else to try to get into the team.

Perhaps mindful that this would probably be his last chance of Davis Cup glory, Connors agreed to play. I was the referee for the match, which was being played on an indoor clay court, and when Connors arrived I could sense that he was even more stressed and agitated than normal. As a player, he carried an air of exasperation and intolerance about him at the best of times, like a gunslinger swinging open the doors of a Wild West saloon bar after a very long and dusty ride. One false move and he would draw. On this occasion, his pistols were already out of their holsters.

The US captain, Arthur Ashe, had scheduled Connors to play in the opening singles match against Mats Wilander. The wiry, laid-back Swede was one of the best players in the world, and although he never came close to mastering the grass at Wimbledon he was a maestro on clay. (He won the French Open three times and lost in two other finals.) Although Connors had won the US Open on clay back in 1976 (he is the only player to have won the tournament on three different surfaces: grass, clay and hard), the dusty orange stuff was not his preferred surface. He didn't mind it, but it was the hard, fast surfaces and the grass he loved.

Before the match got underway I told the British chair umpire George Grime to be as diplomatic and non-confrontational with Connors as the application of the laws of the game made possible. But it didn't take long before the arena echoed to the sound of one of the most spectacular tantrums I have ever witnessed outside of a wrestling hall or a day nursery. A baseline decision had gone against Connors and he went quite mad enough there and then, but when the Swedish captain walked on court to inspect the spot where the ball landed and then trod on it by mistake, the American went absolutely wild. (Of course this couldn't happen now as the rules have changed to state that the captain cannot walk on to the court.) He screamed at the umpire; he screamed at me; he screamed at the Swedish captain. He was given a warning, then a penalty point, then a game penalty, but he still continued to rant and rave. Arthur Ashe was convinced it was just a matter of time before I threw the book at his player. During one change of ends Ashe came up to me and said: 'Alan, if you are going to default him, tell me first and I'll pull him out of the match so that the disqualification doesn't go down in the record books.' I had a certain amount of sympathy with Connors, not just because he had a lot on his mind at that time, with a baby due at any moment, but also because I could see why he thought the Swedish captain might have deliberately obliterated the mark where the ball had bounced. I bent over backwards to be fair and reasonable to him in spite of the abuse he threw at me and at the umpire. Connors lost the match and it was a heavy defeat, 6–1, 6–3, 6–3, which didn't much help his mood. You might have thought he had run out of anger and swearwords by this point, but we soon found out that he wasn't going to let this one rest and he gave us both barrels again shortly afterwards. His four-letter outburst presented me with a second opportunity to default him from the rest of the tie, and I was under enormous pressure to do so, not least from the press.

I returned to my hotel that night and agonised about what I should do. After much soul-searching I decided that I would fine him the maximum amount allowable under the rules and tell him that if he were to step out of line again, then he would be in very serious trouble. Exhausted after one of the most stressful days in my short career as a referee, I descended into a deep sleep only to be woken up by the sound of the telephone in the small hours of the morning. The caller was a Swedish man, but he declined to give his name before pleading with me not to default Connors, insisting that his country wanted to beat a full-strength US team. I told him that my mind was already made up and that he would learn of my decision in the morning. I put down the receiver. I still have no idea of the identity of the caller. I suppose it could have been one of the Swedish team, or even a local who the Americans put up to it, or it could just have been a member of the public who happened to find out where I was staying. It remains a mystery.

The following day Sweden took an unassailable 3–0 lead in the five-match tie after Stefan Edberg and Anders Jarryd beat John McEnroe and Peter Fleming in the doubles. Being no longer of any use to the cause, Connors flew out of Gothenburg, and I breathed a very deep sigh of relief.

Those leading American players certainly made sure that I worked hard for my money during the eighties. On one extraordinary occasion in Key Biscayne in 1986 I had to be given a police escort back to my office after a riot broke out at the end of the match. Connors was playing his old adversary Lendl and the passing of time had definitely not mellowed the bitter hostility between the pair. As I've said, Connors used to delight in taunting Lendl, but it was the Czech who generally came out on top, winning 23 of their 36 encounters (although it should be pointed out that the American's best days were largely behind him by the time Lendl emerged as a major force). There was one line umpire on court that day to whom Connors took great exception, claiming that the same person had made bad calls against him in the past. It was right at the end of a topsy-turvy match and the score was 5–2 to Lendl in the fifth set when the official in question made a line-call against Connors (the other sets had gone 6–1 to Connors, 1–6, 2–6, 6–2). Connors marched over to the chair umpire and said he wanted the line umpire replaced. He then sat down and waited to be obliged. After a while Lendl too sat down, but he said nothing, knowing that he almost certainly had the game in the bag one way or another and was perfectly happy to let his rival stew in his discomfort.

I was the tournament referee, but at most non-Grand Slam events it is the supervisor who has the highest authority. As I arrived on court and walked past Connors, he turned to me and said: 'Ah, Alan, you know what I want don't you?'

I replied: 'Yes, I do and I'll tell you right now that you are not going to get it.' I talked the situation over with the supervisor Ken Farrar, but there was nothing really to discuss and he ordered the umpire to 'start the clock' at which point

Lendl rocketed out of his chair and back to his end of the court. Connors didn't move a muscle and after he was counted out for a fourth time the umpire announced over the public address system: 'Game, set and match to Mr Lendl.'

American crowds can be amongst the rowdiest in world tennis and they were even more so when Connors was playing. The atmosphere at his matches was often more like an English football game or a boxing contest, certainly nothing like the relatively sedate and civilised surroundings you find on the whole at Wimbledon. He was a hero to a particular breed of American male: the tough-talking blue-collar worker. Very often at tournaments in America, especially at the US Open, his match would be put on last in the day so that people could finish work, sink a few beers and then yell him to victory. Until Connors appeared on court it was not uncommon for the arena to be more than half-empty. It was not tennis they wanted to see, it was 'Jimbo'. He was a one-man entertainment show and always gave good value for money.

When Connors packed up his bag and walked off court in Key Biscayne he received a rapturous ovation from his fans, even though he had failed to complete the match they had paid good money to see. I couldn't understand that. If Connors had done that at Wimbledon, he would have been booed all the way back to his hotel room and down to the breakfast room the following morning. Lendl then packed his bags and was given a polite round of applause as he left the court. The supervisor too had left by then – perhaps he was a bit sharper than me and knew what might be coming. I'd never seen a riot at a tennis match and so I was completely unprepared for what happened next. As I waited for the umpire to get down from his chair I noticed that the mood amongst the crowd had changed very suddenly. One or two objects started flying through the air and the jeering became louder and more hostile by the second. The situation was escalating rapidly and I began to feel pretty alarmed by developments. The umpire and I were extremely vulnerable and even though it was mainly at him that their anger was directed, I could hardly desert him and run for it. I saw a policeman standing in the corner of the court and I quickly beckoned him over. 'I have a very ugly feeling about this crowd,' I said to him, and barely had the words left my mouth when a deluge of cushions cascaded down from the seats all around the arena. We needed no second invitation to leave and I confess that I was extremely happy to have a policeman at our side as we were quickly spirited away from the baying mob.

Oddly enough, the only other time I have felt the full force of a seat cushion to the back of the head was at Wimbledon, some time around the beginning of the 1980s, when I was assistant referee. Sue Barker, the darling of British tennis back then, was involved in a doubles match against an American pair on one of the show courts when I was forced to stop the match due to fading light. The crowd are never happy when you have to curtail proceedings for the day, and there was the usual grizzling and grumbling as I led the players away. I was almost off the court when a collective jeer went up, which was quickly followed by a barrage of cushions and other flying objects. I hurried off behind the screens, thinking, 'Wow, they really *do* love Sue Barker!' It was only much later that I discovered that it was not me that they had been targeting but one of the American women who, upset by the partisan support for Sue, had felt moved enough to give the crowd what we in the referee's office term 'a visible obscenity'.

Chapter Four

Thunder in the Air

Rain is the bane of my life at Wimbledon. I would rather spend a day sitting in my office being shouted at by McEnroe, Connors and Lendl all at once than try to solve the logistical conundrums presented by a backlog of matches. The fact that the weather is beyond my control makes it all the more frustrating. I can only sit there and stare out of my window at the gloom, and work out all the options for each hour of rain and pray for a miraculous clearing of the clouds over the 42 acres of the All England Club's grounds. My heart always goes out to the spectators who often travel long distances and spend a lot of money only to return home without seeing a ball struck.

I have a direct line to the experts at the Met Office and we have a special electronic signalling system by which I can communicate with the head groundsman and his staff. At the press of a button I can issue coded instructions which appear in little boxes placed in highly visible positions all around the courts: 1 means be ready; 2 means put the covers on; 3 is inflate the covers; 4 is deflate; 5 is uncover; and 6 is dress the courts (i.e. put the nets up). Getting the covers on quickly is absolutely essential as a delay of just two minutes means you could the lose the court for over an hour, even though all court covers are installed with fans to stop the condensation.

In 22 years as tournament referee at Wimbledon I think we have had just one wet court during the fortnight, and that was owing to exceptional circumstances. This is partly due to the excellence of the covers, but mainly because the ground staff at the All England club are outstanding. My relationship with the head groundsman is extremely important, and I am in constant contact with him over the walkie-talkie, especially if the weather is poor. I have been lucky to work with two of the best in the business: Jim Thorn and Eddie Seaward, the current incumbent. Both are real pros, although their personalities are completely different. Jim Thorn is a very colourful, friendly character with a great sense of humour and a feisty spirit, not bashful about upsetting someone if he feels he's been crossed. Eddie is a quieter character and completely meticulous in the execution of his duties. He's always in the right place at the right time and will take the initiative if I am tied up somewhere else in the grounds.

During the Wimbledon fortnight dozens of temporary ground staff, mostly students, are brought in to help, and teams of eight are assigned to each court. Watching the covers go on seems to take away a bit of the spectators' disappointment at losing play to rain because it is such a slick, well-choreographed manoeuvre. Sometimes one of the groundsmen will fall under the covers because they are running so fast, but the others just keep going because it is imperative they get the court covered. The spectators find it amusing when they see this hump moving around in the middle of the cover, but there was one incident which was not at all funny. A man had slipped under the covers as they raced to put them on and the crowd was beside itself with laughter until it dawned on them that he was not moving.

At first I too thought it was a joke, but after a few seconds I feared the worst and ordered the covers to be taken off immediately. The man was unconscious, having been hit on the head as he fell by the metal bar that runs along the length of the cover. His friends were going to move him to the side of the court so that they could re-cover, because it was now bucketing down, but I told them to leave him where he was in case he had a neck injury. The medics arrived and carried him away on a stretcher to rapturous applause, but he soon recovered and was back working within a couple of days.

I hadn't thought twice about ordering the covers off and I was a little surprised and not overly impressed when a committee member had a go at me about the incident later that night. He complained that my decision had meant we lost the court for the hour or so of play that remained that day and said that I should have sent people under the covers to drag the chap out. Some things were more important than tennis, I responded.

The year 1985 was one of the worst for rain. It was the wettest June for 14 years, the worst-affected start to the Championships since 1969, with the loss of a total of 27 hours of play in the first week alone. On the second day, Jim Thorn removed thousands of gallons from the practice courts, and one journalist likened my office to 'the operations room at the height of the Battle of Britain' after seeing us struggle to work out the right permutations in the order of play to clear the rapidly mounting backlog of matches. The second week was better, but the men's semi-finals were disrupted by a spectacular thunderstorm. Trees were split by lightning and flash-floods swept through the grounds as the storm drains were overwhelmed by the intensity of the deluge. I have never seen so much water at Wimbledon. The tunnel next to the Centre Court, behind the umpire's chair, was so deeply flooded that one of the photographers actually swam through it!

Rain is especially frustrating for the players. If the bad weather is well set in, they still have to hang around, some playing cards, some surfing the Net and some just resting for most of the day before I take the decision to abandon play. It is even worse if there are sporadic showers because they find themselves going on and off court all day, never able to find their rhythm, momentum or focus. The intermittent bursts of rain also leave the courts a little slippery, and many of the players are terrified, understandably, of turning an ankle or tearing a muscle. This was the situation on the first day when only one match out of the 67 scheduled was completed. There was no play on the outside courts all day, but at around 6 p.m. the weather had cleared sufficiently for us to start the matches on the show courts. McEnroe was playing the Aussie Paul McNamee on Centre Court, while Ivan Lendl was against the American Mel Purcell on Court 1. After about 15 minutes, McEnroe called me out to complain that the court was too slippery to play, and he already had his tracksuit on by the time I got there. After treading the surface myself I agreed with him and suspended the match.

Meanwhile, Lendl's match continued on Court 1, where for some curious reason the surface was nothing like as slippery as Centre Court. There was definitely some moisture on the court, but it was clearly playable. As I was standing in the corner, Lendl was obviously trying to indicate his unhappiness about having to play by theatrically knocking the grass off his shoes with his racket and sliding about like an ice-skater. All he had to do was ask me to stop the match, and I would probably have done so. As I watched him cruise to an easy three set win, I thought he would have been happy to get his match out of the way and enjoy a relaxing day or two as the other players hung around waiting for their games to be called.

When he discovered afterwards that McEnroe's match had been suspended, he hit the roof. I was sitting in my office, getting ready to close down for the day, when his agent came in and said: 'Mr Lendl would like to speak to you. He's in the locker-room.' I replied: 'Well my door's always open and I'd be happy for him to come and see me whenever he wants.' There was no way that I was going to down to the locker-room. It wouldn't do much for the authority I am meant to have if I jumped to my feet every time one of the players clicked his fingers. The agent soon returned and said: 'Mr Lendl would like to know the rules about suspending matches. He could have broken a leg. They are worth about 10 million dollars each. He is very unhappy.'

There is no *rule* about suspending matches, but the custom (which Ivan would have known full well) is for the player to tell the umpire that he thinks the court is unfit to play; the umpire calls the referee or the supervisor, who then makes a decision. The agent returned a third time. He said: 'Ivan wants to know why you didn't stop the match. Period.'

'I was never called by the umpire. I did park myself at the side of the court in anticipation of Ivan complaining, but Ivan said nothing,' I said. 'I was ready and waiting and I would never have let players continue if conditions were dangerous. I also have to think about the 10,000 or so spectators who had paid good money and in the end they actually got to see a game of tennis after sitting around all day under umbrellas.'

The agent did not come back again, but Lendl was not finished and laid into me at the subsequent press conference. I think it was all down to the fact that his great rival McEnroe had come off while he played on. His dark mood then, however, was as nothing compared to that into which he plunged after a similar incident on another occasion. In 1990 Wimbledon was on a high state of alert about possible terrorist acts. The day had been running pretty smoothly and I was sitting in my office when the phone rang at around 6 p.m. It was Chris Gorringe, the chief executive, and he asked me to make contact with the chair umpire on Centre Court as a matter of urgency and ask him to stop the match. 'Is this what I think it is?' I asked. 'I'm afraid so,' he said. I called the umpire, Bruno Rebeuh, who immediately requested the players – it was a men's doubles match – to sit down. The weather was fine and the crowd could not understand what was going on.

I raced down to the court as soon as possible, slowing to a walk as I made my entrance so as not to spread alarm. The crowd gave me a huge cheer as I came on because they thought I was about to order the resumption of play. When I asked the players to leave the court as promptly as possible, one of the two Americans, Ken Flach or Robert Seguso, said to me: 'We're not playing that badly are we?' I was tempted to laugh, but when I explained to them what was going on their jaws dropped and they quickly packed their bags and marched briskly off court with the boos of the crowd ringing in their ears.

After I had cleared the officials from the court, Chris Gorringe tried to make an announcement over the public address system but the crowd was in such uproar that nobody could hear a word he was saying. I was waving my arms and vainly trying to get the spectators to calm down when all of a sudden a piercing screech filled the air. It was one of the spectators and he hollered: 'FOR GOD'S SAKE SHUT UP AND LET'S LISTEN TO WHAT'S BEING SAID!!!' It was rather impressive. There was immediate silence and Chris was able to explain that there was a security incident and ask them to leave the court with orderly haste. This is a nightmare scenario for the security people, because if panic breaks out there could be a stampede and an ugly crush, but this crowd behaved with admirable calm and filed out peacefully to the main concourse. It took under four minutes to clear the entire Centre Court of around 13,000 spectators. While this was happening, the ground staff, who were having their tea, realised what was happening and came bounding in to cover their beloved court and protect it in the event of an explosion. I shooed them away, almost having to push them physically out of the court, and I was standing around watching the bomb squad dogs walking through the rows of seats when I suddenly thought, 'What the hell am I still doing here?', and beat my own retreat.

It turned out, thank heavens, to be a false alarm. Someone who had drunk a little too much Pimms had left their picnic basket under a seat and after failing to reappear, a neighbouring spectator grew anxious and contacted the police. The only explosion that day came from Lendl, who was absolutely furious that his match on the adjoining Court 1 was not also suspended. My daughter Penny was working in the office at the time – she and her brother Barry both worked at the Championships for about three or four years when they were students, and it was great having them around – and it fell to her to call the umpire Richard Kaufman, whom she had known from university days, and tell him that the police were happy for Lendl's match to continue.

Afterwards Lendl fumed at me: 'What if it was a bomb? We could have been killed or injured.' Poor old Ivan must have really thought I had it in for him. A couple of years previously he had thought I was trying to get his legs broken on a slippery court, and now he had got it into his head that he was not worth evacuating during a bomb threat. I explained to him that we had it on very good authority from the police that the walls would have been able to contain any explosion and that they didn't want over 20,000 people all crowding into a confined space. But he didn't seem convinced.

I once got stuck in a crowd crush at Wimbledon, and it was a terrifying experience. There is a tunnel that runs underneath the stands between Courts 2 and 3, and I had just descended the steps from the main concourse on my way to one of the outside courts, when the spectators from the match suddenly began to pour in from the court exits above. I think it had just started to rain, so there were also people on the concourse diving in for shelter, including several ice cream vendors with their trays. Within seconds it had become an almighty squeeze and I could feel the air being pushed out of my lungs as we all stood wedged together. The people coming down the stairs were unaware of what was happening and panic soon took hold. People began shouting and screaming, and punches were exchanged as people tried to fight their way out. It was all over very quickly, but for a few moments I began to fear the worst. Thankfully, since the development of the new Millennium building and Court 1, there are more areas for spectators to hide from the rain.

*　　　　*　　　　*

The dreadful weather in 1985 carried with it a raft of associated problems for us in the referee's office, as it always does. It was an especially fraught fortnight for some reason. Perhaps the weather was making everyone feel a little bad-tempered or on edge.

I found myself at the centre of another controversy involving umpires, when I was forced to banish a Welshman called Bob Jenkins from the chair for the remainder of the tournament after he had violated the rule that bars all officials from making comments without permission from my office to the media during the fortnight. Bob, a former traffic engineer and quite a high-profile official, had written an article saying, among other things, that players' fines for code violations should be commensurate with their earnings. It was not so much the content of his argument, but the fact that he had gone into print at all that forced me to send him home. Bob was out on court working as a line umpire when we learned of his article. When I confronted him, he was not exactly thrilled by my reaction. He turned up at Wimbledon the next day, with his uniform, believing that his ticking-off had been the end of it and that it would be back to business as usual. He was wrong and, as it turned out later, his association with Wimbledon was over.

The tabloids, of course, had a field-day with the story, with 'unnamed officials' also putting the boot into Bob. It appeared that there was a certain animosity towards Bob among the umpiring fraternity, probably because of his high profile. He was known in the media as 'McEnroe's Minder' because he had umpired two finals as well as semi-finals and other matches in which the American was involved without any major incidents. There was no doubt that Bob was a good umpire and it was a shame that he had to blot his copybook at the end. The following year he didn't exactly win back the hearts of the people at Wimbledon by publishing a book in which he made a number of stinging criticisms.

Another problem of an entirely different nature arose in that first week when a beautiful young American girl called Anne White appeared on court for her first-round match wearing an all-white, all-tight speed-skating catsuit (or 'an aerodynamic body-stocking', as the manufacturers' blurb put it). It was an arresting sight to say the least, and while the on-court photographers were delighted, the same most certainly could not be said about her opponent Pam Shriver. Pam is an extremely frank, straight-talking woman who likes to call a spade a damned shovel, and she had plenty to say on this occasion, complaining that the blur of white at the other end had distracted her. It was of course a marketing gimmick, and a very clever one it was too, but Wimbledon doesn't like people using the club as an advertising board, and before her match resumed the club officials came down on Anne quite firmly. You certainly could not have accused Anne of breaking the predominantly all-white rule. Short of liming her face and dying her hair, she simply couldn't have been more white. But the rules also stipulate that a player must wear 'regular' tennis gear and it was on that count that she was forced to appear in more conventional dress when their rain-interrupted match resumed the following day.

For all the various distractions and disputes at Wimbledon that year, the tennis was absolutely compelling, especially in the men's draw, and most people seemed to agree that it was one of the most exciting Championships they could remember. McEnroe had arrived as odds-on favourite, but amidst enormous media coverage of his relationship with the actress Tatum O'Neal, he struggled to find his form before crashing out of the tournament in spectacular fashion at the quarter-final stage to South African-born Kevin Curren. His 6–2, 6–2, 6–4 defeat was the heaviest ever suffered by a defending champion at Wimbledon, and inevitably it didn't pass without a major outburst from the New Yorker. I spent a full five minutes trying to persuade him to continue playing after he disputed the validity of a warning for unsportsmanlike behaviour.

Curren was another fiery character, and I had feared the worst when the draw conspired to place them head-to-head in the last eight stage. The South African had one of the biggest serves in the game at that time and he could fire a few rockets off court too. He has the dubious distinction of having earned the most peculiar entry in the annals of Wimbledon's disciplinary history: 'Fined $500 for destroying photocopier.' He came into my office the weekend before the Championships began and asked if he could play his first-round match on Tuesday as he had picked up a minor injury and wanted as much time as possible to let it heal. No problem. He won his match, but the schedule meant that he would have to play his second-round singles as well as a doubles on the Wednesday. Although we do our best to ensure that the players only play one match per day, often it is simply not possible. John McEnroe, who regarded his doubles games as useful practice for his singles, often played twice in a day, as did most of the top women players, whereas very few of the men these days play two events. In 1999, when the weather had been particularly bad, the Indian player Leander Paes played in the men's double final, a mixed doubles semi-final and final – and won them all!

Curren was partnering Britain's Jeremy Bates in the doubles in a match on Court 3, which is situated directly opposite my old office. The pair were two sets to one up and it was getting a bit dark as the match went to a tiebreaker in the fourth set which they lost. Play was immediately abandoned owing to the bad light, and Curren stormed away from the court and marched straight into my office, steaming with fury. 'I want to speak to Alan,' he barked at my colleagues downstairs. I came down a couple of minutes later after hearing a bit of a commotion and found my staff staring in wide-eyed disbelief at what they had just witnessed. Curren had exploded and taken his anger out on the nearest object he could find, kicking it and smashing the photocopier with his rackets so hard that it broke. The referee's office has been the scene of many extraordinary incidents and temper tantrums down the years, but Curren's performance would definitely make the top ten. The official reason behind his tantrum was his unhappiness at having to play two games in a day, but I suspected that it was as much the frustration of having got to within a couple of points of winning his doubles match, only to be thwarted and to have to return the following day to complete it. Time has failed to douse the fire in Kevin's belly, and while most players on the over-45s circuit are happy to get around the court without pulling a muscle, the South African Davis Cup captain remains as competitive as ever.

He was a terrific competitor throughout his career, and in 1985 he was in outstanding form. There were other upsets that year, notably the first-round defeat of the Australian and French champion Mats Wilander, to a big-serving, big-framed Yugoslav youngster called Slobodan Zivojinovic. But Curren's dismantling of McEnroe was followed by an even more dramatic and ruthless annihilation of another former champion, Jimmy Connors, who folded 6–2, 6–2, 6–1 against the mighty power of his opponent's serve in the semi-finals. For the second year running, Wimbledon, it seemed, was nature's way of telling Jimmy that he had slowed down. Curren had also beaten a future champion, Stefan Edberg, but for all his heroics there was only one tennis story that year and it was provided by a rumbustious 17-year-old redhead with a serve like a cannon and the agility of the most athletic goalkeeper.

The tennis world had been given a glimpse of Boris Becker the year before when he had powered into the third round and was putting up a tremendous fight against the American seed Bill Scanlon before he went over on his ankle and left Wimbledon in a wheelchair. The Romanian Ion Tiriac, a former player turned manager, was so impressed when he saw the powerful young German in action in Monte Carlo that he flew to Frankfurt, hired a car and drove to the Becker family home near Heidelberg and there and then offered his parents Karl-Heinz and Elvira a reported $250,000 a year to have their son on his books. When Becker returned to Wimbledon, he came with a reputation as one of the 'promising youngsters to watch out for'. He was not seeded, but the story goes that one British punter with an eye for a thoroughbred and a generous price spotted something special about him and slipped £10,000 on him at 18 to 1 before the tournament got underway.

Becker powered his way through the bottom half of the draw, dispatching Hank Pfister, Paul McNamee, Joakim Nystrom, Tim Mayotte, Henri Leconte and Anders Jarryd to become the youngest-ever finalist and the first German in the final since Wilhelm Bungert in 1967. We had never seen anything quite like Boris Becker. He was a genuine force of nature and we watched in awe as he blasted his opponents off court. He was extraordinarily aggressive and clenched his fists and punched the air like a footballer. Some of his opponents – including Jarryd after their semi-final – claimed that when they passed Becker at a change of ends he deliberately tried to barge them. He certainly carried an extremely intimidating presence and an overwhelming confidence, even at an age when most kids are still hanging around at the local shops and kicking footballs around on the recreation ground. Teenage sensations were nothing new on the women's circuit, but they were rare on the men's. Despite his on-court intensity and aggression I always found him to be an extremely charming, softly spoken and intelligent character. Only once did I have to fine him for a breach of discipline and he was very lucky indeed not to have become the first player to be defaulted at Wimbledon in the Open era. Players are allowed two 'bathroom breaks' in a five-set match, and they are followed off-court by an official to make sure they do nothing other than go to the bathroom. On this occasion, during a match against the Argentinian Javier Frana, Becker went straight to the treatment table in the locker-room and was quickly worked on by his trainer. The official reported the incident to the chair umpire, who failed to pass on the information to me as he should have done. Frana went absolutely mad when he found out about it afterwards, but it was too late for Becker to be disqualified and I could only fine him £2,000.

The 1985 final between two of the biggest servers in the Championships promised (or threatened) to be a demonstration of pure power tennis. The nature of the game was certainly in the process of dramatic change, and it was strange to reflect that just four years earlier Borg and McEnroe had been delighting the Centre Court with a brand of play that now seemed to belong to a distant era. Becker won the contest in four sets to become Wimbledon's first unseeded champion and the first German to lift the trophy. He was also the youngest by some distance to take the title at 17 years and 7 months, eclipsing William Baddeley who was 19 years and 5 months.

Becker was a marked man when he returned to defend his title at the 1986 Championships, which began much as the last had finished – it rained and Kevin Curren was in a very bad mood. The only bright spots on a gloomy, rain-interrupted and ill-tempered opening day were the yellow balls that were being used for the first time. (Yellow balls produce a better image for television, apparently.) Drug tests were also introduced this year, and even the chairman Buzzer Hadingham was forced to undergo one, which inevitably prompted a few jokes in the members' bar.

Curren's composure lost its moorings during a five-set defeat to a little-known, part-time German soldier called Eric Jelen and led to a running row with the umpire Roger Smith. Curren was furious with Smith, an RAF officer, for overruling the line judges on several occasions. He was warned for verbal abuse and handed a penalty point for a visible obscenity before slumping to defeat. Afterwards he slammed the Wimbledon umpire fraternity saying: 'They like to exert their authority more than others and think they are the show.' It's interesting that the vast majority of players who blow their tops after a match are the ones who have lost. Rarely do the winners have an axe to grind, although Lendl was a notable exception. I am surprised it hasn't happened already, but I think it is inevitable that there will be an occasion when an umpire says: 'Right, that's it, I've had enough,' gets down from his chair, punches the abusive player and walks off court. There must be a lot of umpires who harbour dark feelings towards certain players for all the humiliation they have suffered down the years. I have had my fair share of abuse, but it is the umpires who are in the front line and bear the brunt of the blasts. Occasionally I can come to the rescue.

A handful of incidents from 1986 remain vivid in my mind today. Andrew Castle, a British hope, came within a whisker of beating Mats Wilander in the second round and was hailed both as a national hero and as walking proof of the failure of British tennis to nurture its best talent. The night before the match with the No. 2 seed, Castle had been forced to wander the streets of south-west London because he could not afford anywhere to stay. There was a similar outcry a few years later when another British talent, Nick Brown, beat Goran Ivanisevic despite being ranked 593rd in the world. It was the biggest upset since the world ranking system was introduced in 1973, and was all the more impressive for the fact that Brown had been forced to quit the tennis circuit proper, playing only at weekends and working at Marks & Spencer stacking shelves during the week. It is inconceivable that young American talent playing at Wimbledon would ever be in this situation. The truly sad thing was that Brown was no longer even a youngster. He was 30. The question I have been asked more than any other on my travels around the world is, 'What on earth is wrong with British tennis?' and if you can bear with me I'll explain my views on the subject at a later point.

Another remarkable performance that year was produced by the Australian Pat Cash who reached the quarter-finals just four weeks after having his appendix out. The Argentinian beauty Gabriela Sabatini was also causing quite a stir, not least by becoming the youngest player at the time to reach the semi-finals, at the age of 16 years and one month. But her looks were also causing quite an impact and I recall at one stage having physically to restrain a pack of snap-happy photographers who had encroached on to the court to get a close-up of her. From a personal point of view, there was just one incident, and a rather extraordinary one it was too, that stands out from an otherwise relatively quiet Championships in terms of player histrionics. The main characters were the big, brooding Yugoslav Zivojinovic, a nervous umpire and a highly agitated and high-ranking club official. The scene was an extremely tense and close-fought semi-final against Lendl on Centre Court.

The match seemed to have a jinx on it from the outset. Jeremy Shales and Mike Lugg were the umpires for the two men's semi-finals that year, and when they came in that morning I told Mike that he would be doing the Lendl and Zivojinovic match while Jeremy would handle Becker's game against Henri Leconte. I thought no more of it until half an hour before the Lendl match was due to start and Mike Lugg came into my office and said: 'You do know that I can't do Lendl, don't you, Alan?' I felt my blood pressure rise a little and after a sharp intake of breath, through gritted teeth I replied: 'No Mike, I didn't know you couldn't do Lendl. Why not?' He said: 'Don't you remember three years ago I was the net-cord official in Key Biscayne and had a bit of a run-in with Lendl?' No, I didn't and nor would Lendl, I hazarded. If Lendl objected to the appointment of every single chair umpire, line judge or net-call official he had ever crossed, there would a lot of empty chairs around his courts. If a player had had a major confrontation with an official, and generally it has to be with a chair umpire, then we try to keep them apart. But I didn't consider Mike Lugg's spat with Lendl to be especially significant and it had happened so long ago as to be virtually irrelevant. An awful lot of water had passed under Lendl's bridge since then.

To say I was not amused by this development would be an understatement. I was especially angry that Lugg had not mentioned his concern immediately. Why he waited until the eleventh hour to tell me, heaven only knows. He couldn't have just remembered it, if it was such a major event for him. I think Lugg thought that I was simply going to swap him with Jeremy Shales in the other semi-final, and he was quite taken aback when I thanked him for his time and wished him a pleasant journey home.

Umpires, like players, need some time to prepare and focus on the match ahead and it was highly unsatisfactory for Lugg's last-minute replacement, David Howie, that he had to go into this high-profile contest so 'cold'. But it all seemed to be going well enough, the match delicately balanced at one set all, when Zivojinovic reached a potentially crucial break-point on Lendl's serve. The Yugoslav had won the second set on a tiebreaker and this was the first opportunity he had to break Lendl's serve in a game. The court had fallen completely silent as Lendl prepared to serve. The ball rocketed over the net and the line judge hollered 'fault!', but uproar followed in an instant when umpire Howie overruled the call and said the ball was good. I was watching from my office when Zivojinovic went completely berserk and sat down in his chair, refusing to play on. I grabbed my jacket and headed as fast as I could through the labyrinth of corridors and stairs to get to the scene. There was little I could do at this point because the overrule was a point of fact, not of law, and so I stationed myself at the corner of court to see how the drama unfolded. As I stood there I became aware of a presence behind me – quite an agitated presence. It was one of the club's most prominent officials who had come sprinting down to the court when he had heard the overrule. He was as angry as Zivojinovic it seemed, and it was just a shame that he did not follow the Yugoslav's example and stay glued to his seat. The man in question had some strong views on a number of matters, but one of his pet gripes was umpires overruling decisions to which he objected vehemently unless the line official had been demonstrably wrong in his decision.

It was a very tricky situation for me. It was obvious that he was trying to get past me and go on court to tell the umpire to reverse his decision, but this would have been a farcical disaster. He would have made a mockery of himself, Wimbledon and the umpire at a stroke. He had no jurisdiction to go on court and start making decisions about line-calls. It was, as far as I know, unprecedented in the history of Grand Slam tennis for anybody to interfere in a match in this way. So as he stepped one way to get past, I stepped in front of him and blocked his way. When he went the other way, I went too, and so forth. It was extremely lucky that the BBC cameras were trained so intently on the drama on court because my dance partner and I would have looked extremely foolish if we had been seen carrying out our comedy routine in the corner. Eventually, thank heavens, he got the message – or became tired out – and disappeared whence he came.

Zivojinovic, meanwhile, was still rooted to his seat. I didn't quite know what to do at this stage. It wasn't my place to agree or disagree with the decision of the umpire or the line judge. I wanted David Howie to sort out the problem as soon as possible, as the situation was deteriorating with every minute that 'Bobo' refused to play on. Both players were getting cold, the crowd was getting restless and this was just the kind of negative images that Wimbledon and tennis in general could do without. After what seemed like an eternity, and with the slow handclap of the spectators growing ever louder, I decided to walk on and try to persuade Zivojinovic to get on with it. It was the only course open to me. He was, needless to say, not exactly full of the joys of an English summer when I approached him, and he muttered some dark Balkan oaths under his breath, not at me but in a general tirade about the incident. I let him have his say so that he could get it all off his chest and feel that he was being listened to, and then spoke to him as understandingly as I could. I did have a reasonable amount of sympathy for him. Overrules are painful at the best of times, but when you are the clear underdog and they come at a crucial break-point and you are bursting every vessel in your body against the No. 1 seed in a Wimbledon semi-final, then they are especially galling and infuriating. I said he may well have been right, but even if he was, there was simply no legal way the decision could be reversed. I wouldn't say he calmed down, but he resigned himself to the hopelessness of the situation and returned to his end of the court. He ended up losing the match 6–4 in the final set, and I have to say I felt very sorry for him as he trudged off court at the end, with his shoulders slumped and his head down. He was an unseeded player who had taken the world No. 1 to the very brink, only to lose out by the finest margin. Both players were given a well-deserved standing ovation as they walked off after a compelling encounter – a rare treat indeed for Lendl at Wimbledon.

It is impossible to say whether the overrule dispute had had an adverse effect on Zivojinovic's game – who knows, it may even have fired him up a bit more as he went on to win the fourth set – but I was left with an uncomfortable feeling at the end of it all. Although most umpiring decisions even themselves out over a season, they don't necessarily do so over the course of a match. In tennis, one-off decisions can occasionally swing the outcome of an entire match, and in this instance you were left wondering: could Zivojinovic have gone on to take the title against Boris Becker, Wimbledon's only other unseeded champion?

The final was billed as 'The Gloom v. The Boom' and the odds tumbled on Lendl landing his first Wimbledon title. After a rainy first day, the rest of the fortnight had been a scorcher, leaving the courts hard, dusty and fast, giving Lendl some hope against his young opponent whose big serve, clinical volleying, athleticism and speed made him a formidable opponent on grass. Lendl had also won four of his previous five encounters against the German *wunderkind,* but his previous two matches in the tournament had been physically and emotionally gruelling in the extreme. Like his clash with Zivojinovic, his quarter-final against Tim Mayotte, the 'nearly man of tennis' as he had been dubbed by the press, had gone the distance, finishing 9–7 in the fifth set. In total, Lendl had played 108 games in those two matches against Becker's 71, and the fatigue of body and soul could have a significant impact in the final. On a positive note, the sheer guts Lendl had shown in those two matches had led to something of a thaw in his relations with the British public, as represented by the crowd at

Wimbledon. Where once there was just a tremendous glacial indifference to the publicly dour US and French champion, now there was a hint of warmth and grudging admiration. The British love a noble workhorse, and there was nobody in the history of the Championships who tried harder to win the title than Lendl. In the event, though, Becker pummelled his hapless opponent into the Centre Court dust to keep his crown, while Lendl's face grew that little bit longer and darker. It was a grim truth of modern tennis that at just 26 Lendl's chance of winning Wimbledon might already be behind him.

The women's final that year was extraordinary for the fact that it featured two Czech players, Martina Navratilova and Hana Mandlikova, and that nobody in their home country saw a single ball of it. Only those living close to the German border with a powerful TV aerial had a chance of watching the contest. Moreover, as far as the Czech communist authorities were concerned, Martina didn't even exist. She was a defector to the West and the country's newspapers would record the result as: 'Another Player bt Hana Mandlikova, 7–6, 6–3.'

Chapter Five

It's All Gone Bananas in SW19

I start my work at Wimbledon four weeks before the Championships begin, generally on the Bank Holiday Monday at the end of May. I have grown to love the routine of it down the years. Each day I stride through the gates towards my office in that month, something about the grounds has changed as the army of workers hurry about their tasks to get the club ship-shape. The groundsmen are busy trimming every blade of grass on the 19 courts, scaffolders are hard at work installing the extra seats; the BBC teams are laying miles and miles of cables around the courts; the maintenance staff give a fresh lick of paint to all the wood and ironwork; the marquee and catering companies set up their stalls and tents; the gardeners hoe the beds, mow the lawns and trim the edges; and the delivery men begin to arrive with their crates of Pimms and champagne and their barrels of beer. (I understand that the famous strawberries, which come from Kent, are only picked the day before they are to be eaten and are driven up every night of the fortnight.) With the arrival of the 50,000 bedding plants and shrubs the club starts to look ready for business, but every year I think to myself in that final week, 'Surely there is no way we are going to be ready in time.' Yet every Monday morning at the start of the Championships, as the queues start to snake their way up Church Road and Somerset Road, the whole place is completely pristine. Every court is immaculate, every seat is scrubbed clean and the stewards from the three armed services are all there looking spanking smart in their uniforms, as slick and polished as the military operation to get the All England Club fit to face the outside world for another year.

By the time I arrive, my office is already a bustle of activity with ringing phones, buzzing fax machines, beeping computers and gurgling coffee machines. Most of my staff have been there for a fortnight or so, concentrating mainly on handling the hundreds of entries from all over the world for the various events. There is an enormous amount of administration involved, with all the faxes and phone calls flooding in from the players and their agents. In addition to the two singles and three doubles events in the main Championships there are also the junior, senior and qualifying events to deal with. There are a lot of names to process, as well as an awful lot of pidgin English and botched messages to decipher. In total my office oversees the administration, refereeing and umpiring of around 700 matches over the Championships, and I don't know what I'd do without my highly professional friends in the office. We have over a hundred years of experience between the longest-serving six of us. Nothing fazes my office these days. They have seen, heard and faxed it all. Tony Gathercole, my assistant until 2002, started in the referee's office the year before me, and we have always been great friends as well as colleagues. There have been four other stalwarts in the office during my time as referee, all deserving special mention in despatches – Jean Sexton, who was also assistant referee and is now retired, Peter Mornard, Sandy Hughes and Mo Paremain, who was my personal assistant, also retired. Like Tony, they are friends too, and we all go back a very long way (Jill and Jean played in the Surrey Juniors together and Jill was one of the bridesmaids at Jean's wedding). When I was appointed Championships Referee in 1983 I felt it was very important to have a female on my senior staff in what had been until then a predominantly male domain, and Jean fitted the bill perfectly – an experienced referee, a good player in her day and a formidable organiser. It was one of the best decisions I have ever made. Peter is the office manager in everything but name, and a great character to have about the place: a true extrovert who has us all in stitches much of the time. During the winter he does panto and has even appeared at the London Palladium.

The referee's office has always been on two floors, and for obvious reasons we refer to either the 'upstairs' or the 'downstairs' office (but Mrs Bridges and the butler Hudson it certainly isn't). I occupy the upstairs office as it has now, and had before, views of several courts. Working with me in the office are the two assistant referees. Sandy, our computer expert, is also on this floor, along with the IT group, who number around 12. Downstairs there is Peter, Sheila Mercer, Mandy Ripley and Rowena Johnson, who have also been in the team for about 20 years. Since the retirement of Jean, Tony and Mo, Andy Jarrett and Clare Wood have joined us.

The downstairs office is responsible for a wide variety of functions: calling the players for their matches; organising the security to get the players to the courts; dealing with on- and off-court requests for bananas, chocolate, tissues, etc.;

taking calls and questions from the general public and players; and getting the name-cards out to the courts. Upstairs, the primary concerns are: dealing with problems from the previous day; formulating the order of play; fielding requests from players, agents and worldwide television; meeting with the chief of umpires to decide court assignments; answering letters from the public; and, of course, monitoring the weather.

In the build-up to the 1987 Championships we felt a little gloomier than usual, in spite of Peter's best efforts to cheer us all up. The weather seemed to be a little confused, thinking it was November. Down came the wretched rain, day after day, hour after hour. While this is just plain depressing for most of us, it is especially infuriating for the groundsmen trying to get the courts in perfect manicured order. On the Sunday before the start, Jim Thorn pumped an almighty 30,000 gallons of water off the practice area. Under normal meteorological circumstances grass is a very fast surface, but this year the courts would play much slower on the first few days. The rain has innumerable repercussions on the Championships: it dampens morale among staff; it creates a backlog of matches; frustrates the players; infuriates and depresses the spectators; wrongfoots broadcasters; and often encourages some very silly stories in the newspapers. If there is no play on court, there is nothing to write about, so journalists have to dig around for their copy to file by the end of the day. Pat Cash, always an outspoken character, did the press a major favour this year when he described women's tennis as 'junk'. That kept them busy for a while.

There was another reason why I was somewhat apprehensive

that year: 1987 was going to be a landmark moment in the history of the Championships. Our office was never going to be the same again and I wasn't too sure I liked the idea of this brave new world that was about to be thrust upon us. Some character called 'Womble' had been added to our team, and we were told with great confidence that Womble was about to make our working lives immeasurably less stressful. I have to confess that I was not at all convinced by Womble when I first laid eyes on him. He looked suspiciously unreliable and a little temperamental to me. I didn't like the cut of his circuit board one iota.

Womble is about eight foot long and lives on the wall. He is covered in magnetic tiles carrying the names of all the competitors in the various events. Womble is a matrix board connected to a computer monitor. Womble thinks he is cleverer, faster and more efficient than the rest of us in the office, and at approximately £120,000 for three years' work, his services certainly didn't come cheap. It was Womble's boast on joining us that he could spot any mistakes in the draws, make sure that the same player was not assigned two separate courts at the same time and that when a player has to play twice in a day he could guarantee he would get a good rest in between. Well, we would see about that, Womble. With no more technology than a solid, wooden, old-fashioned, no-nonsense 10 pence leaded pencil, I fancied that I could execute the order of play as efficiently and speedily as any machine on the planet.

I hate computers. I'm not just computer illiterate, I'm positively phobic about them. My ignorance of them is so great that I have been banned from touching any buttons in the office, except the ones on my suit jacket and the light switches on the wall. (I'm not even very good with light switches, come to think of it, despite the fact that I was once an apprentice in an electrical engineering firm. Presented once with what I was told was a very straightforward domestic electrical job, I came close to burning our house down after literally getting my wires crossed.) It has been very fortunate for me and our office as a whole that we have Sandy Hughes as our in-house computer wizard. She has been overseeing the increasingly sophisticated IT systems which have become central to our daily life at Wimbledon. Without her brilliance and her team of mini-wizards, we would probably spend most of the Championships lying on the office beating our fists on the carpet.

When I started my job at Wimbledon we would sit down with a pencil, an eraser and a large sheet of white paper and do the order of play by hand. The information was then transferred on to a very long ticker-tape, which we would wrap around someone's outstretched arms and then rush around the corner – generally late in the evening by this stage – to the nearby British Telecom office where it would be fed into a special machine and transmitted to the relevant media organisations. It was a painfully laborious process, but it worked. We always got there in the end. However, I am man enough to admit now that Womble quickly proved to be a fine specimen of a computer and every bit as efficient and intelligent as we were told he would be.

Though it pains me to say it, by the standards of today, Womble, once the very cutting-edge of technology, has become something of an old dinosaur, but he is now linked to a computer system so sophisticated that it is terrifying, and he is still doing a very dependable job for us. Everything in our office is now computerised, including the umpires' scorecards. The chair officials used to score a match with a pad and pencil before bringing their records back to the office where they would be checked by my team and then released to the press and to the various departments around the grounds as an official result. Nowadays, the umpire logs the information on to a hand-held computer, and each time he registers a point it doesn't just go back to the office but heads straight out on to the Internet, allowing anyone in the world to follow a match ball by ball. If the umpire is having technical difficulties he resorts to pen and paper while Sandy dispatches one of her staff to sort out the problem courtside.

From the players' point of view this is a superb development because there are computer screens all around the grounds and in their private area, so they can follow the course of a match and know exactly when they are due on court. Call me old-fashioned, but computers still make me feel extremely anxious. I live in fear of the system suffering a total crash, and so in some respects they have added more pressure to my daily life at Wimbledon. But if there has been one area in which they have been of enormous benefit it is in the transmission of the order of play: nowadays the sun will not even have set by the time Sandy presses the button and the order of play wings its way through the ether to the world's media organisations and to the players eager to know whether they are on court first the following day.

In my first year in charge at Wimbledon, the weather was so bad that we had only two full days' play in the entire fortnight, and the situation was not much better four years later. By Friday we were 140 matches behind schedule and looking at the grim prospect of having to take the Championships into a third week for only the second time in the Open era. One of the unwelcome side effects of the rain is that spectators tend to drink far more heavily than usual as they hang around waiting for play to begin. We had some pretty serious trouble in this respect on the first Thursday, when a huge fight broke out in the walkway between Centre Court and Court 1. As officers and security guards tried to restore order, one unfortunate policewoman found herself being knocked to the ground. There were, however, some lighter moments amidst the deluge. On Court 1 the fans broke out into rendition of 'Singing in the Rain' and all the officials, ball-boys and ball-girls joined in. I love moments like that at Wimbledon and I always feel a shiver of admiration for the fortitude of the British public, putting a brave face on a difficult situation.

Between the downpours, Boris Becker suffered one of the biggest upsets in the history of the Championships when he was beaten in four sets by an unknown Australian called Peter Doohan, who was apparently so hard up he was staying at the YMCA in Kingston for £11 a night. Becker was magnanimous in defeat and put the setback into nice perspective when he said: 'Nobody died out there.' Doohan added an amusing footnote to the story when he revealed that he had ruined the thrill of the moment for his family back home when he telephoned them after the match. Because of the time difference the match was not shown live in Australia, and when Doohan rang the family were perched on the edge of their seats with the decisive set still poised at 3–3!

It was another dreadful year for the British, with all the women tumbling out of the tournament by the second round. Jeremy Bates was the only British player to make it into the second week, to be promptly bludgeoned by Slobodan

Zivojinovic. Jimmy Connors, meanwhile, had suddenly become the darling of Wimbledon after one of the most remarkable fightbacks in Grand Slam history against a plucky young Swede called Michael Pernfors. After losing the first two sets 6–1, 6–1, the old street-fighter was 4–1 down in the third when he suddenly got angry and blasted his way to victory. He was deservedly given a rapturous ovation at the end. Connors, though, succumbed in the semi-finals to the eventual champion Pat Cash, who crushed the unfortunate Ivan Lendl in three sets with as fine a display of serve and volley tennis as you could hope to see – the equal of anything produced by his brilliant compatriots of my generation: Lew Hoad, Rod Laver and John Newcombe.

It was a roasting hot day with temperatures shooting past the 100° mark on Centre Court. After his victory, and under the gaze of Prime Minister Margaret Thatcher and Princess Diana, Cash leapt into the crowd to hug his Norwegian girl-friend and his father. Lendl, meanwhile, sat slumped in his chair, his face longer than ever after a yet another failure to achieve his last major ambition in tennis. There was nothing I could say to him to cheer him up. During his semi-final against Edberg, he hardly invited warmth and sympathy after a string of outbursts and sulks. At one point he sneered at the American umpire Ken Slye: 'Where did they get *you* from?' Lendl said he wanted me to be called out, but with admirable cool Slye stood his ground and told him to get on with it. He was not a pretty sight on court that day, Lendl, but at the end of his defeat in the final, I felt very sorry for him and you wondered what else he could do to land his Holy Grail. He had had a grass court laid in his garden, employed coach Tony Roche, a grass-court expert, and he had practised like a demon to perfect his serve and volley game. He was as fit and determined as anyone on the circuit; he dominated the game on other surfaces; and yet year after year at Wimbledon he just fell short. You couldn't accuse of him not trying, but he was unfortunate to be playing in an era of great grass-court players like Becker, Edberg, McEnroe and Connors.

Lendl was back the following year as grizzly and determined as ever. The weather in 1988 was baking hot which, like the heavy rain, can play havoc with the courts. Normally the grass has a nice spongy feel underfoot, but in extreme heat the courts soon become rock hard and start to crumble. Cracks appear, the ball starts to bounce eccentrically and the players, sweltering in 100°-plus temperatures, become frustrated. As he laboured to a five-set win over an unseeded Dutchman called Michael Schappers, Lendl completely lost his temper and said to the chair umpire Gerry Armstrong, 'I hate your guts.' He also told the former Wimbledon champion Billie Jean King, now a commentator, to 'shut up'. Afterwards he showed his dry sense of humour when he talked about the state of the courts, saying: 'The rough on my golf course at home doesn't look as bad as the grass on this court.'

When the weather is extreme at Wimbledon, the people I have the greatest sympathy for are the groundsmen and their staff, who work all year round to get the courts absolutely perfect only for the weather to wreck their efforts at the end. They are at work by seven o'clock in the morning, work themselves into the ground all day and by the time they get home late at night and turn on the Wimbledon highlights they have to listen to some of the players moaning about the state of the courts. Theirs can truly be a thankless job at times.

Apparently even John Lloyd had to be reprimanded by the All England club for voicing his dissatisfaction with the state of the courts. Meanwhile, Connors, a man never shy of expressing his darker feelings, went even further than Lendl when he stormed off Court 2, calling the ground staff 'f***ing a**holes', after he was beaten by German Peter Kuhnen. He also called a lineswoman 'a blind witch', and was fined for doing so. His behaviour was disgraceful and I was not over-whelmed with sadness to see him pack his bags and leave the Championships.

John McEnroe, who had behaved like an angel in the first round, was back to his old tricks in a second-round defeat to Australian Wally Masur after a two-year absence from Wimbledon because of injury. He was warned for racket abuse after hurling it to the floor, and the crowd gave him the slow handclap as he moaned about a number of deci-sions. But at least he was refreshingly self-critical afterwards, saying he was embarrassingly bad, 'stunk the whole place out' and 'wouldn't have won the women's the way I played'. It was one of those Championships – lots of tantrums and niggles. Even the immaculately mannered Chris Evert suffered a fit of pique during a highly controversial incident right at the end of her semi-final defeat to her old nemesis Martina Navratilova. In what turned out to be the final point of the match, playing down the line her shot hit the top of the net and lolloped over the other side. The line judge said nothing, but there was uproar when the chair umpire Dick Lumb intervened to call the ball 'out' and announce 'Game, set and match Miss Navratilova.' Chrissie was clearly furious and refused to shake hands with Lumb at the end of the match. The crowd too were incensed, and they booed and booed and then began to slow handclap the umpire as he made his way off court.

When we totted up the fines and penalties at the end, it turned out that the 1988 Championships were no worse than any other in that period, but there did seem to be an unusual amount of unpleasantness around that year. The chairman Buzzer Hadingham wrote to Boris Becker apologising for his treatment by the British press, who lambasted him as a 'Sour Kraut' for refusing to pay a £5 parking charge in a club car park. (By mistake he had entered the public car park instead of the one reserved for players and officials.)

I came in for some predictable criticism myself after I put the defending champion Pat Cash on Court 14 for one of his matches. As the man with ultimate responsibility for the order of play, I have always gone to great lengths to avoid creating a 'them-and-us' syndrome amongst the lower-ranked players. I do not think it is a bad idea if one of the top players, at least once in the tournament, is asked to play on an outside court. In my view, that is fair and democratic and in the wider interests of the sport, plus it is good for spectators with only ground tickets. Most of the time, however, it simply isn't logistically possible to put all the top players on the best two courts. What we hadn't really allowed for was the horde of Cash's teenage girl fans who mobbed him on his way to the court and then created an enormous din throughout the match. He needed a six-man police escort to and from the court, and throughout the match there was much screaming and wailing amongst his fan club. There were also dozens of photographers barging their way on to court to get a good angle of the Australian pin-up, and at one point I was summoned to help sort out the chaos. Cash wasn't far off the mark when he described Court 14 as 'a zoo' that afternoon.

Cash was beaten by Becker in three sets in the quarter-finals, but he certainly didn't go down without a fight and a few f-words thrown in Boris's direction. In his press conference after the match, Boris is quoted as having said: 'I certainly learned some new English swearwords out there today.'

After all the crimes and misdemeanours, the tempers and tantrums, the off-court mud-slinging and occasionally loutish behaviour, it was a happy event that the singles competitions were won by two of the best behaved, sporting and delightful characters I have come across on the tennis circuit: Stefan Edberg and Steffi Graf. It was a first Wimbledon win for both of them and their victories were a shot in the arm for the image of the game. The British press could be a little mean about Edberg, cracking jokes about his charisma bypass, but he could certainly play tennis, especially on grass. He was also disarmingly humble and charming.

Edberg always carried himself with great modesty. One incident in particular sticks in my mind and serves as a good illustration of the Swede's character. I was refereeing the Key Biscayne tournament in Florida, and because there were only a handful of practice courts at the tournament many of the players used to practise on the courts at the nearby luxury hotel where they were staying. Often the players, or one of their 'people' would come into our office at the tournament and take away boxes and boxes of balls with which they could practise. As a general rule we never saw those balls again. They were either just left strewn around the court or the player or coach would hang on to them. But on this occasion, Edberg parked his courtesy car a fair distance from the locker-rooms and, lugging all his bags and rackets, went out of his way to come to the office and give back the balls he had borrowed. He even apologised because some of the cans had gone missing!

I have a tremendous amount of time for Edberg, and he tells a very amusing and revealing story about an incident at the Queen's tournament in 2003. He was playing in an exhibition match there, and when he walked into Reception the girl behind the counter didn't recognise him and got a little short with him: 'Well, what are you? A journalist, an official?'

'I'm a player,' he replied.

'Fine, then what's your name?'

'Edberg.'

'Well there we are then,' the girl said, and handed him his credentials on which she had printed 'Mr Ed Berg'.

Edberg's victory over Becker in the final that year was marred by rain and the match did not start until 6.30 p.m., and then had to be carried over to the Monday for the first time in 66 years. It was, the man at the Weather Centre told me, the lowest depression over southern England since 1956. It could just as well have been my mood he was talking about, although that was alleviated somewhat when my daughter Penny plus friends entertained the crowd with an impromptu puppet show from the old scoreboard, which is now the police office. It was rumoured that Edberg and Becker were not the best of friends off court and the press stoked this up over the weekend, billing the match as Big Mouth v. The Quiet Man of Kensington (where Edberg lived). Edberg was just too good for Boris on the day, and the victory denied Germany an historic Wimbledon double following Steffi Graf's success on the Saturday.

Graf's victory ended Navratilova's remarkable run of six consecutive titles and hailed a new era in the women's game as she swept to the Grand Slam – the only person so far to achieve the feat on four different surfaces: grass, clay, Rebound Ace and hard. She also won the gold medal at the Seoul Olympics, and lost just three out of 75 matches in the year. She was one of the most professional and meticulous players I have ever come across, as well as a real pleasure to deal with. Even during the various controversies surrounding her father Peter, she managed to keep a beaming smile on her face. She always used to compete in the indoor event in Brighton, and the other players used to complain that Steffi always got an hour to herself to practise on the one court available. The reply to them was invariably the same: 'Well, if you want to get there at six o'clock in the morning like Steffi, then I am sure you could come to some arrangement.' That was always the end of the conversation. In the final at Wimbledon one year, play was interrupted about six or seven times by the rain, but she never showed any sign of frustration, and every time we called the two players back on court she was always ready to go there and then. She was just the ultimate professional, a model of efficiency, and an extremely popular one too, especially with the people in my office, where she would often pop in for a friendly chat or to say thanks at the end of the Championships.

Only once in all my dealings with Steffi did I find myself in a bit of a tight spot. We were at a tournament in Japan, many years ago, at a time when local chair umpires had not quite risen to the standards of subsequent years. There had been a handful of dubious decisions against Steffi when I was passed a message from her coach Heinz Gunthardt saying that she was going to walk off court unless I changed the chair umpire. This was a very serious situation. Replacing a chair umpire is a draconian measure in any circumstances, but I felt it would be even more so in Japan where loss of face or honour is seen as a profound disgrace. I was caught between a rock and a hard place and racked my brains for a solution over the next couple of games before Steffi sat down again at a change of ends. Finally, I scrawled a note to Heinz in which I said, 'If I do change the umpire, then there is no guarantee that the replacement will be any better. In fact she has got the best of the bunch out there at the moment.' That, thank heavens, was the end of the matter because it could have been a very ugly mess for all of us. Since the advent of professional officials, the standard of officiating has improved worldwide.

When Steffi returned to Wimbledon to defend her crown in 1989, she was odds-on favourite for the title. Becker was the man to beat in the men's singles, but his tournament got off to a bad start when he was prevented by an official from using the practice courts because he did not have his credentials badge with him. Boris was absolutely furious at what he thought was just petty bureaucracy run amok, and I had a good deal of sympathy for him. He was, after all, a former champion, an honorary member of the club and just about the best-known face in tennis at this time. It might have been more helpful if the security guard had simply reminded him to bring it next time, thus avoiding Boris's outburst about Wimbledon in general that the incident provoked. At a press conference, Boris lambasted what he called the 'snobs' at Wimbledon, said the 'two-tier' dressing-room was a disgrace (in fact players earn the right to use the members' dressing-room through their rankings, although not everyone takes advantage of this – Andy Roddick has said he does not deserve to be in the members' dressing-room until he has gained membership by winning the Championship) and bemoaned the fact that there were no shuttle buses for the players' coaches and helpers. During one of his early-round matches, Boris pulled on a green and blue shirt, in contravention of the white clothing rule, and when I had a word with him about it afterwards, you couldn't help but think he was just trying to wind the club up after the incident with the credentials.

But if Boris thought he had off-court problems that year, they were as nothing compared to those of John McEnroe, who was sprayed in the face with an aerosol can by some lunatic as he headed out to one of the courts. For the rest of the tournament, Wimbledon arranged with the police for plain-clothes officers to mingle amongst the crowds while McEnroe was given a Roman-style phalanx of guards wherever he went. The aerosol turned out to be harmless enough air freshener, but the incident highlighted the vulnerability of the players around the grounds. For years I campaigned at Wimbledon for *all* the players to be given a personal escort when they make their way out to court, and I am happy to say that that has recently become club policy. In the past, only the top players were given that privilege and it always made me a little nervous when I saw the other players having to push their way through the crowds with their bags slung over their shoulders.

As the crowds wander around munching strawberries and sipping their drinks, Wimbledon comes across as a comfortable, safe environment – and it is – but behind the scenes there is a huge amount of invisible security activity going on. The club has always been very much aware of the dangers presented by terrorism and random acts of crime, particularly in relation to stalkers following the appalling stabbing of Monica Seles in Hamburg in 1993.

We had a very disquieting incident involving the Nigerian Nduka ('Just call me The Duke') Odizor. It was in 1983 and he had just pulled off a remarkable victory over the fourth seed Guillermo Vilas after being two sets down. Wimbledon was abuzz with talk of his victory, and later that day a large crowd was expected to see him play in a doubles match on Court 13. When the match was called there was no sign of The Duke, and I had sent out people in all directions to find him when I received a message from the chief executive Chris Gorringe to come to his office. Chris explained that Wimbledon had received a very specific and credible letter saying that Odizor was going to be killed. The Duke was sitting in a chair looking terrified and he was understandably extremely apprehensive about heading out on court. The police were there too and after a lengthy consultation it was agreed that they would swamp the crowd with plainclothes detectives and the match would go ahead. Odizor, to his credit, went out on court but he never looked comfortable and he and his partner lost their match.

Generally, though, cxccpt for organising the escorts for players to courts, I have no idea about the day-to-day details of security operations, except each morning we have a visit from the 'sniffer' dogs and their minders, who patrol the grounds, and I am only informed if an incident, generally a bomb scare, affects the playing of the matches. In 2003 for instance, I discovered at the very end of the

Championships that the club authorities, in consultation with the security services, had placed a fire officer at each end of the court whenever a French national was playing. The reason being that shortly before the tournament began two Iranian women had set themselves on fire outside London's French Embassy in protest at the arrest in Paris of 150 members of a group suspected of involvement in terrorism. We were taking no chances. It's amazing what goes on behind the scenes at Wimbledon – no one knows the half of it.

Despite the shock of the aerosol incident, McEnroe was producing some of his best tennis at Wimbledon for years. In his first match he battled back from two sets down against Australian Darren Cahill and was ahead in the match only for the last six minutes. He reached the quarter-finals for the first time since 1985 with an ill-tempered win over John Fitzgerald, who later accused him of gamesmanship and abuse. Nothing changes . . . Then, watched by Princess Diana and the Duchess of York, he beat Mats Wilander, prompting the memorable tabloid headline: 'The Brat Sat On The Mat'. On his way to the court, a young girl was knocked to the ground by a TV crew trying to film, and suffer a bleeding nose. Showing his softer side, McEnroe later invited the girl to the players' lounge, where he and his wife Tatum O'Neal comforted her.

The most controversial incident of the entire Championships, however, came from the most unlikely of sources – Tim Mayotte. The American had a number of nicknames including 'The Springfield Rifle', 'The Nearly Man Of Tennis' and the 'Eternal Quarter-finalist', but perhaps the most accurate was 'Gentleman Tim'. He was a truly well-mannered and gracious player, one of the most decent characters you could hope to meet anywhere, not just on the tennis circuit.

But the only time I have seen Mayotte lose his cool, he lost it in truly spectacular fashion. After years of biting his lip when decisions had gone against him, perhaps all his frustration came flooding out in one almighty deluge of temper. Boy, was he cross! It happened in the tiebreaker of an extremely tense quarter-final encounter against Stefan Edberg. The Swede was serving, and just after Mayotte had returned the ball into the net, the line judge called 'out'. The chair umpire John Frame ruled that the ball was good, but Mayotte assumed that the point would be replayed because he thought the line-judge's call had come *before* he returned – and so did Edberg, it seemed, because he stayed on the same side of the court and turned to a ball-boy and asked for another ball. John Frame deemed the point to stand because, to his mind, Mayotte had played the ball before the line judge had shouted 'out'. Mayotte went as mad as I have ever seen anyone at Wimbledon, bawling at Frame in the chair and then destroying his racket, for which he was given a code violation. My jaw dropped as I watched the scene on court – not even McEnroe at his most volcanic had erupted quite like this.

When players have tantrums on court, the crowd generally boo and heckle or slow hand-clap them, but in this instance they were right behind Mayotte, as were the BBC commentators. One of them, John Barrett, is a close friend under whose Davis Cup captaincy I had served, but I became rather annoyed when I heard his commentary going on about what a poor decision it was. Because the awful thing about the incident was that the umpire was absolutely right. Mayotte ended up losing in three sets, but it was far closer than the result suggested because two of them had gone to tiebreakers. After the match, Mayotte refused to shake hands with umpire Frame who was roundly booed as he made his way off the court and then, under escort, back to the office. There was such a hullabaloo that we decided to smuggle Frame out of the ground and put him into an official car to take him on the short journey to his digs in Southfields.

In a scene straight out of an Ealing comedy we gathered together about a dozen other umpires, all dressed in exactly the same uniform as Frame, and then had them file through the crowds in the hope that nobody recognised the man who had suddenly become Public Enemy No. 1. I put him in the car and breathed a sigh of relief as I headed back to the office. Later, however, I was told that he had endured a terrifying journey. The car was sitting in heavy traffic when someone in the crowd recognised him and all of a sudden there were people banging on the roof and the windows and hurling abuse at him, as if he were a serial killer being driven away from the Old Bailey to a maximum security unit. Who, I asked myself again, would be an umpire?

The following day I insisted, for the sake of clearing John Frame's battered reputation, that the BBC replayed the incident and that John Barrett apologised for his comments, which he had the good grace to do.

I'm sure he won't mind me reminding him, but curiously enough it was John Barrett, when he was Davis Cup captain, who lay behind the one time in my own playing career when I felt close to losing my cool. I played in four Davis Cup ties in all, two of them against Luxembourg and two against Austria. My first match against Luxembourg remains a source of modest pride to me as I earned a place in the record-books as the only man to win his Davis Cup début 6–0, 6–0, 6–0. The fact that I also managed to relieve John Barrett of a few pounds, due to the bet he made during the match that he didn't believe I could win without losing a game, makes me prouder still. But the rubber that stands out in my mind far more vividly than any other was in one of the contests with the Austrians.

There were four of us in the team: Mike Sangster, Bobby Wilson, Billy Knight and myself. When the matches got underway, we had gone 1–0 up, when Mike Sangster suffered a dreadful decision against him. There had been a number of poor calls throughout the day and various contretemps with the umpire. We were growing a little bit annoyed as we looked on from the sidelines. When the match was stopped due to bad light, I don't know what possessed me but I marched on court straight over to the linesman who had made this partic-ularly awful call. I was absolutely furious, and as I strode towards him, the others thought I was going to hit him because I had raised my hand and the line official cowered a little. In fact, I just went to shake his hand and said sarcastically: 'Well done, that was a great decision.' By the standards of today, my gesture was the equivalent of hurling a racket to the ground and shouting, 'You're the pits of the world!' I am not especially proud of that moment, but I always felt very passionate about representing Britain in the Davis Cup. When I came to deal with angry players as a referee, my own flash of temper on that occasion is always somewhere at the back of my mind, reminding that passions do and will run over sometimes.

On the Sunday, we took an unassailable 3–1 lead, which

meant that with just one match left to play the rubber was now dead. I was the fourth member in the team and because I had not been pencilled-in to play, I went and had a vigorous warm-up with one of the other members of the team, wearing the only set of tennis clothes I had brought with me to the stadium. As soon as we had won the match, we all headed to the club bar to celebrate, except Mike Sangster who was scheduled to play the last singles match. I had had about three or four reasonably sized glasses of lager when John Barrett came in and told me I was playing. I spluttered into my glass and said: 'You must be joking. The clothes I'm wearing are soaking with sweat and I'm on the wrong end of a few beers. I can't possibly play.' But he insisted. His reasoning was that Sangster was new to the team and that he didn't want to see his confidence destroyed by Austria's leading player, who would be determined to salvage a bit of pride for the home team. I could understand his reasoning but I was terribly disappointed.

It was every bit as terrible as I had feared and I lost the first two sets 6–0. I was in a really bad mood: my limbs were heavy after a long practice session; there were a couple of pints of lager swilling around my stomach; my clothes were sodden, cold and clammy when I stepped out on court; my head was a bit woozy; I was being annihilated. It was undoubtedly one of the lowest points of my playing career.

I managed at least to get three games in the final set, but for a while it looked as if I was going to be in unique position of having won and lost a Davis Cup match by 6–0, 6–0, 6–0. Afterwards the press got hold of a statement, purportedly coming from me, saying I was never again going to play under John Barrett. We immediately issued a counter-statement saying that was rubbish, but it was too late to stop the story making some of the first editions. I don't know how the statement was concocted because I had not said anything of the sort. Certainly, John and I had exchanged words and looks before and after the match and everybody knew that I was upset, but I would never have abandoned the opportunity to play for my country. Despite all this my friendship with John has not suffered in any way, and we remain very good friends to this day.

When Mayotte was blowing his top on court all those years later I was reminded that player anger was nothing new to tennis. The only difference was that we bottled it up. It was an extraordinary episode, but if nothing else it highlighted the tension and strain on the modern professional tennis player and showed that even the most angelic characters could be consumed by demons every now and then. The following morning Mayotte's coach called me to apologise on his behalf and said how very out of character his behaviour had been, but he did not need to tell me or anyone else that.

The four semi-finals in 1989 had a familiar air about them: Becker *v.* Lendl and McEnroe *v.* Edberg, probably the four dominant Wimbledon players in the 1980s. Lendl, of course, had never won the title, but he was always there or thereabouts and only once in seven years had he failed to get as far as the semi-finals. There was an historical parallel which gave his followers hope that 1989 would be his year: this was his 11th attempt to win the Championships just as it was for his fellow Czech Jaroslav Drobny when he triumphed back in 1954 (when, *vis-à-vis* nothing at all, he became the first player to wear glasses in a Wimbledon final). Once again though Lendl was to be denied, as Becker rallied from 2 sets to 1 down to reach the final, where he crushed Edberg in three sets to avenge his defeat by the Swede the previous year.

Becker's triumph made him only the third man, after Borg and McEnroe, to win the title three times in the Open era and it also completed a remarkable German double as Steffi Graf beat Martina Navratilova in the women's final. As I watched Boris walk up to collect the trophy from the Duke of Kent, it seemed incredible that he was still only 21 years old, while Steffi was just 20 years old. Tennis had certainly become a very young person's game. Since McEnroe took the third of his titles in 1984, no one over the age of 22 had won the men's singles title. In my playing days, we were just starting to make an impression at that age and the best players were by and large the ones closer to 30 than 20. In 1908 Britain's Arthur Gore actually won the title at the age of 41, but nowadays he might be considered too old even for the over-35s senior tour.

The year 1990 was quieter and I suppose I must have been immensely pleased about it at the time for, as far as I am concerned, no news during the fortnight is generally good news. News at Wimbledon means temper tantrums, downpours, bomb-scares and other security incidents, tension between the press and the players, grumbling umpires, the death of etiquette, streakers, letters of complaint, etc . . . But 1990 appears to have been remarkably uneventful in all these respects. The relative peace and quiet was reflected in the crowd figures which were down quite sharply, even though the weather was dry and warm. This, however, had nothing to do with lack of spectacle or interest at the All England Club and everything to do with the World Cup in Italy, which coincided with the Championships. If sports lovers thought that was unfortunate, they were spoilt for choice on 4 July 2004, when the men's singles final took place on the same day as the Euro 2004 football final, an England–New Zealand one-day cricket international and the French Grand Prix.

Just two entries stand out in my notes for the 1990 Championships and they read 'grunting' and 'bananas'. In the absence of any major on-court histrionics, 'grunting' became the talk of the Championships over the following few years, at least in the media, and there were calls for it to be stamped out as a new blight on the modern game. The tabloid newspapers even introduced machines called 'gruntometers' by which they could measure the decibel level of the players as they played their shots. The game had seen a handful of impressive 'grunters' in the past, not least Jimmy Connors, whose vocal performance on court was once memorably described as 'like that of some monolithic Russian female shot-putter'. But the undisputed champion of the grunt, without any question, was Monica Seles, who was rapidly emerging as a great player of the future at the turn of the decade.

You could not hope to meet a lovelier person off court than Monica Seles: one of the few leading players who always takes time to stop and talk to people less celebrated than herself. Although she was quiet and humble off court, the same could not be said of her when she had a racket in her hand. One commentator likened the noise she made to an express train going into a tunnel. Many of her opponents and several commentators claimed that Monica grunted deliberately in order to put off her opponent, but I have always doubted that. For a start you have to make a bit of an effort to grunt if it doesn't come naturally, and to grunt deliberately during every shot of every point of every game of every match would be some achievement. I also doubt whether Monica was capable of being that devious. Moreover, today, there is probably more grunting around than there ever has been and I think it has a lot to do with coaches telling players to inhale when the ball is approaching and then exhale when they strike. I don't think it's any more malicious than that.

Today tennis has a tremendous new grunter in the teenage Russian girl Maria Sharapova. She doesn't just grunt, she positively screams, and it has clearly upset a number of her opponents. At the French Open in 2003 she was obliged to go and talk about the issue with the tournament referee, but officials can only act under the 'hindrance' rule if it can be shown that the player is making the noise on purpose, which is virtually impossible to do. I believe the opponent of a grunter will not be as distracted as much as players on a neighbouring court because he or she will be able to adapt to the rhythm and monotony of the grunts. Many of the non-grunting players are very unhappy about the noise pollution and a kind of 'counter-grunt culture' has emerged in recent years whereby the offended parties ape their opponents' noises as retaliation. Grunting has done Sharapova no harm, mind you, what with winning both Wimbledon and the WTA end of season championship in Los Angeles in 2004.

Bananas also seemed to be a hot topic of conversation that summer. You would have thought Britons had never seen a banana before, judging by the amount of press coverage surrounding the fruit. It really must have been an extremely quiet, controversy-free Wimbledon if the press were forced to write articles headed: 'The Dawn of the Banana' and

'Wimbledon Goes Bananas!' Becker, Edberg and Michael Chang were amongst the keenest munchers, but the media craze became so bad that reporters for one of the tabloids were asked to count how many bananas they saw a player eat in a match. (For the record, the American David Wheaton finished top of the banana charts with nine in a match.) From hindsight, though, silly as it was, at least it was all just a bit of light-hearted fun and I'd rather that any day than all the muck-raking of the players' private lives we had had in the past.

It had been a relatively quiet Championships tennis-wise as well and there were only a few matches which stayed in the memory for long, but at least the fortnight came to an end with a couple of crackers. First of all, Martina Navratilova beat Zina Garrison to win her ninth and final Wimbledon singles title to surpass the record set by Helen Wills-Moody back in the twenties and thirties. The achievement was all the more remarkable because she was now in her 34th year. Martina was always a great one for keeping her emotions in check, but on this occasion she was clearly overwhelmed by the moment and bounded into the crowd to hug her partner. Afterwards she said she planned to get drunk for the first time in her life and I don't think there would have been a single person in the crowd that day who would have denied her that indulgence. She was a terrific champion, a model professional, and has done wonders for the reputation of women's tennis.

The men's final between Becker and Edberg was predictable only in that it was the third year running that the two players had faced each other in the final. On this occasion, Edberg, now a relatively old man at 24, got the better of his old adversary in a thrilling five-setter which he edged out 6–4 in the decider.

The only other event of outstanding interest that year was the passing of the All England Club's chairmanship from Buzzer Hadingham to the dynamic and forceful John Curry. Buzzer, a former head of Slazenger, was one of the old school: a perfect English gentleman. Sadly, he died in January 2005. I always had a very good relationship with Buzzer and he showed he was the right man for the job at the right time. He was a regular at the club for many years, but more recently to be found at the bridge table rather than on the tennis courts. He was considered a safe pair of hands and deserves praise for helping to steer Wimbledon through a fairly turbulent period for tennis in general, resisting all the ridiculous calls for getting rid of the club's grass and showing an even hand in his treatment of the players. The eighties were also a period of unbridled commercialism, but Buzzer was at the forefront of ensuring that Wimbledon did not surrender its traditions to the various temptations and pressures.

Wimbledon seems to have an uncanny knack for appointing leading officials who, like Buzzer, turn out to be the right people for their time. There are, of course, factions of traditionalists and modernisers at the club, but the vast majority of members lie somewhere between the two and take a view on each issue based on its merits. In the 1990s vast changes would sweep through Wimbledon, and the club was lucky to have the bullishly impressive figure of John Curry at the helm. It is widely agreed among members that Curry was one of the best chairmen the club has ever had, and it was under his supervision, together with the chief executive Chris Gorringe, that the long-term plan – an enormous modernising and building programme – swung into motion. The result of this monumental programme was a new Court 1, as well as extensive new facilities for the players, the members and officials in the 'W-shaped' Millennium building. John Curry was not an easygoing chap in the mould of Buzzer, but he had very sound judgement and if he thought something was good for the club he would endeavour to push the proposal through the various committee stages. Under his chairmanship, Wimbledon, without ever losing its traditions, was well and truly catapulted into the modern era.

Chapter Six

A Day to Remember,
a Time to Forget

After the calm of 1990 came the storm of 1991. Any hopes
that the tennis and weather gods were going to shine their
favour on me for a second year were soon washed away. When
it rains for me at Wimbledon, it seems to pour and, heavens
above, did it pour in 1991! It was one of the wettest first weeks
Wimbledon has ever experienced, and the wettest overall for
80 years. There was no play at all on the opening Monday
and by Thursday evening there had been just over nine hours
of action, with only 52 of the 240 scheduled matches
completed. The atmosphere was proportionately gloomy in
our office as we surveyed the wreckage that the deluge had
wrought upon our best-laid plans. There had also been torren-
tial rain in the build-up to the fortnight, wiping out the straw-
berry crop in Kent and forcing the caterers to import the
hallowed fruit from Belgium and France.

One particularly frustrating effect of the rain is that the
press, understandably desperate for something to write about,
always manages to wheel out one or two big names in the
game, generally former players, who proclaim that it is high
time Wimbledon drags itself out of the Dark Ages and gets

a roof for the Centre Court. In 1991 it was Billie Jean King's turn. Personally, I'm not wholly convinced. My main objection to the proposal is that a roof would be very unfair on all the players except a handful of what you might call the 'marquee' names. You can only play four matches a day on a court, five if you are lucky, so while one of the top seeds might get his match over and done with and enjoy a relaxing day or two back at the hotel, his unseeded opponent in the next round would have to hang around at Wimbledon waiting to play and would then miss his rest day because the whole schedule will have been concertinaed by the delays. Then there is the cost: all the rough estimates we have heard being bandied around the club suggest that the installation of a roof is an astonishingly expensive business, running into millions. You have to ask yourself whether that money might be better spent elsewhere, say perhaps on a fresh initiative for youngsters in the game.

There are also the groundsmen and the court preparation to bear in mind. Getting a court in perfect shape is a delicate enough operation at the best times: the balance of light, air and water has to be spot on if Wimbledon's courts are to reach their pristine best. A roof would present serious difficulties and challenges to the groundsmen.

Whenever I am asked about Wimbledon getting a roof, I always recount a story told to me by the German player Michael Stich. After the grass-court tournament at Halle back in his homeland put a roof over their main court he was asked to play there as part of his build-up to Wimbledon. When he arrived at the All England Club a week later, he told me how disappointed he was with the state of their Centre Court. During the qualifying rounds in the week before the main draw it had rained so hard that no play was possible on the outdoor courts and so they closed the roof and played all the matches on the show court. By the time the main draw got underway there was little grass left on the court and Stich said it was like playing on clay. There is a possibility that this might happen at the All England Club, which would make a mockery of Wimbledon's unique status as the only major grass-court championships left on the circuit. Grass is a central part of Wimbledon's appeal and tradition, and to abandon it for the sake of playing a handful of matches, and at such an exorbitant cost, strikes me as folly. For me, the addition of a roof would kill some of the spirit of Wimbledon.

The argument I can see in its favour – and I admit it's a fairly persuasive one – is that it would allow about 15,000 people (a welcome increase from the current capacity of 13,800) who have paid good money for their tickets and a day out actually to see some tennis. Fair enough, but what of the other 20,000 left trudging around under their umbrellas outside clutching their sodden tickets? I can see both sides of the argument, and the pressure from television, which brings so much money into the game, is enormous. The ideal compromise, in my judgement, would be to install the roof but only bring it into play from the quarter-finals onwards when *all* the matches could be played there. That would be logical and fair, but then if it rained earlier in the tournament there would be an outcry I suppose. It's a no-win situation.

The roof is likely to become a reality in 2009. It will require a lot of building work, but as I have said, increasing the capacity to 15,000 with more comfort and improved facilities for players and spectators has positive elements. The proposed material for the roof is reported to be very strong, waterproof (obviously), flexible and translucent, with enough light coming through to give you the impression you are in the open air. It will take ten minutes to close, which means that the court coverers, all too commonly seen today, will still be used while the roof is closing. Getting the covers over the court is quite an art and there is always a certain amount of competition between the teams on all courts to see how quickly it can be done.

While there might be an iota of good sense in the idea of a roof at Wimbledon, another frequently raised proposal that Wimbledon should get rid of its grass is lunacy as far as I am concerned. There have always been vociferous campaigners calling for Wimbledon's lawns to be replaced with some form of artificial surface. To me, this would be absolute sacrilege. Wimbledon on any other surface than grass would not be Wimbledon. I don't think I could even bring myself to watch it and I imagine there would be a huge rebellion against such a move if anyone at the All England Club seriously considered the notion. For what is it that is particularly distinctive about Wimbledon if not its grass? You could get rid of the strawberries and cream and the Pimms and the Royal Box and the whites, and Wimbledon would still be Wimbledon – perhaps only just – but it is the grass that makes Wimbledon unique and distinctive. When people turn on the television at the start of that last week in June and see the lush green, perfectly manicured courts, they experience not just a thrill of anticipation but a reassuring sense of continuity as well. Wimbledon has become part of our culture, a national institution, even for those who do not ordinarily show an interest in tennis, and this is because it has preserved its most important traditions.

If you plan to replace the grass, why not be done with it altogether and move one of the world's premier sporting events to a utilitarian, soulless concrete complex in Milton Keynes or Telford? That, apparently, is exactly what the former chairman John Curry threatened to do during a row about planning permission with the local council. At some point in the negotiations he reportedly said something along the lines of 'Well, do you really want to force us to relocate the Championships to Basingstoke?' That was the end of the matter.

The anti-grass lobby, and it is a very small minority it should be stressed, complains that as there is no longer any meaningful grass-court season as such and players don't get a chance to prepare properly for the Championships, Wimbledon should ditch its distinctive heritage. But since the Australian Open abandoned its grass, it seems to me that now more than ever it is important to keep the surface at Wimbledon. It has become unique. Today there are four different surfaces in Grand Slams, providing a genuine all-round test of a player's ability, and anyone in any doubt about whether Wimbledon should uproot its famous courts should just ask the players, even the ones whose natural game does not lend itself readily to the surface.

There will always be some people who like to challenge Wimbledon's traditions year after year. One of them in 1991 was Andre Agassi, who returned to Wimbledon for the first time in four years after reportedly boycotting the event for, among other things, the fact that he was obliged to wear predominantly white clothing. Whether this had been his personal choice or had been made under pressure from his manufacturers or marketing people I couldn't say, but there was much speculation about what his attire would be when he stepped out on court. I fired a warning shot across his bows before the Championships by announcing that he would not be allowed on court unless he was dressed properly, and the American, in turn, stoked the fires of curiosity by refusing to reveal to the media what he would be wearing. Agassi is in every respect one of the most colourful characters in the game, his outrageous, often garish, clothes in the past reflecting the flamboyance of his play and character. He was then rapidly emerging as one of the great players of his generation – as well as a marketing manager's dream with his good looks and great personal charm – and all eyes were trained on him as he walked out on court for his first-round match with Grant Connell of Canada wearing an immaculate white tracksuit. I was watching him like a hawk from the side of the court, but he maintained the suspense and had the crowd muttering and giggling when he kept his tracksuit on for the pre-match warm-up. Finally, he sat down and took off the bottom half of his tracksuit to reveal a pair of gleaming white shorts and socks and then slowly peeled off his top to reveal a perfect white shirt. Agassi beamed a cheeky grin, the crowd laughed and I breathed a great sigh of relief and slipped away.

Wimbledon keeps a whole room full of spare white clothing because year after year, deliberately or not, players break the whites rule. It's a particular problem, however understandable, in the junior events, as the youngsters and their families are less familiar with the protocol. But I am forever amazed at the number of senior players, many of them well off, who come out wearing unacceptable clothing just, it seems, to get their hands on the official Wimbledon shirts that are brought out to them. Many players used to ask for three or four shirts, claiming they got 'oh so sweaty', but the sheer volume of shirts the club were doling out led to strong suspicions that the players were just trying it on. Difficult as it may be to believe, the club also had a similar problem with its official towels. Some of the players used to take the towels from the dressing-room, hand them to friends in the crowd as they came on court and then call an official to ask for some more to be brought out. I wouldn't say that this practice exactly brought the club to its financial knees, but each year a tidy fortune was lost in this way and the club was forced to take action.

In an effort to put an end to the mischief, the club decided to give the players a guest pack which, among other things, included a Wimbledon towel. But that didn't make the slightest difference and still the towels were being dished out in their hundreds. The club's policy ever since has been to give the players plain old white towels in the dressing-room and the Wimbledon ones are issued on court by officials, who are under orders to try to get them back. They don't always succeed, however, and often the player has got the towel safely stuffed into his bag and is hot footing it off court by the time the official has cleared his throat. Apparently they are a collector's item.

In spite of his run-in with Wimbledon over its whites policy, Agassi quickly became the darling of that year's Championships as he swept through to the quarter-finals where he suffered a surprise defeat to the unseeded David Wheaton. (Perhaps it was the bananas!) Agassi may have had a prickly relationship with Wimbledon when he was younger, but I have always had a tremendous amount of affection and admiration both for the man and the player. You cannot help but like him. He is one of the good guys, and Jill and I were absolutely delighted when we saw that he and Steffi Graf had found romance together. I only had one major incident with him at Wimbledon when he put on a bit of a prima donna exhibition about the state of the court and became quite angry with me. He was by no means the only leading player to resort to play-acting in order to make his point – Lendl for one was an absolute master of the theatrical form – but on this occasion Agassi had the good grace and humility to call me the following morning and apologise for the way he had behaved. He didn't agree with my decision but he did recognise he had been 'out of order' in his actions.

The Agassi show was a welcome diversion in 1991 as the rain put a dampener on the whole atmosphere in that first week and British gloom was deepened by the annual culling of our players in the opening rounds. Just one British man and not a single woman made it into the third round. Jeremy Bates, Britain's leading player at this time, was 1,000–1 with one of the main bookmakers to win the Championships: the same odds they were offering for the Archbishop of Canterbury to announce the Second Coming of the Lord. Incredibly, the bookmakers took two bets on the latter but none on the former, which reflected the sense of hopelessness and crisis enveloping the national game.

Two of our players came up against Goran Ivanisevic, the rangy, big-serving Croat who was just starting to make a name for himself – and both matches were highly memorable for different reasons. Goran has always been a very colourful, amusing, big-hearted player, and I was happy for him when he pulled off his remarkable Wimbledon triumph in 2001. I'm sure, however, he would be the first to admit that, in his early years especially, he could often be something of a pain in the proverbial while on court. He had burst to prominence the year before by reaching the semi-finals, and if there were some amongst the British tennis public who were still unaware of him at the start of the 1991 Championships they certainly knew all about him by the time he had stomped away in a fine Balkan bate by the end of the first week.

In the first round he was playing Andrew Castle, a tough cookie and a battler who had the insolence to push the No. 10 seed to the wire in tiebreakers in the first two sets. Ivanisevic had perhaps been expecting a pleasant little workout against Castle, a gentle loosening of the muscles to get him into shape and rhythm for the bigger game awaiting him further into the draw. But roared on by a partisan home crowd, Castle was having none of it and worked Ivanisevic into something of a froth at the other end. Finally, Ivanisevic snapped and went completely berserk. He had already received a penalty point for smashing a ball into the canvas surrounding the court when he began to complain to the umpire about the state of the court and promptly sat down refusing to play, just as his fellow Yugoslav Zivojinovic had done a few years earlier. I was tied up elsewhere while this was going on and as the match was being played on one of the outer courts my assistant and old friend Tony Gathercole had the task of dealing with him. With the crowd baying, Ivanisevic sulking and the umpire nonplussed, we had once again found ourselves in a scene of high farce at Wimbledon. Tony, though, was firm and cool, and after telling Ivanisevic the court was playable he ordered him back on court and the Croat moodily peeled himself off his chair and returned to action. The fact that he clinched victory in the third set suggested it was not so much the state of the court as the state of Ivanisevic's mind which had not been fit for play.

Ivanisevic's second-round match was no less dramatic, for this was the famous occasion when he crashed out to Nick Brown, then ranked somewhere around 600 in the world. The predominantly British crowd delighted in his demise as much as they did in Brown's victory. Ivanisevic was not the most popular man in SW19 that week, and no one could have imagined that almost exactly ten years later this surly Croat would have many people in the Wimbledon crowd weeping tears of joy at his success.

But Ivanisevic was not the only one throwing the toys out of his pram in the early rounds, and amidst the showers and bad light, McEnroe was behaving as badly as he had done ten years earlier with his 'pits of the world' tirade. The shaggy hair and incredible athleticism of 1981 had now gone, replaced by a shorter crop and a slightly less willing and able body, but the temper certainly showed no signs of the ageing process. Perhaps it was the weather, perhaps the frustration of his fading abilities, but whatever the cause, he was in a mighty stink that fortnight. In one of his early-round matches, he had tried to have a line judge removed, announcing that the man had been 'bugging me for years'. He screamed at the umpire Richard Kaufman, and then gave the supervisor Ken Farrar and myself a thunderous ear-bashing when we came on court to try to defuse the situation. At one point he hurled his racket from the baseline to his chair and altogether he crashed his racket into the turf on six occasions, while his wife Tatum looked on nervously from the crowd.

He was only marginally better in his next match, but it was in his fourth-round defeat to Stefan Edberg that he really let fly and forced me to fine him the maximum $10,000 after he blew up at a line judge out of earshot of the umpire. In a ten-second outburst he managed to slip in the f-word no fewer than six times – a feat that might have won him an entry in the *Guinness Book of Records* under different circumstances – and unfortunately for him an ITN camera crew was on hand to record the diatribe.

It is possible, although uncommon, to get away with swearing on court. One incidence of this, once again involving Mr McEnroe but as the innocent party, occurred in a 1992 Davis Cup match between the United States and Argentina. The match was being played in Hawaii and I was very pleased to be asked to referee. Jill accompanied me and we invited our friends Mary and Hugh Stewart as well. Hugh had actually played for the United States but Mary had never been to a Davis Cup match. We had a wonderful time and the backdrop of the beach and accommodating whales in the distance when the draw was made has to be one of the most picturesque I have ever seen for a cup-tie.

Not that things were quite so relaxing on court. This was one of McEnroe's last Davis Cups, albeit as a doubles player, and during his match one of the Argentinians swore in his native tongue. The umpire failed to notice, and by the time I had realised, play had continued. McEnroe, however, had heard the phrase and complained that the player had not been warned because the umpire had not understood. I did my best to explain that it was now too late to do anything about it, but McEnroe felt it was most unfair as he was always warned or penalised – as he had been the previous year at Wimbledon – just because he spoke in English.

*   *   *

I truly could have done without all the temper tantrums of the 1991 Championships. The weather had caused such an immense backlog of matches that Wimbledon was forced to contemplate the unprecedented move of playing on the middle Sunday. Although the other Grand Slams play straight through with no break, the Sunday had become something of a sacred institution at Wimbledon and gave all the players and many of the staff a welcome rest. With more rain forecast, the programme looked fairly bleak as I ran my eye over the great list of matches that still needed to be played. Players need as much time as possible to relax between matches and I was trying to be as fair as I could to all of them as I battled with the various permutations. On this particular day we had finally managed to get the women's singles just about back on track, but the men were still a day behind. We had just issued the following day's order of play in which I had the women playing first, with the men to follow – the idea being that the women could have a rest day – when there was knock on my door and in walked Ion Tiriac, Boris Becker's coach. 'The red-haired wonder would like to have a word with you,' he said.

'Fine. My door is always open,' I replied, and with that in came the wonder himself. Becker sat down and then very politely and eloquently explained that he felt I had made a mistake with the order of play, saying that I should have had the men playing first so they could at least rest up for half a day before they came back the following day, rather than finish up late in the evening, rush back to the hotel and then come straight back in the morning. What he said had some merit, but I had made my decision on the basis that the women's final was a day earlier than the men's, and therefore in my mind the women had priority. The weather gods had got me into the hole in the first place, but for once, thank heaven, they came to my rescue and all scheduled matches were completed.

On the Thursday evening of that miserable first week I had a meeting with the chairman John Curry to discuss the previously unthinkable – opening the gates on Sunday. This was the nuclear option, but the pile-up of matches was stacked so high that the idea was now very much on my radar screen. The logistical and security problems of such a move were immense. No tickets had been printed; many of the 6,000-strong staff working at Wimbledon during the fortnight had already made plans for the day off; caterers needed time to order in more supplies; the police and local council would have to be informed and possibly even persuaded to let it go ahead; and there were also fears that traffic might clog the area as the punters shunned the Sunday version of London Transport, taking their cars instead. John Curry was not at all keen on the idea, but he understood that I knew better than anyone else what was needed to get the Championships back on course. Unfortunately the weather forecast was not good and privately I had pretty well made up my mind that we would have to break with tradition and play on the Sunday. However, on the Friday the weather lifted and we managed to clear in excess of a hundred matches in the day, encouraging the chairman to think that all was now well. All the staff and everyone else related to the Championships had been alerted to the possibility of Sunday play, so it was just a matter now of announcing the decision one way or the other.

Two factors persuaded me that we would have to have the

extra day. Firstly, the forecast was poor and secondly we would not have a 'clean order of play' the following week, giving the players the necessary amount of rest, if we did not clear the backlog once and for all. The matches would simply have been too close together. John Curry was never a man to shy away from speaking his mind. His honesty was one of the keys to his success as chairman and I certainly felt the full blast of his frankness when I told him that we would have to play. He was very unhappy indeed.

By ten o'clock on Sunday morning a queue almost two miles long had formed outside the grounds as tens of thousands of 'real' tennis fans descended on the grounds for the cut-price tickets. There were 11,000 Centre Court and 7,000 Court 1 tickets on sale at £10 each, plus 5,000 ground passes for the outer courts at £5. I watched as the gates opened and the spectators streamed into the courts to bag the best seats in the house. I will never forget that Sunday and I will go so far as to say it was one of my happiest days ever at Wimbledon, as a player, club member or referee.

It was the only time I have ever seen Centre Court completely full from the moment the first ball was struck to when the covers came on at the end of the day. This was partly because there were no corporate tickets involved that day and so no businessmen shunning the seats in favour of a long lunch in one of the marquees, but it was mainly down to the sheer enthusiasm of the crowd. I have never known an atmosphere like it at Wimbledon. It was like a good-natured football crowd or the Last Night of the Proms on the two main show courts, and there was endless cheering and even the odd Mexican wave, which seemed appropriate in this carnival atmosphere. Gabriela Sabatini was first up on Centre

Court, and I remember watching the mixture of sadness and joy on Martina Navratilova's face as she walked past her favourite court before heading out to Court 1 for her own match. Navratilova stopped outside Centre Court for what seemed like an eternity, as if she were trying to soak up the atmosphere and take some of it away with her. Jimmy Connors also appeared on Centre Court and was given a highly emotional standing ovation at the end of a three-set defeat to his fellow American Derrick Rostagno. Most people thought his 19th Wimbledon would be his last, but the old warhorse was back for more the following year.

At the end of a wonderful day, many people on the way out came over to shake my hand and thank me, and I was positively glowing with contentment when I was driven home that night. Over my coffee the following morning, I read a headline along the lines of 'Wimbledon Public Should Thank Mills', and to this day I feel very proud of my part in what became known as 'People's Sunday'.

I generally don't get many positive headlines – at best they are neutral – and I don't get that many pats on the back. For some reason, people just don't feel the compunction to come up to me and say: 'Congratulations, Alan – the way you squeezed that doubles match on to Court 14 at the end, there was an excellent piece of scheduling . . .' Mine is not a job in which you expect to receive plaudits. To most members of the viewing public I'm the spoilsport in the grey suit who pops out of the corner to order the covers on, or to administer a rap over the knuckles to the men behaving badly. In truth, the vast majority of our hard work is done behind the scenes, juggling the interests of a host of different groups of people. No one really knows about the pressures and challenges of our office, which are as varied as they are manifold: we are at once ACAS negotiators, private counsellors, ambassadors, policemen, magistrates and schedulers trying to compile the equivalent of a national railway timetable. I have loved it all and that has been reward enough in itself down the years. But on that one wonderful Sunday it was particularly gratifying that for once I seemed to have made a lot of people very happy.

For a long time it had seemed inevitable that the Championships would spill over into a third week, but by playing on the Sunday, together with a succession of 11 a.m. starts, a reduction of the men's doubles matches to the best of three sets and the long-awaited appearance of the sun in the last five days, we were able to complete the programme on time. The improvement in the weather was reflected in the behaviour of the players and you could not help but conclude that, in some small way at least, the two issues were linked. If the players spend hours cooped up inside in the competitors' area listening to the drumming of the rain, seeing the dark clouds set fast over London and on some days trooping on and off court, their adrenalin levels going up and down like yo-yos, it is no wonder that they grow frustrated. There is plenty of tension building up in the players in any event, but by the time they get on court after days of kicking their heels the more volcanic amongst them are rumbling loudly.

The players were not the only ones erupting. There was an almighty punch-up at the gates after six burly businessmen stepped out of their stretch limousine and presented their Centre Court tickets, for which they had paid £1,000 each on the black market, only to be told they were counterfeit. I wish I had been there to see their faces, but I was quite happy to have missed the 'discussions' with the security guards that followed.

Amidst all the hullabaloo of an especially eventful and difficult Championships, it is quite easy for us in the office to lose sight of the very point of us all being there in the first place – that is, the drama and excitement of the tennis itself, and there was certainly plenty of that during those final few days. Princess Diana was in the Royal Box to see Agassi's glorious procession through the draw brought to a heart-breaking end by Wheaton, while Navratilova quite literally ran out of the grounds in tears after losing to the 15-year-old Jennifer Capriati. (It was difficult to take on board the fact that by the time the youngster from Florida was born, Navratilova had already played in three Wimbledons.) Gabriela Sabatini came agonisingly close to lifting the women's trophy when she lost 8–6 in the final set to Steffi, but the biggest surprise came in the men's final where the 40–1 German outsider Michael Stich beat his compatriot Becker in three sets in what, in all truth, was not the most captivating final I have witnessed at Wimbledon. Big, booming, Teutonic serves were the order of the day and so predictable was the progress of the play that the first two sets were settled by tiebreakers. Still, it was good for tennis that the Becker–Edberg stranglehold on the Championships had been broken and better still that it was achieved by an outsider, something that would give inspiration to a new generation of players starting to make an impression on the game. The old order had had its day: Connors and McEnroe would be back for one more year and Lendl would have two more stabs at the title that was always to remain just out of reach, but this great triumvirate were effectively history. Becker and Edberg, meanwhile, were also on the wane. The curtain was starting to come down on an extremely colourful era in the history of men's tennis and a new cast of performers was waiting in the wings to take the stage. The players' behaviour over the coming years would be nothing like as rowdy as it had been over the previous decade or so, but from where I sat in the referee's office, that would not necessarily be such a bad thing. The tennis, though, would be just as absorbing.

Every summer, for close on half a century now, I have walked or driven through the gates at Wimbledon either as a player, an official, a member or on one memorable occasion, as a father going to his son's wedding reception. I competed in the Championships for 17 years in all, in the singles, the men's doubles and the mixed doubles; for six years I came in my capacity as assistant referee and since 1983 I have been there as the referee. Throughout the year, when we are not travelling, Jill and I go up to the club for meetings or for a game of tennis, or perhaps some lunch or a drink with friends. I must have walked through those gates over a thousand times and although the club has undergone sweeping changes during that time, the essence and atmosphere of the place has remained virtually unaltered. The ivy is still climbing the walls and the steeple of the church at the top of the hill still dominates the view over the clusters of ancient trees and the rooftops of the splendid properties of what the estate agents now like to call 'Wimbledon Village'. The layout of the courts to the left of the main entrance as you walk in from Church Road past the statue of Fred Perry are much as they were when the man himself graced the lawns. Even the old water tower towards the back of the grounds is still there, a monument in its own way to the most famous tennis club on the planet.

Sometimes when I pass through the gates, my mind wanders back to the very first time I came to the club in 1955 as a nervous 19-year-old Lancashire lad. I was upset not to have been invited the year before because, although it would be a lie to say I was setting the British tennis scene on fire, I had had some good results and on paper was worth my place in the draw. If you came from up North in those days, you could not help but feel that there was some real substance to the talk of a North–South divide. If you came from the North it was certainly more difficult to catch the eye of the national selectors.

Like most players, I remember my first day vividly. I had travelled down the night before and, unlike today, there was no luxury hotel or chauffeur-driven courtesy car waiting to pick me up. I arrived in Wimbledon by train and then hopped on the bus carrying all my bags and rackets. I remember feeling a goose-pimpling shiver of pride when my fellow passengers looked at all my baggage and equipment, knowing that I was on my way to play in the world's most celebrated tennis tournament. I was so nervous that I left as early as possible to get to the grounds, but when I arrived there at about 10 a.m. the old guard on the gate refused to let me in. Like the paying public, I had to be a good lad and wait until the gates were opened at the scheduled time, thank you very much. It was more than his job was worth to let me in, was the rough gist of his explanation. So for the next two hours I sat down on a bench near the club, thinking about my match against a veteran Australian called Jack Arkinstall and waiting for the big iron gates to swing open.

The atmosphere was so much more casual in those days and once inside, there was no one to tell you where to go or what to do. It took several enquiries and wrong turnings before I found my way to the locker-rooms. I was so over-whelmed by the occasion that I could not eat and barely even speak, especially once the crowds had flooded into the grounds and the whole place was a-buzz with anticipation. The sight of the great names of the era hardly helped to soothe my nerves: the No. 1 seed Tony Trabert, the brilliant young Australians Ken Rosewall and Lew Hoad, Jaroslav Drobny, Vic Seixas . . .

I was on Court 10, down by the water tower, and my legs were like jelly and my stomach a butterfly sanctuary as I made my way through the crowds for my showdown with Arkinstall. In those days there were no chairs for the players to sit on, so I just dropped my bags, shook hands with my opponent, muttered some meaningless vapourings about what a super day it was and how the courts looked just super, took a gulp of the Robinson's Barley Water and headed out on court for the warm-up. I was very nervous, and from hindsight I had lost the match even before I got anywhere near the court. The right amount of nerves can be a good thing – it gives you a bit of edge and concentrates the mind, but in excess things can be severely debilitating. The mind wanders, the wrist wobbles, the legs shake and the mouth dries up. I was simply overawed by the whole experience. I am sure that had I met Arkinstall at my local club in Formby without knowing who he was – he was not one of the favourites, just a good solid player – then I might have given him a half-decent run-around. I was fit, I had a good backhand and although my serve was a little weak, my all-round game was fairly reasonable. As it was, the Australian barely broke sweat as he dispatched me in straight sets 6–2, 6–3, 6–2, and to be honest, once I realised that I was going to be given a bit of a pasting, I was pretty keen to get the whole thing over and done with and put it down to experience.

I knew fairly early on in my career that I was never going to be one of the greats. I was never defeatist, but I understood my limitations. Other players were just more gifted than I was. End of story. Only a handful of people are born to greatness, but I was never frustrated by the knowledge that I would not reach the summit of the game. I just loved playing and I loved the thrill of travel and the camaraderie of the circuit. After my national service with the RAF, I landed a job with the soap manufacturers Cussons (organised by the LTA), who were heavily involved in the sponsorship of tennis. They gave me a pretty reasonable salary to act as a sales representative for the company when I was travelling on the tennis circuit and between tournaments. My brief involved going into local chemists to promote the latest range of soaps and other goods and although it was by no means the most exciting or glamorous employment, I wasn't going to complain if it paid me a salary and allowed me to pursue my life on the tennis circuit. Later during my playing days, I was taken on by the sports manufacturers Dunlop and I performed a similar job for them, contacting local sports shops while on my travels and then working in their London office for most of the winter. That too paid me good money for the day and I also had a company car, a light blue Hillman Minx. My mother said to me when I was starting to head out into the world, 'The day you get a job for £1,000 a year and a car of your own I will be very happy woman.' That's exactly what I had by my mid-twenties and I think she was very proud.

The highlight of my career was beating probably the greatest player the game has ever seen. Unfortunately, my moment of glory came at a pre-Wimbledon tournament in front of a few dozen spectators rather than at the All England Club before a packed Centre Court. Still, how many other people can say they have beaten Rod Laver? It happened at the Hurlingham Club, an exclusive private club set in beautiful grounds in Fulham on the northern banks of the Thames, and I remember it was a grizzly old day and Laver was not in the best of moods. This was the biggest moment of my career to date and I wasn't going to let it pass without making a good fight of it.

Predictably, I was little nervous at the outset and he won the first set pretty easily. Until Laver arrived on the scene most left-handers used to lob or slice their backhands, but he was the first to be able to hit them flat or with topspin, and he certainly hit some blistering ones in that first set. I had the impression that the whole thing was a bit of a bore for him and he just wanted to get it out of the way as quickly as possible, but for me this was one of those moments of a lifetime, something to tell the grandchildren (but now that we have them I am not sure they would be interested!) and I wanted to hang in there as long as possible.

It was perhaps partly that I never imagined for a moment I could beat the great man and partly because he wasn't whitewashing me, that I began to relax and grow in confidence, especially when I took the second set. Laver seemed distinctly underwhelmed about the prospect of the match going to a third set, and his frustration grew even more visible as I played really well in the third set to take the match. The organisers were furious. They had hoped to sell lots of tickets on the virtual certainty of a final between Laver and another excellent Aussie called Martin Mulligan. But while I was beating Laver my friend and doubles partner Bobby Wilson was beating Mulligan and the crowd weren't exactly breaking down the gates to see us face off in the final the following day.

There are two other triumphs in my career which will remain vivid in my memory forever and they came against former Wimbledon champion Drobny and a very good Italian player called Nicola Pietrangeli, one of the top seeds at Wimbledon for several years at the start of the sixties. Drobny, to be honest, was past his best when I met him in the first round in 1959, but he was still some scalp and the victory was all the sweeter because my mother, who had never been to Wimbledon, was in the crowd on Court 1 that day. There was a wonderful atmosphere and because I was British, all the spectators were firmly behind me. (At this point in his itinerant life Drobny was Egyptian. Originally a Czech who had fled the communist rule of his homeland he later became a British citizen and also represented somewhere by the name of Bohemia-Moravia!) It was an incredibly long match and although it only went to four sets, the scores will give you some idea of how hard I had to scrap for this moment of glory: 14–12, 3–6, 10–8, 8–6. I remember seeing the glow of pride on my mother's face after the match and that was more satisfying even than beating one of the great players of his generation. My parents had done so much to help me pursue my ambitions as a tennis player at a time when most people just wanted their children to get as good an education as possible and quickly settle down into a sensible, steady job.

Tennis, of course, was amateur in those days and so there was no money to be earned directly from it. It was not a career but an enjoyable pastime that might, if you were lucky as I had been, win you a job in a related line of work. But in spite of all this, my parents even remortgaged the house to help meet the costs of travelling on the circuit. If it hadn't been for their kindness, I might still be working as an electrical engineer or a soap salesman up on the Wirral.

The British always used to relish playing the overseas players, especially the ones from Europe, because they hardly ever played on grass and were at an obvious disadvantage when they came over. But I would have been the rank outsider when I came up against Nicola Pietrangeli in the third round of the 1962 Championships. I have got to know Nicola very well since and we are good friends, but he wasn't best pleased with me that day on Court 3. He was the No. 7 seed and he must have rubbed his hands with glee when he looked at the draw and saw the name A. Mills. It should have been a walkover for him. The match had been reasonably close for a couple of hours, but I was trailing two sets to one and facing match point at 5–4 in the fourth with Pietrangeli serving. My memory of the next few seconds are crystal-clear: he served and rushed the net, looking for the killer volley and I passed him with as sweet a backhand as you could hope to strike.

The shock of the moment, together with a wild crowd roaring their support for me, seemed to puncture any confidence he had, and I went on take the set 7–5 and the decider 6–1. Although the victory lacked the kudos of beating Laver, or the emotion and doggedness of my encounter with Drobny, that triumph, in purely competitive terms, was probably the most impressive of my singles career. He was an excellent player, somewhere close to the peak of his game, and after hanging in there for dear life I was so inspired by the support of the crowd that my game reached previously unscaled heights. You often hear players talking about the crowd lifting them, and though it may sound like a cliché, it's absolutely true. You feel like a sailing ship with a strong wind behind you.

The 1962 Championships were one of two in which I managed to reach the last 16, and I was a bit disappointed (to put it mildly) to discover that my match against a Mexican called Rafael Osuna was scheduled for Saturday and not Monday. I had assumed that as I had played on Friday afternoon I would have the whole weekend to rest up and wallow in a bit of glory before my next challenge. As it was, I was pretty flat the following day and subsided to a straight-sets defeat without ever threatening to make a contest of it. As referee it is one of the virtues of being a former player that I understand the importance of having as long a rest as possible between matches. The order of play committee and referee were responsible for putting together the programme for each day and I certainly didn't appreciate their decision that evening.

I imagine the order of play was generally far easier back then than it is today. In the amateur era it was largely just a matter of making sure a singles match didn't clash with a doubles in which the same individual was playing. There were no requests from international television companies, no queue of players, coaches and agents asking for matches to be played at certain times on certain courts and no chair umpires making themselves unavailable for particular matches because they had fallen foul of players X, Y and Z. There was, of course, the rain to contend with, but there would not have been a great outcry if a player was obliged by the revamped schedule to play twice in a day in order to clear the backlog. Players may have grumbled amongst themselves, but they wouldn't have gone crying to the referee's office or to the order of play committee, and they certainly wouldn't have dared launch a scathing attack on the Wimbledon authorities in the newspapers.

For the first ten years of my time as referee, getting the following day's order of play out was, without question or qualification, the most trying aspect of my daily responsibilities. For all the reasons mentioned above, together with occasional computer problems and the rain, it was a logistical – and diplomatic – nightmare. The pressure to publish it is intense and it comes from all quarters – and with good reason because everybody connected with the Championships naturally wants to know what is happening the following day so that they can make their plans accordingly. Players need to be informed as early as possible so that they can prepare the build-up to their match. Long gone are the days when players had to check the *Daily Telegraph* each morning to see when or whether they were playing that day. Most of them nowadays live by strict diets and fitness regimes; they warm up, they warm down; they are given massages to loosen and soothe the muscles. Nothing is left to chance. If, for some reason we are unable to produce the order of play until close to midnight, the players will either have to wait up for it or get up earlier than their bodies might have wished to discover whether they are playing or not. Then there are the newspapers to consider and they too are extremely keen to get hold of the order so that they can inform the readers of what was happening that day, while television companies, especially those broadcasting to different time-zones, need as much advance warning as possible, especially if one of 'their' players is still in the draw.

The order of play was the bane of my daily life in my first few years as referee at Wimbledon. I enjoy the mathematical challenge of it – it's like a massive Rubik's cube, but the pressure could often be overwhelming, especially when the order of play committee used to file into my office towards the end of the day.

'I've searched all the parks in all the cities and found no statues of committees', the author G.K. Chesterton once observed. At about 6 p.m. on each day of the Championships my heart would sink as I heard the door open and the voices of the committe members drift up the stairs into my cramped office. This was the busiest time of my day (and still is). We are trying desperately to get the order of play completed and published as quickly as possible, while at the same time making quick decisions about whether to cancel scheduled matches for fear they may not be completed in time or, if we have rattled through the programme that day, whether we should try to slip a few more matches on to various courts, from the 'order of play' that states 'matches to be arranged'. That involves keeping a close eye on the scores from around the ground and then calculating what time might be left to us. Heaven knows what else might be going on as well. It is a case of juggling a lot of mental balls at the same time, like a performing seal, but when the eight or so members of the committee careered into the office, the balls tended to get scattered in all directions. In those distant days we used to have a mini-bar in the office, and as the members descended on us, within moments there would be the cry of 'Gin and tonics, please!' (Alcohol, by the way, has been banned for many years for all on-court officials including referees, chair umpires, supervisors and line judges. There is a ban on drinking for 12 hours before start of play, and of course while play is in progress.)

With the ice clinking in their glasses, the committee would then wander over to the window from where they could watch the matches taking place on Court 3 across the concourse. If it was an interesting contest they would stand there and chat away, all bunched together as if they were on the Tube during the rush-hour on the way to the City, while I put the final touches to my proposed order of play. Then they would slowly sidle over to my desk, some behind me, some at my side, and start pointing at the order of play sheet in front of me. They all craned and jostled and looked over each others' shoulders as I sat there claustrophobically, hemmed in by eight pairs of legs, biting my lower lip and trying to keep my temper in check.

I'm sure they all had the best interests of the Championships at heart, but they were often very clumsy and thoughtless in the way they went about it. A committee, as the joke goes, is a thing which takes a week to do what a man can do in an hour, and the order of play, of all things, cried out for the patience and expertise of just one man, someone (i.e. the referee) who had an overall understanding of who was playing when and in which event; someone who had fielded the calls from the various television stations and handled the myriad requests from the players and the coaches. Furthermore, if anything ever went wrong with the order of play, it would be the referee not the committee who got it in the neck.

How I managed to keep my composure at those infuriating meetings I don't know, but my way of dealing with it was to

When I appear at court side I know sometimes I can be the least popular man in the Champions|

But I do sometimes get a round of applause for walking off.

Always a happy moment. And a great relief. I'm sure the Duke will be saying, 'Well done, it seems to have all gone very smoothly this year.'

Tennis has afforded Jill and me some wonderful opportunities to travel. That's Pat Rafter (*above*) in an Arabian outfit, in Dubai.

Below Me with the legendary Fred Perry in 1981. Britain's last men's Wimbledon champion and '. . . the only Englishman bloody-minded enough not to want to lose'.

**Being a tennis lover, I have relished the opportunity
to see many great champions and gallant losers.**

1985: Unseeded Boris Becker burst on to Wimbledon centre stage like a force of nature. He was at the vanguard of a dramatic change in the men's game.

Two of the greats, Chrissie and Martina's on-court rivalry brought the women's game to life in the seventies and eighties.

1989 saw a remarkable German double and confirmed, if it were needed, that tennis was now a young person's game.

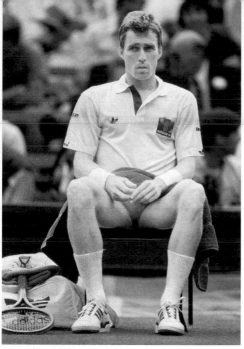

The Wimbledon title remained out of Ivan Lendl's reach despite his repeated and determined efforts.

1990: Martina's ninth and last singles title. Quite simply the greatest women's player of all time.

1992: With his first ever Grand Slam win, Andre Agassi proved wrong the merchants of doom, who were predicting the dominance of the power game over skill and artistry. I think he was quite pleased.

At his peak, Pete Sampras, whose game was perfectly suited to grass, dominated the Championships with seven wins out of eight between 1993 and 2000.

The 2001 semi-final was an epic. I have no doubt that had the rain not come down on the Friday, when Tim was two sets to one up and playing dazzling tennis, he would have reached his first final. As it was, the stop-start, rain-interrupted Saturday saw his momentum and chance slip away.

If the 2001 semi was an epic, the final was a classic. Wild card entrant Ivanisevic defeated Pat Rafter in five gripping sets. At the end of it all, Ivanisevic's joy in victory and Rafter's dignity in defeat will live long in my memory.

The astonishing story of Venus Williams and her sister Serena has inspired a new generation of inner-city kids to take an interest in tennis.

Roger Federer's victories in 2003 and 2004, achieved with a mix of artistry and all-round skill, were a joy to watch.

keep pressing my point. What particularly used to set my teeth on edge was when a member appeared to push for a match to be played on a particular court at a particular time for his own personal enjoyment. I should stress that this did not happen very often, but sometimes the members would be bringing important guests for the day and it seemed that their priority was to give those guests the best possible entertainment.

On one occasion, one committee member insisted that the last match on Court 4 had to be a better one than normal, which I thought was very curious. I smiled politely and said I would see what I could do, but then instantly discarded the request into my mental dustbin. I thought there was something odd about his motives and sure enough, it turned out that he was entertaining guests that evening on the members' balcony overlooking Court 4. In a further instance, a committee member was very keen to see a match involving a player called Scott Davies in a singles match on Centre Court following the women's quarter-finals. This match was due to be played the following day, and I said that would not be possible because Scott was behind on the doubles and as he was scheduled to play his match later that evening, he couldn't possibly be third up on Centre Court as well. 'But that's the match I really want to see,' he insisted. 'Why can't the chap play two doubles the day after. That's what we used to do in our day!'

Eventually I replied: 'Well, if you feel that strongly about the Scott Davies match then you can go and tell Scott in person that he will be playing two doubles matches in a day.'

The man replied: 'I certainly won't – that's your job,' and then walked out of my office. I never had any intention of carrying out his ridiculous and selfish request, but I spoke to

Scott about it and when he finally stopped laughing he said that he would have kicked up an almighty stink if he had been obliged to play two doubles in a day.

The whole procedure was farcical and infuriating and I had to come up with a way of putting an end to it without upsetting too many people inside the club. It was a very delicate situation. I didn't want to cut off the branch I was sitting on and risk losing my job, but equally the existing arrangements were unworkable and intolerable. I decided to have all my proposals ready by the time they came into the office and then tell them that they were free to change the courts but not the time-slot they were in. With that, I would disappear downstairs as fast as possible and try and get on with the rest of the day's work. By the time I returned to my office, most of them had gone having left a list of changes they wanted.

For the last ten years or so the production of the order of play has become even less stressful following the reappointment of Mike Hann as chairman of the committee. He had seen the fine old mess of the earlier years and came up with a very sensible proposal that the committee members should write down their recommendations, for the show courts only, and then give them to him or the vice-chairman before presenting them to me. The office has since been a far happier place as a result, and coupled with the improvement in the computer system, the production of the order of play, though still a laborious task, has been largely trouble-free. It is certainly beneficial to have the opinion of the committee in order to see what they consider to be the important matches. The chairman of the order of play committee is my link to the club chairman and management committee if there are difficult decisions to be made, such as cutting a whole event from five to three sets due to rain or deciding on the possibility of play in the middle Sunday, as occurred in 2004.

Chapter Seven

It Takes Two to Tarango

It was a happy twist of fate for me that resolving the little problem with my colleagues on the order of play committee happened to coincide roughly with the retirement of the big trouble-makers in the men's game. Tennis was entering a less colourful and eventful period in the early nineties, and from a purely tennis point of view I was sad to see these characters disappear to count up their phenomenal career earnings and spend some more time with their families. But I would be lying if I said I missed that well-trodden path from my office out to the show courts, the knot in my stomach, the slow handclapping, the snide comments of the players and their boorish and childish behaviour. Players would still behave badly at Wimbledon, spectacularly so in 1995, but the eruptions were less frequent and less intense. Thus it was with a lighter heart and a spongier spring in my step that I would make my familiar way through the club gates and head into the office during those years.

It was a period dominated by two of the greatest players of all time: Pete Sampras and Steffi Graf. Sampras won the title seven out of eight times between 1993 and 2000, while Graf won five out of six between 1991 and 1996 to add to the two titles she had already won in the 1980s.

For all the promise he showed, the hype surrounding him

and the fact that his game was perfectly suited to grass, Pete Sampras had failed to deliver at Wimbledon in his first three years, only once making it to the second round. In 1992 he was a different proposition entirely, bulldozing his way to the semi-finals before he was blasted off court by Goran Ivanesevic under a barrage of booming aces. But the Championships that year were destined to belong to the crowd charmer Andre Agassi, who lay on down on the Centre Court grass and cried tears of joy after overcoming the Croat in a pulsating five-setter, which the American won 6–4 in the fifth. Agassi, who had never won a Grand Slam event having lost in three finals, produced some astonishing tennis over that fortnight, taking the fight to the big servers by standing on or close to the baseline and taking his returns unbelievably early. The doom merchants of the day had predicted that the big servers with their graphite rackets – a wooden one had not been used since 1987 at Wimbledon – were slowly killing off tennis, spawning a generation of robots, but Agassi's cavalier and revolutionary tactics squashed that theory at a stroke. In doing so he also proved that you did not need to perfect the traditional serve and volley game to win Wimbledon.

Steffi Graf lifted the women's trophy, and it is curious to reflect now that the two champions who dined together at the Savoy that Sunday evening are now husband and wife, and raising a family. Agassi was not the only American to end the Championships in tears that year – McEnroe, of all people, also broke down. I thought I had seen the full range of the New Yorker's emotional repertoire down the years, but it was moving to see the now slightly balding maverick reduced to a sentimental jelly after he and Michael Stich pulled off a remarkable win in the doubles. The final, against Jim Grabb and Richey Reneberg, had to be carried over to the Monday and there was a noisy, youthful crowd there to see McEnroe and his German partner battle to a nerve-fraying 19–17 victory in the final set. McEnroe immediately leapt into the arms of Stich, with all the enthusiasm and joy of a young teenager experiencing triumph for the very first time. His young son was in the crowd to witness his father's heroics, and perhaps aware that this was the final hurrah of his extraordinary career, he broke down and wept. It was a curiously affecting moment as the crowd cheered him to the rafters and for all the anguish he had caused me down the years I couldn't but help feel moved. It had been an incredible championship all round for McEnroe, who evoked memories of his glorious magic back in the early eighties and defied all the odds to reach the semi-finals where he finally succumbed to Agassi.

In an earlier round, McEnroe did something uncanny which still makes me shiver a little at the memory of it. As the light had begun to fade I had come down on to Centre Court and taken up my customary position at the corner of the court assessing the conditions. I could only have been there for about two seconds when McEnroe, who had his back to me and had not seen me enter, put his hand behind his back and stuck up a finger as he prepared to receive serve. At first I thought he was presenting me with his middle digit and was telling me in his own frank fashion that my presence was not appreciated on court and why didn't I just go away and mind my own business. But what he was actually doing was telling me he wanted one more game so that he and Stich could wrap up the set before having to retreat to the locker-room. It was a weird moment as there was absolutely no way he could have actually seen me.

McEnroe would never again play singles at Wimbledon, although he has been back almost every year since in his capacity as a television pundit, a job to which he brings the same intensity, precision and flair that characterised his play. His behaviour in his swansong year on the whole was fairly good, but I still had a few run-ins with him. On one occasion I had ordered play to be suspended due to bad light during his doubles match on Centre Court against Anders Jarryd and John Fitzgerald. 'That's the most asinine decision I have ever heard,' McEnroe said to me, and while Jarryd and Fitzgerald packed up their bags, the American continued to argue. After a while, Fitzgerald interrupted us and said wearily: 'Millsy, can we go now?'

The biggest controversy of the Championships that year occurred off court when the young Dutchman Richard Krajicek sparked an uproar by casually describing his colleagues on the women's circuit as, and I quote, 'fat, lazy pigs'. It was an unfortunate and spectacular lapse of diplomacy and manners on Krajicek's part, and I could barely believe my ears when I heard his disgraceful insult. The journalists, of course, loved it. It was manna from heaven and gave them a great story that they could spin out for the whole Championships. Very handy indeed when the rain came down and there was no action on court to report. Pat Cash, a few years earlier, appeared to have stretched the boundaries of decency and tact when he called the women's game 'junk', but Krajicek managed to make that comment seem positively flattering by comparison.

From a personal point of view, I have always enjoyed watching women's tennis just as much as men's. It's not a question of gender as far as I am concerned. So long as the two players are evenly matched and are producing a competitive, close-fought match, then I am happy to sit and watch. I would rather go to the local park and watch two players of the same standard battle it out than sit at Centre Court and witness one of the big names in the game demolish an inferior player. There is no fun or sport in that.

It is unfortunate that over the last couple of decades the gulf between the top players in women's tennis and the rest has been fairly pronounced. For some reason there hasn't been the depth that you find in the men's game, especially in the early rounds, but women's tennis is now getting stronger and stronger at every level.

A glance at the Wimbledon results in the modern era provides compelling evidence of this inequality, and the paying public will often be lucky if many of those early-round matches last longer than 45 minutes. For that reason, and that reason alone, I don't think that the women should get the same amount of prize money as the men, yet. The issue is raised every year and Wimbledon is forced to defend itself against accusations of chauvinism, but in my view sexual politics have got nothing to do with the nub of the matter. It's simply a question of the money reflecting the amount of entertainment provided by the players, and as the men play the best of five sets and their games are often closer as well as far longer, it seems only right and fair that they should get slightly more money – and it is only slightly more. In 2004 the men's champion Roger Federer received £602,500, while Maria Sharapova received a cheque for £560,500 in the women's; a first-round loser in the men's earned £9,040, while the women were given £7,230. Wimbledon has carried out a number of surveys over the years, asking spectators as they come through the gates who they were coming to watch, and the overwhelming majority say that it is the men they are most interested in seeing.

There is another factor, too. As the women only play three sets in the singles and doubles, it is much easier for them to play in both events. These days you rarely find the leading players in the men's also entering the doubles – McEnroe was the last of the very top players and today only a few including Jonas Bjorkman from Sweden and Max Mirnyi from Belarus commit to both draws on a regular basis. Thus if you add up the money the women earn from both then they are roughly on a par with the men and although they are playing in two different events to achieve that equality, if you totted up the total amount of time all the players spent on court at the end of a Grand Slam fortnight, you will find that the men and women are roughly even in that respect.

What I would like to see is the introduction of partial parity by making the prize money equal from the quarter-finals onwards, because there is enough depth in the women's game to provide plenty of close-fought contests from that stage. For me, if Wimbledon surrendered to the calls for complete parity between the men's and women's events, they would be merely pandering to tokenism and political correctness and I believe it would be an injustice for the men. Krajicek's comment that year was as crass and baseless as it was unhelpful and it brought the debate of a serious issue so low that it was difficult for people to look at the facts with a cool head.

The Australian and the US Opens both offer equal prize money and in 2005 the sponsors of the Dubai Open, Dubai Duty Free, announced they would be joining them when they raised the prize money of the women's tournament to $1 million, matching the men's event which is held a week earlier.

This is one of the most glamorous tournaments in the world and I have been lucky enough to be the referee for the women's event since its inception five years ago. All the players and officials are looked after very well indeed, some 'roughing' it in five-star hotels, while the top players stay in the magnificent seven-star Burj Al Arab – where this year Andre Agassi and Roger Federer could be found playing tennis on the helicopter pad at the top of the hotel (they were both very careful indeed when approaching anywhere near the back of the court – the drop would have been rather long!). The tournaments are taken seriously and both titles were won by the world's No. 1 players, Roger Federer and Lindsay Davenport.

Serious it certainly is, but it is also a huge amount of fun. The players' party is incredible, offering the opportunity to have a henna tattoo, hold a falcon, watch belly dancers, wear Arab dress and ride a camel. There is almost constant sunshine and golf is on offer, as is a trip (or two) to the gold souk. One year we were invited to a small golf clinic given by Seve Ballesteros which was followed by a wonderful barbecue lunch and a walk round nine holes watching Tiger Woods, Colin Montgomerie, Thomas Bjorn, Mark O'Meara, Lee Westwood and Darren Clarke play an exhibition match. My only regret is that with all that golfing greatness around me, not enough of it rubbed off on my game.

In truth, the Wimbledon Championships of the early nineties, in both the men's and women's tournaments, were nothing like as dramatic as they had been in earlier years. Graf and Sampras were simply too dominant, while the power of the big-hitters like Courier and Ivanisevic had undoubtedly killed off some of the finer skills and artistry of the men's game.

Sampras was so methodical, smooth and robotic in his play, his demeanour so hangdog and undemonstrative and his triumphs so lacking in surprise or emotion, that it took him years to win over the British public. He was undoubtedly one of the greatest players ever to take up a racket, and his record at Wimbledon provides a persuasive argument that he was perhaps the best grass-court player of all time, but he certainly had to work hard to win the plaudits that his outstanding achievements so deserved. From a purely selfish point of view, Sampras was a delight to deal with and although he spent more time on Wimbledon's courts than any other player over the decade, not once did he cause a dispute that I had to resolve.

Where once I used to spend much of the Wimbledon fort-night shuttling back and forth between my office and the show courts, like a world-weary UN diplomat, during that period my peace-keeping missions were few and far between. The only time I had any difficulties with Sampras came in 2002 in what turned out to be his final appearance at Wimbledon, and it was only afterwards when he let fly to the press that I had any idea that there had been a problem. It was all a bit strange. I had very little direct contact with Sampras over the years and most of our communication was carried out through his long-serving coach Paul Annacone, but on the night before his second-round match against the Swiss Georg Bastl, who had only qualified as a lucky loser following the withdrawal of the injured Felix Mantilla, the seven-times champion called me himself to ask when and where the match was to take place.

I had put the match on Court 2, known to many as 'the graveyard of champions', because I felt there were other, potentially more entertaining contests worthy of the two main show courts. Sampras thanked me and hung up, but 15 minutes later he called back and asked if there was any chance he could be switched to one of the 'inside' courts (i.e. Centre Court or Court 1), to which I replied that once the order of play had been released, it could not be altered. Again, Sampras said nothing to me and there was certainly no hint of pique or resentment in his voice – he was as softly spoken and demure as ever. About 30 minutes later there was a knock on the door and in came his new coach José Higueras, who asked me why his player had been put on Court 2, and whilst I was explaining my reasons and reassuring him that of course Pete would feature on the two main courts later in the tournament, I saw him eyeing up the order of play on the board behind my desk. Then he turned to me and said: 'Fair enough, I can see looking at that, that the matches you have put on Centre Court and Court 1 are more appealing than Pete's game.'

Like Sampras himself, Higueras was perfectly reasonable and did not kick up the slightest fuss, and so I was a little surprised to say the least when Sampras's agent swept in shortly afterwards and said: 'Wahooh! I bet your phone has been buzzing hot these last few hours, Alan!' I said that I had not noticed any appreciable rise in the temperature of my handset (perhaps not as pompously as that but I was certainly a little cool with her) and I was beginning to feel a little bit peeved at having to explain, for the umpteenth time, why his match had been put on that particular court. I wish I had been given a pound for every time a player, or one of his or her 'people', asked why they had not been put on the show courts.

'I have spoken to Pete twice and he understands the situation,' I explained wearily. 'He may not be delighted – nobody ever is – but he told me in person that he understands the reasons. I have spoken to his coach, who was the same, and apart from that no one else has mentioned anything to me.'

In the event, Sampras lost to the unknown Bastl in five sets, and at the end he looked the perfect picture of misery as he sat motionless in his seat for about two or three minutes before shuffling off court very slowly, his shoulders even more slumped than usual. I could not possibly have known that this was going to be his last ever match at Wimbledon. It would have been great to have put him on Centre Court for his final match so that he could have been given the send-off that his remarkable achievements deserved. But who could have forecast that the great man would be beaten by a young player who had only scraped into the tournament owing to a last-minute withdrawal?

It was a very sad end to a glorious Wimbledon career, and it was regrettable that he was unable to bow out with greater ceremony and dignity on the court he had made his own for the best part of a decade. Afterwards, he complained to the media that he felt Wimbledon (i.e. me) had treated him shabbily, and the following day I found myself buried under an avalanche of criticism by the press and complaints from the public. ('How could you do this to Pete – he's been so good for Wimbledon down the years . . . you should be ashamed of yourself,' etc.) The moaning didn't bother me especially – you become numb to it after a while – because there was simply no way I could put him on Centre Court in every single match he played. All the greats – Borg, McEnroe, Connors, Lendl, Becker and Edberg – had had to play on Court 2 as well as the outside courts on occasions, even when they were at the peak of their games, and there was no precedent or justification for giving Sampras special treatment. I suspect there wouldn't have been a single whimper of discontent had Sampras won the match, as everyone expected he would.

That incident, though, was the only bit of unpleasantness I experienced with Sampras, who was in all respects a model of exemplary conduct. In fact, all the leading Americans of that generation – Agassi, Courier, Chang, Martin and Sampras – in contrast to their immediate predecessors, were a sporting and honourable group of players.

Courier was exactly as you found him, an easygoing, straightforward, all-American boy, and I only had one moment of controversy involving him at Wimbledon. It came in 1993 in a third-round match against Jason Stoltenberg of Australia. I was sitting in my office when the phone rang and I was asked to come out to Centre Court where a possible default situation had arisen. In my 11 years as referee at Wimbledon, I had never been forced to disqualify a player and I was running through all the scenarios that may have occurred as I hurried out to court. As I arrived I saw Courier deep in conversation with the chair umpire who informed me that the American had told him to 'f*** off' and that there was a line judge to corroborate his claim. If true, then indeed I would have had to default Courier, but I wasn't convinced, especially as the player himself insisted with great conviction that he had simply cried 'F***' in frustration. It was another tricky moment for me and although I was reluctant to cast doubt on the umpire's version of events, it was possible that he could have misheard Courier as there was, after all, little difference between the two oaths.

I gave Courier the benefit of the doubt and told the umpire to issue a code violation for a verbal obscenity, but as with all these close-call decisions I went away with an uncomfortable feeling about it all. Had I done the right thing? Should I have gone with the umpire? Was Courier lying to me to save his skin and avoid the shame that would have befallen him? I was still turning it all over in my mind when Courier wrapped up victory and so to set my mind at rest I headed straight to the locker-room to confront him. It was water under the bridge now and I did not have the authority to default him retrospectively. Courier was the only one in the room as I entered, but moments later his coach Higueras burst in and said, 'What was all that about?' – which immediately reassured me because it meant that whatever Courier had said, it hadn't reverberated around the whole court.

I did say to him, 'We have known each other for many, many years and if you did say what the umpire claimed you did, you have obviously got away with it but for my own peace of mind, I would be grateful if you could tell me the truth.' Over the years of listening to players give their version of events over a disputed decision, I have developed fairly strong antennae when it comes to telling whether someone is being truthful or not. In this case I have no doubt Courier was being honest when he continued to plead his innocence in the locker-room. (It's a strange state of moral affairs when a man who admits to shouting f*** all over Centre Court is standing their pleading his 'innocence'!) But equally I could see how the umpire might have thought the abuse had been aimed at him. Courier was convinced he had served an ace down the middle and when the line judge called it out he looked to the chair umpire to overrule it. When the intervention never came he blurted 'f***!' as he headed back to the baseline to serve again, and because there had been eye-contact the umpire thought it was directed at him personally. It was an understandable misunderstanding, so to speak, and although I believe I was right not to default him, it was an ugly moment and I am sure that some in the umpire fraternity took a pretty dim view of my actions. Still, I had long since stopped expecting to make all of the people happy all of the time. Upsetting people, unfortunately, was an inescapable part of my job and I have just had to roll with the punches, painful as some of the blows have been on occasions.

As with Courier, my association with his compatriot Andre Agassi was a largely happy one and only once did we lock horns. Agassi, the No. 2 seed, was playing Todd Martin on Centre Court late one evening, and with the light starting to fade it was a question of when, not if, play was to be abandoned for the day. Martin, a real battler, was pushing his opponent to the limit, but neither of them had complained about the light and Agassi, in particular, seemed more than happy to continue when he won a tiebreaker in the third set to go 2–1 up. He was on a roll, but his mood changed very quickly when he lost his serve in the opening game of the fourth set and immediately walked over to the chair umpire to ask how much longer they had to play on. I was called out on court and as I arrived – to the predictable murmur of boos around the crowd – there was an odd moment when Martin, for some reason, playfully threw a ball at me from the baseline. Instinctively I threw it back and smiled before I realised what I was doing and, quickly putting my serious face back on, I approached the chair to talk to Agassi and the umpire.

I told Agassi I was surprised that the two of them had carried on playing so long into the deepening gloom, but reminded him that it was up to him, or his opponent, to call for play to be stopped and carried over to the next day. From the crowd's point of view, it appears that I am just being a spoilsport if I order play to be halted when the players themselves seem perfectly content to continue. I told him that as we always stop on an even number of games in the interests of fairness, they would have to play one more before coming off. Agassi was not at all pleased about this, and amidst a wide-ranging tirade of complaints and threats told me that he looked forward to suing me for every dollar I had if he fell over on the increasingly dewy surface and injured himself. He gave me a thunderous look before stalking off to receive Martin's serve.

Shortly afterwards, Martin played the ball to one side of the court, and although Agassi had no chance of reaching it, he made off in pursuit before theatrically crumpling to the turf like a newborn deer on a skating rink. It was a comical moment, although Agassi for sure wasn't seeing the funny side of it, and it was all laid on for my own personal enjoyment. 'See what I mean?' his face was saying as he got to his feet and looked over in my direction. Agassi was now 2–0 down in the set and he looked as though he could have happily strangled me there and then as he stomped off court, his bad mood following him to the locker-room like vapour trails off an airliner. I had never seen the usually sunny American in such a state, and I thought it spoke volumes for his decency that he telephoned me the following morning to apologise for his display of petulance. He still didn't agree with my decision, but he said he had no right to express his disapproval in that way. Occasionally, a coach or publicity-sensitive agent calls me in the office to say sorry for the behaviour of their player, but that is very rare, and it is rarer still to hear contrition from the man himself. In spite of the ear-bashing he gave me, Agassi went up in my estimation after this episode. Some of the top players are so consumed by their own importance, it would never cross their minds to lower themselves by admitting any wrongdoing.

Agassi is a veritable angel by comparison with some of his colleagues on the circuit – fame and vast wealth can have a curious effect on some people. The most appalling example of player arrogance I have come across in all my years on the circuit involved a player from Eastern Europe. It was at a tournament in the United States in which the car-manufacturers Mercedes Benz were heavily involved, and as part of their sponsorship deal they provided cars to the leading players over the week. This particular player had pranged his courtesy car, and when he was told by the woman in charge that he would not be given another, he was outraged. What he said to her would have shocked even a parade ground sergeant-major.

The most surprising and depressing aspect of this episode was that the player involved is by and large a decent character, but it happened not long after he had shot from obscurity to international prominence with a string of impressive displays. In trying to fathom what might induce an essentially good person to behave in such a way, you cannot help but conclude that it is the celebrity and the money – and all the grovelling and toadying that comes with it – which lies behind it all. One day you are a nobody, battling for recognition in the backwoods of the international circuit, and the next you are headline news with a bulging bank-balance, surrounded by a swarm of people eager for a bite of the spoils. You do not even have to be a household name to earn a vast fortune in modern tennis – there are plenty of millionaires on the circuit who will never be household names.

It is no wonder perhaps that some of these players, cocooned for much of their young lives in the weird parallel universe that is the international tennis circuit, are occasionally given to unfortunate lapses in their conduct. To spend the greater part of your late teenage years uprooted from your family and friends, shuttling around the world from one hotel and tournament to the next, is to be deprived of a more traditional upbringing. The great wealth and fame that follows for some will inevitably have an immense impact on a player's lifestyle and character, and although it might be difficult to extend much sympathy to a young millionaire, you can at least understand how some might come to develop an ego the size of Jupiter and a paranoia to match. If you are constantly told you are marvellous and the whole world seems to want your picture or your autograph, you could be forgiven for thinking that yes, perhaps you are a terrific human being and not just someone who happens to excel at hitting a small ball over a net. There is no telling how the pressures of the international tennis circuit will go to work on a player, but some of them at some point in their careers do suffer a major lapse of judgement or collapse of self-discipline. (This is, however, rarely the case with the women players.)

Without wishing to cast myself in the role of a charity worker for distressed tennis millionaires, I do try to make a point of talking to as many of the players as I can when I come across them on the circuit. I tell them that I am always available for a chat about anything that might be worrying them, but in recent years I have found that it has become increasingly difficult to get close to the players. Nowadays they all have their 'team': small travelling circuses that pitch camp around the players and which can sometimes cut them off from the outside world. Players used to come and see me fairly often, but today it is generally their 'representatives' who do their talking and listening for them and I conduct hundreds of conversations through an intermediary who shuffles back and forth like a courtier relaying communiqués from his over-lord. I'm sure that some of these functionaries perform impor-tant roles in the lives of the players, but the interest in their 'client' is usually first and foremost a commercial one and I cannot help but feel that the players themselves would benefit if they had greater independence from their advisers. It cannot be natural and healthy to spend all your life in a hotel room while others do your living and decision-making for you.

By the time the Wimbledon Championships got underway in 1995, I liked to think that I'd pretty well seen and heard every-thing there was to see and hear on a tennis court: riots, sit-down protests, countless explosions of tempers, four-letter outbursts, smashed rackets, snoozing line judges, flying cush-ions, bomb scares, plain-clothes police officers, keeping foxes off the grass, weeping players, unconscious groundsmen, drunken spectators and hysterical teenagers. In subsequent years I saw Cliff Richard get to his feet and lead the Centre Court in a merry song-and-dance; I listened to former President of the United States Bill Clinton address the crowd from his seat like a Roman emperor; I have helped smuggle Barbra Streisand into the grounds to avoid the crush of the crowds; and I heard that an elderly club member once turned to Charlton Heston and said 'So what do you do?' With toe-curling embarrassment I once watched Elizabeth Taylor wave and smile to the crowd who had had risen to their feet to applaud the entrance of Princess Diana to the Royal Box at the other end of the Centre Court. Nothing, I thought, could surprise me any longer, but my experiences at Wimbledon in 1995 were a powerful reminder that in my job, anything, no matter how outlandish, is possible.

There were three major incidents that year, all of them utterly extraordinary, dramatic and traumatic in their own way. The first involved a young Tim Henman, then playing in only his second Wimbledon. I had known Tim since he was a young teenager when I was refereeing junior tournaments in Surrey. Although he was largely unknown to the British public at this time, he was a player of outstanding promise and those who had watched his development, with the help of Jim Slater and David Lloyd, were convinced that Britain had finally managed to produce a player of truly world-class potential – the best since Perry, many claimed. In my association with him up to that time, I had found Henman to be an impeccably courteous, even-tempered and good-natured character – the last person on a tennis court you would expect to have to throw the book at for a breach of the rules.

Henman, who had lost in the second round of the singles to the defending champion Sampras in straight sets earlier in the day, was involved in a doubles match out on Court 14, now situated outside the new broadcasters' complex between Centre Court and the new Court 1. He was partnering his fellow Briton Jeremy Bates against a Swede by the name of Henrik Holm and a live-wire character called Jeff Tarango who I would get to know all too well by the end of that fortnight.

It was late on Wednesday evening in the first week and we were all winding down in the office after a relatively smooth, uneventful day when I received a call on my walkie-talkie from one of the supervisors telling me to hurry out to the court because they had a possible default situation on their hands. I had heard similar claims in the past, but on this occasion, the tone of the supervisor's voice led me to believe that something very serious was afoot. I couldn't for the life of me imagine what might have happened, although I did harbour what soon proved to be some utterly groundless suspicions. Marching briskly through the crowds outside Centre Court, I tried to work out which of the four players was the most likely offender and, based on their disciplinary records, my prime suspect was Tarango, whom you might describe as one of the more emotional players on the circuit at that time. Second favourite was Jeremy Bates, a player of great intensity and determination, whose feelings might very occasionally spill over in his desperation to succeed. But as for Henman and Holm – a well-mannered Home Counties boy and a Swede for heaven's sake – I didn't even give them a thought.

I entered the court from the corner, and as I made my way up to the tramlines, some of the crowd pleaded with me to be lenient on the culprit. 'He didn't mean to do it . . . it was just an accident . . . Go easy on him . . .' As I approached the chair to talk to the Australian umpire Wayne McKewen, I saw Henman deep in conversation with him, and my first thought was that the young Briton must be pleading someone else's case on their behalf, or was perhaps just giving his version of events. As the umpire began to explain what had happened it dawned on me fairly quickly that I was going to have to make one of the most controversial decisions in the history of the Championships. My heart sank and my pulse raced, and no matter what way I looked at it, the rules were perfectly clear – I was going to have to throw Tim Henman out of the Championships – the first man to be defaulted since the Open era began in 1968. I then listened to Henman's explanation and to his great credit he didn't try to excuse himself or underplay what he had done. He seemed as shaken as anyone by events and he hung his head in embarrassment and his voice croaked a little as he talked me through his unfortunate moment of madness.

The match had a reached a crucial juncture in a tiebreaker when a shot from one of Henman's opponents had struck the tape on the net and dropped over the other side. In his anger Henman took a ball from his pocket and looked up to smash it somewhere. Careful to avoid the other players and the line officials, he took aim at a spot on the other side of the court – this all happened in a split second – and then let fly. At that moment, a young ball-girl called Caroline sprung from her haunches to collect the ball sitting at the foot of the net and was hit on the side of the face. She burst into tears, more in shock than agony though a ball in the face at that speed must have really stung, but once she had recovered she pleaded with me not to take any action and, bless her heart, even said she was the one who had been at fault. But my mind was made up: the rules state quite clearly that a player has to be in control of his emotions at all times and that if he strikes a ball in anger and it hits someone, then it is a cut-and-dried default situation. If the ball-girl had been in the wrong place when she was struck, then there might have been a bit of room for doubt, but she hadn't, and with great reluctance I told Henman that he – and Bates – were out. Henman was superb: he comforted the girl as best he could, accepted my decision like a man and apologised to everyone involved for his uncharacteristic rush of blood to the head.

It was not, as you can imagine, the most popular decision I have ever made at Wimbledon, and as soon as the players began to pack up their bags, mutterings of discontent could be heard all around the little court. It was just as well that this was Wimbledon and the offender was Henman, not Key Biscayne and Jimmy Connors, or Santiago and Marcelo Rios. As I left the court with the eyes of the crowd burning into my back, I drew a deep breath and braced myself for what promised to be an extremely stormy 24 hours. My gloom was momentarily lifted when Jeremy Bates came up to me as I was leaving and said: 'Does that mean I can't play in the mixed doubles now?' I reassured him that he was OK because he had not been the perpetrator, to which he joked: 'Damn it! I thought at least some good might have come of this.'

The uproar was every bit as tumultuous as I had expected. This was a front-page story (headlines: 'Tantrum Tim') and was slotted into the evening news bulletins on television somewhere between earthquakes and ministerial resignations. The members' lounge at the club was buzzing with comment and I was forced to bite my lip when I heard that one character had blustered: 'What the devil does Mills think he is doing defaulting the son of a member of the club? It's an outrage.' Tarango's contribution to the flood of opinion I felt was also worth ignoring – he claimed the ball-girl could have been killed and that, had he been the offender, he would have been thrown out of tennis altogether.

The following day I was given a fearful grilling by the BBC anchorman Des Lynam live on television and I began to feel a mounting sense of impatience as he waded into me as if I had been Pontius Pilate himself. Of course, it wouldn't do for me to start getting tetchy and so I played all his bouncers with a dead bat and tried to appear as unruffled as I could. Afterwards, Lynam was as nice as pie and said that it was part of his job to play devil's advocate, which, from hindsight, was fair enough I suppose. Public opinion, as always, was divided, but most people seemed to accept that I had little option but to apply the rules as they had been laid down. Henman himself couldn't have been more reasonable and understanding. He posed for pictures with the ball-girl the following day, giving her a kiss and a bouquet of flowers, and he never once moaned about his fate.

I felt fairly shaken up by whole incident and the inevitable furore it triggered, but by the end of the first week the tremors had just begun to subside and some sort of normality to Wimbledon life had been restored. Without warning, the Championships were struck by an even greater upheaval. If the Henman incident had registered fairly high on Wimbledon's Richter scale, what happened on Court 13 that Saturday broke all the records. It was by far the most spectacular controversy in which I have been embroiled in my 20-odd years as a referee, and I can still barely think about it without an inward groan and a shudder. At the centre of the storm was the afore-mentioned Jeff Tarango, a 26-year-old philosophy graduate from California with a notoriously fiery temper. Off court, I had always found Tarango an intelligent, thoughtful and generous character, but there was a touch of the Jekyll and Hyde about him, and once on court he could be as truculent and feisty as any player I had come across – as highly strung as one of his rackets and liable to snap at any moment.

Although he was a very accomplished doubles player, he never progressed further than the third round in the singles of a Grand Slam event; his highest singles ranking was 42 and he won two ATP tournaments over his career, in Tel Aviv and Wellington. Nor had Wimbledon proved a happy hunting-ground for him, and in his six previous appearances he had gone out in the first round each time, winning just one set and losing 18.

It was a third-round match down in the bottom southern corner of the grounds by the water tower, and Tarango's opponent was a German called Alexander Mronz. The chair umpire was a Frenchman, Bruno Rebeuh, who had given me no indication that he had had any significant problems with Tarango in the past. To be honest, it would have been difficult to find a leading chair umpire who hadn't at some point in their career crossed swords with the volatile Californian. At the start of one tournament, I recall Tarango handing me a catalogue of officials he did not want in control of his games which was so long that he might just as well have handed me the official international directory of chair umpires. 'If this is truly the case, then I'm afraid we're going to have to put inexperienced local amateurs in the chair for you,' I told him. 'Which would you rather?'

'The locals,' he replied.

All had seemed well when Tarango arrived at the court with his French wife Benedicte and caught sight of the supervisor Gilbert Ysern – a man who then held the equivalent of my post at Roland Garros. All the 1,600 seats around the little court appeared to have been taken and so Tarango asked Gilbert if he could find a place for his wife, which he duly did. I think Tarango got on pretty well with Gilbert, or at least knew him to be a high-ranking and experienced figure, and he imagined that the Frenchman had been detailed to oversee the match because he was an official of some stature. In fact, Gilbert just happened to be there when Tarango arrived; he was not actually assigned to the match and would soon disappear on a roving role around the grounds. Had he known this, Tarango would probably have asked for the chair umpire Rebeuh to be replaced.

The match stood at 7–6, 3–1 in Mronz's favour, when Tarango exploded – and it had taken the merest spark to ignite his notorious and well-stocked tinderbox. Rebeuh had actually overruled a line judge in Tarango's favour, but ordered the American to retake the serve because he felt the original call might have distracted Mronz as he went for the return. Had it been a clean ace the point would have been awarded to Tarango. You can only speculate what might have been going through the philosophy graduate's mind at this stage – he may just have had a bad night's sleep for all I know – but whatever it was, something extremely ugly consumed him over the following few minutes. Incensed that he had been asked to replay the point, Tarango immediately approached the chair to challenge the decision. As he did so, a couple of spectators, perhaps mindful of his reputation, started to heckle him, shouting: 'Come on, get on with it, Tarango!' The American was infuriated and told them to shut up, prompting Rebeuh to issue a warning to him. Tarango spun around, snapped back at Rebeuh and demanded to see the supervisor. It was not Gilbert Ysern who stepped on court, as he had expected, but Stefan Fransson, one of the other supervisors, and this seemed to upset Tarango even more and he immediately launched into another tirade at Rebeuh, who responded by docking him a point as a second code violation.

The situation was quickly spiralling out of control, and Tarango, now in the thick of a deep red mist, then did what no other player has done at Wimbledon – he disqualified himself. 'Right, that's it. I've had enough,' he exclaimed. 'You are the most corrupt official in the world and I'm not playing any more.' I had seen young boys in playgrounds tuck their football under their arm and stomp off home to Mummy, but I had never heard of a tennis professional acting in such a way. Tarango packed up his bags and with the crowd roaring and hooting, partly in disbelief and partly in derision, he tramped off court, with just one destination in his mind – my office. In doing so, he had just walked himself out of the Championships and into some very serious trouble. Had I imagined for one moment that Tarango would have had taken such drastic action, I would have been out there in a flash and would have stayed on court until the final ball was struck.

I was utterly oblivious to the commotion raging outside and was probably feeling pretty relieved that the Henman storm had largely blown over and it was business as usual again in the referee's office. My peace was violently shattered as Tarango burst through the door of the office downstairs and stormed up the stairs to see me. I wouldn't say that it was exactly like a scene from a horror movie, but I did jump a little at the sight of this very angry, disturbed-looking man glaring at me. At roughly the same moment, Tarango's wife Benedicte was barging her way through the crowd in pursuit of Rebeuh and when she caught up with him, just yards from the sanctuary of the umpires' office, she grabbed him by the arm and then delivered a stinging slap across his face. When word reached the media centre of these extraordinary events, you could almost hear them standing on their desks, whooping and cheering their delight. Rarely can a story have presented itself on a silver plate in such a way. This was going to be ten times more fun than writing about Pete Sampras for the umpteenth time. One journalist used to like to say that certain less colourful players could clear Centre Court quicker than a thunderstorm, but by the same token Tarango, particularly after that day's events, could fill a press conference quicker than Anna Kournikova.

Shortly after he arrived, another equally irate man burst into the office below, accompanied by a sobbing child. The young boy had been knocked over by the great bag slung over Tarango's shoulder as he buffeted his way through the crowds on the way to see me, and his father was demanding that the American came to apologise. Neither of the men knew of the other's presence in the office and when one of the girls rang up to tell me the man was waiting for me downstairs, I told her to try to persuade him to come back later. The prospect of these two raging bulls locking horns in our poky little office was too grim to contemplate.

If there was one venue where you would not want to meet Jeff Tarango in a fury, it was my old office. More of a cupboard than a room, it was claustrophobic at the best of times. It would be almost four hours before we parted company, and throughout that entire time the media pack were virtually bashing down the door to get to him. Rarely have I been more delighted to inhale the outdoor air than I was when I finally felt it was safe to release Tarango out of my sight and into the hands of the baying mob of the international press corps. Although 'counselling' is not one of the terms that features in the job-description of my contract with the All England Club, the task of offering support and advice to players is one I have grown used to down the years. And counselling was exactly what Tarango needed because I don't think the full magnitude of his actions struck him until the flood of adrenalin coursing through his veins began to subside as he sat facing me in the office. He never shouted at me, but he was extremely agitated and fidgety, running his hands through his hair, standing up and then sitting down, his eyes darting back and forth.

All his anger was focused on the chair umpire Rebeuh and he made some highly inflammatory comments about him. It was all totally unsubstantiated, and I had the feeling that the poor chap was trying to match the enormity of his own actions with proportionately extreme allegations in order to vindicate what he had done. There was clearly some history between the two of them, although I don't think that Rebeuh felt the animosity quite as keenly. I believe he would have been the first to tell me when the day's matches were signed off if he thought that their relationship was too poor to allow him to umpire the match.

The allegations flowed freely, and for what seemed like an eternity I listened to the American's tirade. I was desperately keen not to put him before the press until he had completely calmed down, because there would have been the most almighty stink if he repeated half the things he was telling me. With me in conversation with Tarango trying to defuse the worst dispute I had experienced at Wimbledon, the others in the office were left with the responsibility of printing the following day's order of play. Unfortunately Sandy and her staff were stuck in their office at the other end of the corridor and were unable, or unwilling, to interrupt my discussions with Tarango, resulting in some comical scenes – desperate to get the order of play released they ended up having to dangle a computer disc out of the window on a piece of string for their colleagues in the office below to take away.

When Tarango finally appeared to have regained his composure I sent him on his way, telling him it was vital he said as little as possible, that he regretted his actions, that he was sick of his bad-boy reputation, etc., and that under no circumstances would he be wise to start throwing around the highly derogatory allegations he had been making to me. Be calm, be humble, be apologetic, be remorseful, was the thrust of my advice. The press had been bombarding the office with enquiries about when Tarango would appear, and when he finally made his entrance to the most packed press conference I have seen at Wimbledon, you could almost hear the gnashing of teeth and the scraping of claws. I sat back in the office to watch the conference on television and within seconds I had my head in my hands and was shaking it back and forth in disbelief at what I was hearing. Far from keeping a lid on his thoughts, Tarango had launched into a dreadful rant about Rebeuh.

I cringed as I watched and listened to him digging himself into an even deeper hole while the press sat back, barely able to contain their glee, and lapped it all up as if Christmas had come early for them. They already had a great story, but it was just getting better and better the more Tarango raved. Just when it seemed it couldn't get any worse, the door of the press room was flung open and in marched Tarango's wife Benedicte. Even her husband seemed a little taken aback by this turn of events. And was she angry! She shouted about the injustices and conspiracies against her husband, and said that she had hit Rebeuh because Jeff himself would have been banned from tennis forever if he had done so himself. (The police, incidentally, asked Rebeuh if he wanted to press charges against her, but he declined.)

Watching this all unfold, I felt an ever-tightening knot in my stomach and not a little frustration that half a day's worth of gentle advising had gone up in smoke in a matter of seconds. I had had a certain amount of sympathy towards Tarango at first – he was clearly very troubled that day – but after watching his performance before the world's media, that modicum of compassion evaporated pretty sharply. When he returned to my office shortly afterwards my heart sank a little and I heard myself saying: 'Jeff, I've done all I can for you but after that I'm afraid you're on your own now.' He stayed for a while longer, repeating much of what he had said earlier before I told him, as politely as possible, that I had plenty of other work I should be doing.

Perhaps the worst aspect of the whole sorry saga was the moment when Rebeuh came into the office and asked to see a recording of the press conference. It was positively awful watching him take it all in, as we listened to the American hurl insult after insult and allegation after allegation. Rebeuh was absolutely mortified. He went as white as a sheet and was clearly in a state of total shock.

It had been a dreadfully depressing and exhausting day, and I was desperate just to get home, pour myself a stiff nightcap and settle into bed for a good long lie-in the following morning as it was the rest day of the middle Sunday. But just as I was putting on my jacket to leave the office, I was handed a message from Tarango, and I was not exactly overjoyed as

I read it. Tarango wanted to have a meeting with Bill Babcock – the ITF administrator responsible for player punishments – and myself at 11 a.m. on Sunday. I was beginning to spend so much time with the American I was tempted to call him up and invite him to come home with me and sleep the night on my sofa.

Jeff brought a friend along to the meeting back at the All England Club, and then the four of us settled down around a conference phone and listened to his lawyer in the United States effectively submit a plea in mitigation before he was sentenced. It was all fairly standard stuff: 'Jeff's a great guy; Jeff had done an enormous amount for the game back in the States; it was a moment of madness; it was completely out of character . . .'

At the end of it, Bill and I said we would go away and discuss all the facts before announcing what disciplinary action would be taken. We ordered Jeff and his friend a cab, and as we waited for it to arrive I took the opportunity to remind him to avoid talking to the press, a couple of dozen of whom were doorstepping the main gates to the club. The only media inside the grounds that morning were an NBC television crew, who were supposedly filming footage for a documentary about Wimbledon, but as we stepped down the steps from the main entrance, they jumped out of the shadows and went straight for Jeff. There was a bit of a scuffle as I tried to block the cameraman's line of vision and he gave me a pretty spicy volley of abuse as I asked him to move out of the way. Jeff seemed to have finally taken on board our advice about holding his tongue and as he stepped into the cab he said something impressively statesman-like, along the lines of, 'We've had a very frank and cordial discussion.'

Just before they set off, I leant in through the window and said: 'Don't forget Jeff, that for your own good, the less said the better. Don't throw any more fuel on the flames.' I watched the black cab pull up to the gates and within seconds it was surrounded by reporters and Jeff had the window down and was chatting away as if he were greeting some old friends from school. There's just no helping some people, I thought.

Tarango was fined the maximum $15,500 at the tournament, but that was increased to a total of almost $44,000, when the ITF's Grand Slam Committee imposed their sanction. In what amounted to the toughest ever punishment imposed on a player, Tarango was also suspended from the following year's Wimbledon as well as another Grand Slam. Later on, on appeal, the fine was reduced to the total of his prize money, which was approximately $28,000, and suspension from Wimbledon the following year. You might have thought, as I watched Tarango drive away that Sunday morning, that I would never want to set eyes on the man ever again, but curiously enough we have become pretty good friends. Ever since that awful day, he has always gone out of his way to seek me out. No doubt, most people who follow tennis will remember him for his spectacular outburst that day, but I will always have positive feelings for him and thoroughly enjoy his company. He is essentially a good man, clever, funny and kind, who just happens to have a devil of a temper. It is one of my biggest regrets that I was unable to get out to the court in time that fateful Saturday to talk him out of walking himself into one of sport's most famous controversies. All the subsequent hullabaloo flowed directly from that one quick flash of temper, the snap decision in the heat of the moment to storm off. In order to justify the extremity of his actions he maybe felt in some way he had to provide equally extreme reasons for doing it.

By the start of the second week, I was starting to feel a little world-weary with all the controversies raging around Wimbledon. The tennis had become a mere sideshow to all the action happening off court, but in truth it was not the most captivating of Championships as Sampras and Graf took the singles titles just as everybody suspected they would. Sampras beat Becker in four sets in the final, while Steffi was given a surprisingly tough game by the clay-court specialist Arantxa Sanchez Vicario and only clinched the title 7–5 in the third set.

There was one other major controversy that year, more of a mystery in fact, and today I am not that much wiser about what happened than I was at the time. A colourful all-American, rock'n'roll character called Murphy Jensen, a French Open doubles winner, with his equally flamboyant brother Luke, was scheduled to play in a mixed doubles match with the Dutch player Brenda Schultz-McCarthy. The pair had practised as arranged that morning and, according to Brenda, there didn't seem to be any problems with her partner, who was his usually bubbly, cheery self. But when the match was called and Brenda and their opponents arrived on court, there was no sign of Murphy. He was called several times but without any joy and so I despatched a handful of people from the office around the grounds to try to find him, but they didn't have any luck either and reluctantly we had to default him – and Brenda – which made it the third disqualification of the Championships (although Tarango had effectively disqualified himself). As news of his disappearance spread, wild rumours began to circulate around the club as the press set off in a pack to hunt down the AWOL American. As far as I knew, no player had ever failed to turn up for a match at Wimbledon without first notifying the club that they were injured or sick or otherwise indisposed. Who could tell what might have happened to him? The person I felt especially worried for was his mother, who grew increasingly anxious as the day wore on.

Someone said they had seen him in the Wimbledon transport office from where the players' courtesy cars are sent out and there were various other wild and unsubstantiated newspaper reports. Some said he was suffering from depression, while one report claimed he had simply decided to go fishing in Scotland. He was a keen fisherman apparently, but that theory, like all the others, seemed way off the mark. Still, there must have been some reason behind his vanishing. If you forget to turn up for a match at Wimbledon – or anywhere else for that matter – you might at least offer an explanation.

The Jensen family, together with Brenda Schultz-McCarthy, were staying in a house at the top of the hill just a few hundred yards from the All England Club and they were very soon under siege from the world's media. It was impossible to get through to the house on the telephone because a journalist had somehow got hold of their number and within an hour or so, the whole world was jamming the line trying to get through. I had to make contact with Murphy's mother in order to try to find out what had happened so that we could issue a statement and put an end to the mystery as soon as possible. The police drove me the short distance up the hill in an unmarked car and when we arrived at the house, we could hear doors slamming and the phone ringing. As we walked down the drive towards the front door, dozens of reporters and cameramen leapt from the bushes and trees and descended on us, sticking microphones and dictaphones under my chin as I struggled to push past. I completely ignored them and we dashed inside after Brenda's boyfriend opened the door and ushered us in before quickly slamming it shut. Mrs Jensen was understandably worried sick, and every time the phone rang she picked it up immediately in the hope that it was Murphy, only to slam down the receiver as yet another a journalist tried to elicit some information from her. She too had no idea what had happened, but there was little hope of Murphy getting through to her with so many journalists jamming the line.

We did our best to reassure her and asked her to get in touch as soon as she had any news of Murphy, but by the time the Championships were wrapped up for another year a week later, we still had no idea what had become of him. A week or so afterwards, I received a letter from his brother Luke saying that Murphy had turned up safe and well at their home in the United States, but he offered no explanation of his sudden disappearance. I saw press reports saying that he had fallen asleep in the transport office and when he woke up and realised he had missed his match, he was so mortified that he fled the Championships and went on a fishing trip before boarding a flight to the United States. It was all very peculiar, but to be honest, by the end of the 1995 Championships nothing would have surprised me.

Chapter Eight

Barefaced Cheek and a Split Personality

The 1996 Championships were nothing like as fraught and stormy as the year before, but they were no less strange for that.

The competing interest of Euro '96 in the first week and rain on four days of the second conspired to bring down overall attendances and put a bit of a dampener on the tournament. Not all the members were that pleased about the plan, but the club erected a giant screen and kept the gates open past 10 p.m. on the first Wednesday evening in order that spectators would be able to watch England's epic semi-final with Germany. Interest in Wimbledon that year was further undermined by the scattering of the top seeds in the early rounds: Agassi, Courier, Chang, Kafelnikov and Boetsch all fell at the first round, Stefan Edberg and Thomas Enqvist in the second, Becker was forced to retire injured in the third, while Sampras crashed out to Krajicek in a rain-wrecked quarter-final, bringing to an end his remarkable run of victories at Wimbledon.

Only one seeded player, Todd Martin, No. 13, reached the semi-finals in the men's singles, while the final itself was contested between two players whom the majority of the British public had never heard of: the Dutchman Krajicek and a charming American character called Malavai Washington, the first black finalist in the men's singles since Arthur Ashe. The final, which nobody in their wildest moments could have predicted, was a pretty disappointing affair as Krajicek eased to a comfortable straight-sets victory, and most of the excitement came in a few extraordinary moments before play began. By now, of course, I was braced for any eventuality at Wimbledon, but I almost had a turn when something caught my eye as the two finalists were posing for the traditional pre-match photographs.

After running through the protocol with the two players the master of ceremonies led them out on to court once the television people had given us the thumbs-up. We had all turned around at the service-line nearest the Royal Box to make the customary bow and then, as the photographers gathered to take their pictures, I saw a young girl clamber over the perimeter hoardings wearing what looked like a waitress outfit. With one quick tug she tore it from her body, leaving herself wearing nothing but an apron and a grin. She then proceeded to skip about in front of the royals and the other dignitaries before jumping into the clasp of two police officers. Krajicek and Washington, like the rest of us, were utterly dumbfounded by the sight, but shock soon turned to laughter and I remember looking up and seeing the Duke of Kent positively guffawing at the spectacle. The girl was led away. I read the following day that her family had all been sitting around having their Sunday lunch while watching the tennis on the television and almost dropped their plates when they saw her cavorting about the court.

I certainly wouldn't want to see streakers replace the

traditional military band performance at the Wimbledon final,
but I suppose as a one-off occurrence it was a fairly amusing,
harmless incident. There was no smile on my face six years
later, however, during a similar incident in the 2002 final
between Lleyton Hewitt and the Argentinian David
Nalbandian. In fact, what happened that day was probably the
lowest moment in my time at Wimbledon, or at least the most
humiliating by some distance, and I can barely recall the scene
now without feeling a deep burning sensation in my cheeks.

There had been a rain delay and I was standing in the
corner of the court and the players had just sat down and
were preparing to resume play when I saw a man leap out of
the crowd opposite the umpire's chair. He was fully dressed
– and my first instinct was that he was a dangerous madman
hell-bent on some act of violence or political protest – but he
had barely stepped on to the court when he pulled a string
and all his clothes fell from him in an instant. Nothing was
left to the imagination. Everything was on full display and he
immediately began to prance and cavort around the court. I
don't know whether it's some form of chauvinism, but
somehow the sight of this ludicrous man, with his body covered
in writing, failed to amuse the crowd as much as the girl had
done in 1996. The Duke of Kent certainly wasn't rolling
around in the aisles on this occasion and nor was I when I
realised that nobody was doing anything to have the prankster
removed from the court. If streakers are funny at all it is in
the first few seconds that they have emerged – it is the shock
of it I suppose – but the hilarity soon wears off. This particular clown must have been on for several minutes, although
it felt like the whole fortnight, and the joke was dying fast as
he continued to leap about like a mad salmon.

I was astonished that nobody had come on to put an end to the nonsense and was starting to feel a little annoyed. I approached two police officers who were just standing there rooted to the spot with their arms folded, laughing their heads off. 'Well go on then, get him off now,' I snapped. It transpired later that the man was a self-confessed 'serial streaker' with over 150 credits to his name and who had bared all on an outside court during a doubles match involving Anna Kournikova two years earlier. But nobody, least of all the police, knew that as he gallivanted around the court and I asked them, with barely disguised impatience, why they weren't doing anything. He could, after all, have been acting as a diversion while his accomplice perpetrated a more serious crime – an unlikely scenario, I confess, but I was desperate for somebody to act and if a policeman can't help you in a situation like this for heaven's sake, who can? The police said something along the lines that they had no jurisdiction to apprehend him unless he presented a threat of bodily harm. Marvellous! The streaker seemed every bit as surprised as I was that he had been granted the freedom of the court and the undivided attention of tens of millions of viewers around the globe, and he even seemed to get a little bored by it all himself. It crossed my mind for a moment that, tired of his own performance, he might even just put his clothes back on and calmly walk to his seat.

I was absolutely furious, and as nobody else seemed moved to take any action, I decided to get rid of him myself. I was in such a state of agitation that what followed is all a bit of a blur, but I remember somebody thrusting a red blanket into my hands as I stepped out on to the court like a comedy matador. Everyone was guffawing with laughter, except me of course, but the one thing I wasn't going to do was make even more of a fool of myself by chasing him around the court. I made a tentative move towards him and then stopped hoping he would come to me, but this was a bit of sport for him now and he ran away and leapt over the net as gales of laughter swept around the Centre Court. I thought my head was going to pop with anger and embarrassment when, to my utter relief, I saw one of the service stewards beckon to his colleagues to come and help. He was a great character who I had got to know very well over the years, and I was never more pleased to see him when he marched on to court with the others and finally led the clown away.

I was still hopping mad about the episode, and as soon as the tennis was underway I stormed over to the office of the chief executive Chris Gorringe to find out why the dozens of security people present had failed to take any action. Chris had no idea what had been going on because his television had been turned off, but after a few phone calls it turned out that 'streakers' were something of a loophole where security was concerned. The service stewards were under strict orders not to go on to the court unless there was some kind of major emergency, while the employees of the private security firm retained by Wimbledon were instructed only to protect the players from possible harm. As a result of the incident, security measures were reviewed and the service stewards now have the responsibility of dealing with a similar incident in the future.

There were a lot of people at the club, needless to say, who found the whole episode a big laugh and I had to smile weakly at all the inevitable giggling and ribbing from my esteemed colleagues over the weeks that followed. No doubt I too would have struggled to suppress a laugh if it had happened to somebody else, but it was an appalling experience, and other members were spitting fury over it because they felt that it was not just me but the entire club that was made to look foolish. Every time I see a rerun of the incident on the television, or a photograph of me standing there clutching that red blanket with a face like an angry beetroot, I just want the earth to swallow me up.

It may have come across as just a harmless caper to many of those watching but, setting aside my own personal embarrassment, the incident also raised worrying security issues. It was the second time during those Championships that a member of the public had been able to slip through the protective cordons aimed at guarding the players. In the first week, two men wearing tennis clothes calmly walked out on to Centre Court between matches and hit a ball back and forth for about 30 seconds before strolling away and out of the grounds without anyone raising an eyebrow, let alone a finger. These incidents always send a shudder down my spine. In 1993 Monica Seles was stabbed in the back at a tournament in Hamburg by a maniac obsessed with her rival Steffi Graf (I was officiating at the men's event there). It was a horrifying incident and shocked the entire world of sport. Although the attack led to a fundamental overhaul of security at all professional tennis tournaments, the streaking incidents at Wimbledon highlighted the continuing threat. If a harmless fool can walk on to court as easily as if he were walking into his own kitchen, so too can a maniac determined upon a far more terrifying act than running around without any clothes on.

It would be a sad day for tennis if it was ever forced to go the former route of football by installing metal cages around the court, but if there was ever a repeat of the Seles incident, calls for radical security measures, not least from the players, would become deafening. It is my own view that there should be more security personnel on court regardless of the steep costs – there is enough money in tennis – and that greater protection should be given to the women who are potentially more vulnerable. For instance, I do not know of a male player who has been troubled by a stalker, while there are a number of women who have had to suffer the trauma.

Stalkers are nothing new: Chrissie Evert once returned to her Florida home from Wimbledon to discover that an obsessed man had been living in her bedroom wardrobe for three days, while Martina Hingis, Anke Huber, Steffi Graf and, most recently, Serena Williams, have all had problems with obsessed followers. Serena now has a personal bodyguard wherever she goes, and whenever she is on court you can see him standing in the corner ready to intervene in the event of trouble. Several of the other players have also hired personal body-guards, but tournament organisers have been reluctant to provide individual security to the players because the costs are considered to be prohibitive, with 256 players in the singles of Grand Slam tournaments.

Security at Wimbledon, or any other tournament in which I am involved, does not fall within the remit of my job description, but usually I will be one of the first people to be informed if there is some kind of major incident going on. The two biggest threats to safety during my time as referee have been stalkers and bomb scares, which were a frequent problem before the IRA called its ceasefire in the mid-nineties. In addition to the incident stopping play on Centre Court that so upset Ivan Lendl, two alerts remain especially vivid in my memory. On one occasion, the air was filled with the sound of screeching sirens as the bomb squad arrived to investigate a suspect package sitting in the middle of the concourse between the main steps to the club and the courts on the left as you enter by the main gates.

A public address announcement ordered the spectators to clear the area as the police taped up either end and play was stopped on the four courts abutting the concourse. While dozens of heavily armed police officers with their robots and dogs calmly went about the business of inspecting the suspect device, the crowds munched away on their strawberries and supped their Pimms without the slightest air of alarm. On this occasion, I remember the Spanish player Arantxa Sanchez Vicario walking past the suspect package into my office after her match on Court 3 was halted with the contest poised at match point. Moments later we witnessed an extraordinary sight when a bomb-disposal expert in a gas mask and heavily padded body-suit strode down the deserted concourse looking for all the world like an alien in a science fiction film. Live footage of the event was going out on the world's television screens and I recall wondering how the families of the London bomb squad people must have felt had they been watching pictures of a man who might have been their son, father or brother approaching the holdall. It turned out, like all the other incidents at Wimbledon, to be a false alarm, but it was a heart-stopping moment all the same.

Around the same time, there was another incident involving a suspect package on the concourse by the tea lawn, the area to the right as you enter the main gates where most of the food and drink stalls are situated. On hearing the news, I went out to see what was going on and found the whole area completely deserted but for a police car with all its door opens. As I approached, a police officer shouted 'Quick, get down! Over here!' and I rushed to join him crouching behind the door of his car. The urgency in his voice set my heart racing and I don't mind admitting to a few nerves as I watched this *Star Wars*-style robot buzzing and beeping its way around the package before the all-clear was finally given.

In the wake of the September 11 attacks in the United States, security at Wimbledon has been tightened up and spectators' bags are now searched as they enter the grounds. This is a sensible development but it can also be a logistical nightmare as the queues to get in are bad enough in any event, and going through the personal belongings of upwards of 30,000 people can take an very long time. They have speeded up the searches since, but at first it caused a few problems and in 2002 I got caught up in it all when the public's frustration at the long delays outside erupted. I was standing on the concourse near the main gates talking to one of the supervisors when two ladies up from the shires, both bearing an uncanny resemblance to Sybil in *Fawlty Towers*, marched over and started haranguing me about the dreadful wait they had had to endure outside. As the most 'visible' Wimbledon official during the fortnight, I suppose I should have learned my lesson by then and laid low in my office, as these two went at me as if I was the devil himself, all but bashing me over the head with their brollies and thermos flasks. I was beginning to wonder whether they would ever stop and I would be able to return to my duties, but I couldn't get a word in edgeways as they tore strips off me for making such a frightful hash of the security arrangements, and I should be ashamed of myself, etc., etc., before my supervisor friend cut them short, explained I that I had nothing to do with the bag searches and wished them a pleasant day.

It may be an illusion arising out of the confidence and experience I have accumulated over the years in my job, but in the recent past Wimbledon has felt a far quieter, more relaxed place than it was in those earlier years. It may have something to do with the great changes which swept through the club after the long-term plan was launched a decade or so ago – the whole place now has a more comfortable and professional feel about it. There is more space around the grounds, so it no longer feels so crowded, and my office is now like a ballroom compared to the rabbit-hutch that was our former place of work. That in particular has made an immense difference to the pressure on me during the fortnight. The suffocating atmosphere of the old office, the changeover to computers, the bomb scares, 'the brat-pack' of players on the men's circuit in the eighties and early nineties – all conspired to create a sense of urgency, or impending emergency, as I went about my duties. During those turbulent years, I was like the proverbial swan, giving an outward appearance of easy calm (at least I hope I did) while all the time thrashing around beneath the surface.

But I suspect this change of atmosphere has its roots in something far more fundamental than mere building works and changes to working conditions. Tennis itself has undergone a remarkable transformation since I first sat down at my new desk in the assistant referee's office in 1977. The prize money at Wimbledon has increased by almost 40 times since then, way above the rate of inflation, and that in itself tells a story about tennis – it is less a sport or pastime now and more a multi-million pound business. When McEnroe triumphed for the first time in 1981, it was the last time Wimbledon was won by a man using a wooden racket. So ended over a hundred years of tradition, and a new era of cutting-edge technology, with much of the old artistry and skill of the game removed, was ushered in. It is not for me to say whether tennis is any poorer for these developments and 'advances', but I am merely pointing out that the world of tennis has become a different planet to the one I used to inhabit as a young official. There is, of course, still plenty of drama and excitement to be had, but the big serve does play a large part in the men's game, and some of the women's, which leads to shorter rallies.

That said, there was one occasion in recent years when Wimbledon undoubtedly shook with drama: the 2001 Championships when Goran Ivanisevic became the first wild-card entrant and only the second unseeded player after Becker to win the men's singles. It was a stupendous achievement, and although his victim that Monday afternoon was Pat Rafter – possibly the most delightful man to pick up a tennis racket in the modern era – the day will forever stick in my memory as one of the most joyous I have experienced in almost half a century of Wimbledons. The day became known as 'The People's Final' because it was held over until the Monday of a third week, owing to dreadful weather at the back end of the tournament, and all 14,000 tickets went on sale on a first-come, first-served basis. Over 7,000 spectators had camped out overnight on Church Road, many of them Australians and Croatians, and when I arrived at the club early in the morning, Wimbledon looked and sounded more like a street carnival than a tennis tournament, a happy riot of noise and colour. I sensed that it it was going to be a very special day, whatever the result.

A decade earlier I had felt very proud of the role I had played in pushing for 'People's Sunday', and I hope you will excuse me again if I recount the small part I played in this other extraordinary Wimbledon occasion. After his victory Ivanisevic thanked the All England Club for daring to give him a wild card, but it was only as a result of my intervention that he was granted one at all. Wild cards, which were introduced in 1977, are awarded by the committee to eight players who are not ranked high enough to qualify automatically. We generally give them to British players in order to drum up national interest in the Championships and in tennis as a whole, and by and large only one or two are given to overseas players, which is usually more than any other Grand Slams.

When the committee sat down to consider the applications in the build-up to 2001 there was a general reluctance to give one to the temperamental Croat. His form had been pretty wretched in recent seasons and, dogged by a chronic shoulder injury, he had tumbled down the world rankings to around the 130 mark. The year before he had been eliminated from Wimbledon in the first round and in 1999 he had gone out in the fourth. Applying roughly the same guidelines Wimbledon adopts for the seedings, the committee could not see an especially powerful prima-facie case for the Croat's inclusion this year. When he folded limply in the first round of the Queen's tournament to an unknown Italian called Cristiano Caratti, his case became even less convincing.

I, and a couple of the committee members, were insistent,

however, arguing that though his current form was poor, he was a confidence player who could suddenly hit his stride. He had also made an outstanding contribution to the Championships down the years, reaching the final on three occasions only to lose to Sampras twice (1994, 1998) and to Agassi in 1991, and I thought it was only right and fair that he should be given another crack at the title he had come so tantalisingly close to winning. I did not imagine for a minute that he would actually win it but I thought he would be good for a couple of rounds and could entertain the fans with a performance or two of his own peculiar brand of tragi-comic drama. In the end I got my way, but the bookmakers were no more upbeat about his chances than the committee members and he was installed at 125–1.

What happened over the following fortnight is one of the great stories of tennis. After seeing off the Swede Fredrik Jonsson in the first round, Ivanisevic then bundled aside a host of leading names to set up a titanic and highly contro-versial semi-final clash with Tim Henman. Carlos Moya, Andy Roddick, Greg Rusedski and Marat Safin had all been blasted off court by the big-serving Croat, but it wasn't until he came up against the darling of Wimbledon that the real drama began – and this is where I come into the story again. Some of Henman's fans still haven't forgiven me for what they see as my role in what unfolded after the rains began to fall on the Friday.

As I explained earlier, I have always done my best to try to accommodate the requests of international television networks whenever it has been practicable and reasonable. On this occasion the Americans had asked that Agassi's semi-final against Rafter be played first so that people over there could see some of the match (or all of it, depending on the time zone) before heading off to work. At the same time, the BBC had submitted a request for Henman's contest with Ivanisevic to be scheduled second as people returning from work here would be able to tune in to it. I had no hesitation in agreeing to the requests which seemed completely logical to me. To have switched them around would have been perverse.

Rafter's semi-final with Agassi was, in its way, every bit of an epic as the other would turn out to be, and he finally broke the American to take the fifth set 8–6. All seemed well enough when Henman's match got underway about half an hour later, and the crowd had worked themselves into a fever of excitement and expectation when he came from a set down to lead 2–1. When the rain started to come down and I was forced to abandon play for the day, Henman looked well set to reach his first Wimbledon final after producing some truly dazzling tennis against the Croat. After speaking to my friends in the Met Office that evening I was not at all optimistic about the likelihood of play the following day, and my heart still further sank when I rose early the next morning, drew back the curtains and saw the heavy rain slanting out of the steel-grey clouds.

If I could choose when the rain came at Wimbledon I would always opt for the first week because although there are hundreds of matches to schedule in the early rounds, there are at least plenty of contingencies to clear the backlog, including starting play earlier, using the middle Sunday and reducing the doubles from five sets to three. But if it rains at the end of the second week, there is no Plan B. Wimbledon is in the hands of the gods. That Saturday was a nightmare as the weather played its usual havoc, and it was Henman who suffered the most as the tremendous momentum and confidence he had built up the night before was washed away with the rain. Ivanisevic, meanwhile, took the opportunity to rally himself, and it was my old friend Tarango, Ivanisevic's occasional doubles partner, who later claimed some of the glory for talking the moody Croat out of the gloom that had descended upon him overnight. During one of the rain-breaks that afternoon, Tarango went into the locker-room and needled his friend with a string of provocative comments designed to rouse him into a fury, taunting him that he had crumbled pathetically after losing a tiebreak the night before. Whether Tarango's words had any effect or not I couldn't say, but Ivanisevic, the man dubbed 'the Split Personality', was certainly a different player when the action resumed later in the day, battling back to square the match at two sets all. When rain forced the match into a third day, the initiative lay with the Croat, who led 3–2 on serve, and it was Henman who was now under pressure.

I was having my own personal nightmare as we tried to work out what we were going to do about the scheduled final on Sunday. In the interests of the players and the television networks we had to make a decision as quickly as possible as to whether we would play it on the Sunday, at some point after the completion of the semi-final, or carry it over until the Monday and open the gates to the public. If we decided upon the latter, it would have been the first time that the men's singles final at Wimbledon had ever *started* on the Monday, and most people inside the club seemed dead set against it. There was a lot of argument amongst the committee members behind the scenes that afternoon about the best course of action to take, and the pressure began to mount as the media

harangued us for an answer. I was in a minority of club officials who wanted the final to be played on the Monday and
I had a devil of a job persuading some of my colleagues of
the good sense behind my position. I was determined to press
my case, however, as I believed my plan would prove the best
for all concerned.

There were two main reasons why I wanted the final on
the Monday, and they both centred around the interests of
the players. It was, after all, going to be one of the most
important days in their lives and as far as I was concerned
we had a responsibility to ensure that they were as best
prepared for it as possible. Firstly, I thought it would be unfair
on the winner of the Henman–Ivanisevic semi-final because
there was always the possibility that that final set, with no
tiebreak, could go on for a long time, and though it might
not exhaust them physically it would be emotionally draining.
Secondly, and just as importantly, it would be unfair on Rafter
because he wouldn't know when the final would get underway
and would thus not be able to prepare himself properly. Many
of my colleagues on the committee, including some of the
most powerful figures at the club, remained sceptical, however.

A media conference featuring myself, the chairman Tim
Phillips and the chief executive Chris Gorringe had been
scheduled, but we had yet to reach a decision and were still
arguing amongst ourselves when we entered the packed audi-
torium. Tim was superbly evasive and non-committal and
played the barrage of questions with characteristic cool and
diplomacy, but when someone shouted from the floor 'So what
does the referee think?' I saw my opportunity to press my case
for the Monday. Careful to stress that it was my own personal
opinion, and not that of the Club, I said I would rather see

the match held over because it was only fair on the three players in the equation. 'But what I will do,' I added, 'is ask the two semi-finalists themselves what they would like. They may well want to play on Sunday.' I was doing this with the players foremost in my mind and I was as good as certain that Henman and Ivanisevic would want to go for the Monday option. I knew that this might not delight everybody but I was prepared to put up with their annoyance because I was convinced I was doing the right thing.

I was about to get to my feet when the old chestnut about Wimbledon installing a retractable roof was raised and I was asked for my views on the subject. I said: 'I'll let you sort that out amongst yourselves, if you don't mind, as I better be getting on with my job. I will go and contact the players and get back to you as soon as I have the answer.' A few cards in the crowd started shouting: 'Hear, hear, let the referee do his job!' but I knew as I walked out of the press conference that the Monday final was as good as in the bag.

Tim Henman had just driven out of the grounds moments earlier. When, shortly afterwards, I managed to get hold of him at his home in Barnes, he said: 'I thought this might be you. I heard on the radio that you were about to call me.' I finally managed to track down Goran Ivanisevic too, and the response of both players to my question was exactly as I had expected. In fact their answers were almost identical to the word: 'When I win tomorrow, then I would like the final to be on Monday.' So that was that: Monday it was. Although some of my colleagues at the Club may not have thought too highly of me when the decision was finally announced, by the end of that wonderful day there was not so much as a whisper or snipe of criticism from any quarter. It was one of the great days of sport and although I had played only a very small part in it, I feel very proud and happy that I stuck to my guns.

Sadly, from a British point of view at least, Henman was unable to rediscover the rhythm that had ebbed away from him on the Saturday, and Ivanisevic had little difficulty in wrapping up the final set. It was of course a great disappointment not just for him but for the British public who had been shouting themselves hoarse over the previous five years in support of his efforts to rid the country of the embarrassing fact that the last time one of our compatriots had lifted the men's trophy at Wimbledon, King Edward VIII was mulling over his abdication.

The acute disappointment of his defeat, if that is what you can call getting to within a few shots of a Wimbledon final, was soon blown away by the tumultuous events of the following day. The atmosphere on Centre Court that day was as good as, better perhaps, than on the People's Sunday ten years earlier. Some of the more traditionalist members of the Club may not have enjoyed the sight of all the Croatian and Australian flags draped around the arena, nor the deafening roars of encouragement for the two protagonists who soon became locked in a colossal battle of wills, but if that was the case I for one certainly didn't hear any complaints from anyone that day or in its aftermath. Everybody was united and transfixed not just by the compulsive spectacle on show but by the electric atmosphere it generated around the Centre Court.

It was one of those rare occasions when the goose-pimples and the adrenalin did not subside until hours after the event, and even the people were still buzzing and glowing with the heart-lifting excitement of it all. Because this was not just the story of one man's victory in an important tennis match –

there was also a fascinating context to it. Ivanisevic's remarkable progress through the draw as a wild card was part of it, and his three previous failures in the final added even more emotion, but he was also carrying the hopes of a young nation trying to make its mark on the map after all the horrors of the most recent Balkans war. On the other side of the court, you had Pat Rafter, the most popular man on the tennis circuit, a character you wished nothing but the very best for, and he, like his opponent, was also facing what was realistically his last chance to win a title that had eluded him in a tight contest against Sampras 12 months earlier. The presence of the Australian Test cricket team in the crowd only seemed to add to the drama.

Like most neutrals, my loyalties were torn right down the middle. You simply didn't want either of them to lose, and it was that perhaps which lay at the heart of the tension. It was almost unbearable as the match swung first this way then that, all the time buffeted by the raucous cheering of the 14,000 fans perched on the edges of their seats. The ferocity of the support was almost alarming, and although there had not been a single unsavoury incident as far as I knew, I took the precaution of putting some contingency security measures in place. As the match drew to its thunderous conclusion, I had the security people place some of their men around the perimeter of the court, just in case there was a spontaneous invasion in the heat of the moment. Amidst all the commotion, you never knew what might happen, especially if a controversial call was to enrage one set of supporters.

The tension was certainly getting to Ivanisevic, and when he was foot-faulted I looked on nervously as he completely lost his temper, kicked the net, smashed his racket and abused the umpire before, thank heaven, the red mists evaporated. When the match entered the final set, the smart money was on Rafter because he had just swept the fourth 6–2 and he seemed to have a fair wind behind him while Ivanisevic was becalmed in the doldrums. Mr Ivanisevic Snr, who had a serious heart condition, had defied his doctor's advice to join the Centre Court crowd that day and it was perhaps his presence that lifted his son to one mighty last effort in that final half-hour or so. Trailing 6–7, Ivanisevic was three times within two points of defeat, but he somehow pulled through and in the very next game he succeeded in breaking Rafter to go one game clear. Like the rest of the crowd, and no doubt the millions of viewers around the world, I could barely watch as Ivanisevic tried to steady his famously volatile spirit and serve out for a glorious triumph. When he double-faulted three times in that final game and squandered two match points, you began to fear that you were watching one of the most painful acts of 'choking' in the history of sport, but finally his booming serves found their range and the giant Croat slid to the Centre Court grass and lay face down in ecstatic relief.

Amidst the wild celebrations that ensued I tried to keep a cool head, but any fears that the emotion of the moment might turn ugly or stupid in some quarters of the ground proved utterly baseless. Everybody behaved beautifully until the awards ceremony was over and Wimbledon was put to bed after one of the most memorable days in its very long history. Bed, however, was the last thing on the minds of Ivanisevic and his rowdy followers who had gathered outside the entrance to the players' area and filled the air with Croatian folk-songs before accompanying their hero on what reportedly was an extremely noisy, colourful and good-natured pub crawl around Wimbledon village.

As the Croats danced and drank themselves crazy in the pubs and bars, you couldn't help but feel heart-broken for Pat Rafter – not that the man himself was showing the slightest signs of despondency, self-pity or bitterness. More than any other player I have come across, Rafter has lived up to the Kipling ideal of treating the twin imposters of triumph and disaster just the same. 'I had my chances to win it, but I just didn't take them,' he said to me, as I commiserated with him before the award ceremony got underway. 'Great game, though, wasn't it?' Almost exactly 12 months earlier he had said words to roughly the same effect after he came within an inch here and a shot there of beating the great Sampras, who had just equalled William Renshaw's record of seven Wimbledon men's singles titles. Though the match only went to four sets it was far closer than the score-line suggested. Having won the first set on a tiebreak, Rafter lost the second the same way by the agonisingly close margin of 7–5, and it would have taken a truly monumental effort on Sampras's part to come back from there had the Australian won the set.

If there is one group of tennis players I have a special fondness for, it is the Australians. You come across a few prima donnas and bigheads on the international tennis circuit, but rarely will you find an Australian among their number, and that has been my experience of them from my playing days right through to today. When the Woodies, Todd Woodbridge and Mark Woodforde, won their sixth Wimbledon doubles titles in 2000 I went to congratulate them on their achievement. I have known them for years and they said: 'I tell you what, Alan, we are off to a restaurant up the hill with the family and a few pals for a bite to eat and a drink. Please would you and Jill come and join us?'

I love that about the Aussies. In the serious world of modern tennis they are a breath of fresh air – tough as you like on court, but easygoing and down-to-earth away from it. The 2002 champion Lleyton Hewitt plays with a fury and intensity to rival any of the greats, but I have never had so much as a squeak of trouble from him in the few years he has been coming to Wimbledon and in the other tournaments in which we have both been involved. On the contrary, he has been one of those players who just gets on with it, even when things don't go his way, as when he relinquished the defence of his title in 2003 in a shock first-round defeat to the Croatian Ivo Karlovic. The men's title that year went to Roger Federer, who fulfilled his dream of becoming Wimbledon champion by defeating the big serve of Mark Philippoussis with artistry and all-round skill. It was a joy to watch. Philippoussis is another Australian who, although criticised in his own country for being a little glum and difficult on occasions, has always been easy, polite and straightforward in my dealings with him. Serena Williams defeated her sister in the women's final that year and Todd Woodbridge edged towards another record when he won the doubles with Jonas Bjorkman. But the tournament perhaps belonged, once again, to Martina Navratilova who, at 46 years old and in the last match of finals day, won the mixed doubles title with Leander Paes and equalled Billie Jean King's record of 20 Wimbledon titles. It is an extraordinary achievement and it is fascinating to watch the incredible determination that goes with success of that magnitude. It was a wonderful moment for both of them, and when

Leander finished the match with a smash he turned to Martina and bowed and she fell into his arms in tears.

Perhaps one of the reasons that Pat Rafter is one of those Australians who is so confident, modest and sociable is that he comes from a family with eight brothers and sisters. I think it was in 1997, one of the wettest first weeks on record, when we lost the whole of the first Thursday and Friday to rain and everybody connected with Wimbledon was going out of their minds with frustration. We were all sitting in the office kicking our heels and fielding calls from all sorts of characters wanting to know what was going to happen to the playing schedule, and so on. (You would be amazed by some of the questions we are asked when the weather has forced play to be suspended, but my personal favourite has to be: 'I was wondering if you could tell me when it is going to stop raining.' Incredibly, we get that one fairly often. The really stupid questions can provide a little comic relief, but generally sitting in the office during these times is a miserable experience.) Pat came in to see us and stayed for the better part of the two days, taking it upon himself to answer some of the telephone calls. He was extremely amusing with his replies to all the questions and had all of us in stitches. 'How the hell do I know when it's going to stop raining for God's sake? – I'm just a dumb player,' he shouted down the phone on a few occasions. Other players come into the office from time to time, not often to socialise but perhaps to ask that a match be played on a particular court or scheduled at a certain time. Pat is a truly delightful character and I was very sad to see him retire, even more so because he never managed to win Wimbledon.

I remember his final against Sampras in 2000 vividly,

because I came within a minute of having to make what would have been one of the most unpopular and controversial decisions in the history of Wimbledon finals. Rain had disrupted play all day and it was well past 9 p.m. and the sun had long since disappeared when the match reached a critical juncture with Sampras leading two sets to one and 4–2 in the fourth. I was standing in my usual position in the corner and, no exaggeration, it was so dark I was having difficulty picking out faces at the other end. Neither player had lodged a complaint to the umpire and so I had to let them continue, but it was now as gloomy a scene as I had ever come across on a professional tennis court and I knew that I would have to intervene. With the policy of only stopping play with the games on an even number it was looking as though I would be forced to walk on with the scores standing at 5–3, assuming that both games went with serve. I could hardly dare to imagine the reaction of the crowd if I had had to call an end to it for the rest of the day – it would be a bit like stopping the FA Cup final a minute from time with a player racing in on goal.

The spectators had been there all day long dodging the showers before finally getting the chance to immerse themselves in a thoroughly absorbing contest, only for that wretched referee Mills to call it all off just when it was reaching a thrilling climax. I could almost feel the thump of the cushions on the back of my head as I stood there picturing the scenario that would follow. When the American succeeded in breaking his opponent and then served out for the match, I breathed an immense sigh of relief mixed with sadness for Rafter. As soon as the winning ball was struck, the Centre Court was lit up by a blaze of a thousand flashbulbs around the court – one of the most amazing sights I have witnessed there, and it was so dark by the time the award ceremony got underway that those at the back of the stands could not even see it. It was typical of Pat Rafter not to have asked to go off for the bad light when he was losing. When I asked him why he didn't complain about it, he replied matter-of-factly: 'Well, it was the same for him, wasn't it?'

Another contemporary character who I have never heard bemoan his ill-fortune is Tim Henman, even after he was overhauled by Ivanisevic in that rain-wrecked semi-final in 2001 when he appeared to have the match in his pocket. That was the closest he had ever come to winning Wimbledon and he must have felt desperate after the event. It's not Tim Henman's fault that it's been so long since a Briton has won the Wimbledon's men's title, but reading the papers you sometimes get the impression that it is our divine right that he does so on our behalf. The British tennis reporters are by and large a first-class bunch of writers, but the judgement of some of their number always seems to get a little scrambled at the sight of Henman at around the end of June and early July. Henman's record at Wimbledon is truly exceptional, especially when you compare it to the other three Grand Slams where he had never progressed further than the fourth round until 2004 when, in perhaps the best year of his career, he reached the semi-finals of both the US and French Opens. Between 1996 and 2004 Henman reached the Wimbledon semi-finals on four occasions, likewise the quarter-finals and the fourth round once. Only Sampras himself can hold a candle to those achievements, and it has been Henman's bad luck that in two of those semi-finals, each going to four sets, he found himself facing the great American, perhaps the most accomplished and ruthless grass-court player of all time. In the other, against Ivanisevic, it was the rain (and not me, as some people would have you believe) that torpedoed his chances. I have no doubt that had Henman not been thwarted by the rain that Friday he would have reached the final, and then who knows what might have happened with a full house roaring him on. To regard Tim Henman as anything other than a hugely successful and talented tennis player is nonsense. As I have said, 2004 was an exceptional year for him, finishing up as he did at No. 6 in the world rankings. It is also worth bearing in mind that in 2003 he beat Sebastien Grosjean, Gustavo Kuerten, Roger Federer and Andy Roddick on the way to winning the Paris Masters.

I always feel my blood pressure rising and my brow furrowing when I pick up a newspaper during the second week of Wimbledon and I see headlines to the effect: 'Henman fails again!' Is it only in Britain that a man can have as outstanding a record as Henman and lift his game to exceptional heights year after year only to be dubbed a failure and a bottler? It says a great deal about the man's grace under pressure that he manages to maintain his composure in the face of that kind of criticism. Instead of celebrating the fact that Britain can boast its first truly outstanding player since Perry himself, he is pilloried for the country's shame of no longer being able to produce a Grand Slam winner. What makes the criticism all the more ironic and galling is that Henman has achieved what he has *in spite of* rather than because of the way British tennis conducts itself. I almost choked on my cornflakes not long ago when I read one of our leading boxers, who has won nothing of the slightest consequence in the professional code, saying that he was heading to the United States to ply his trade because he 'didn't want to be a loser like Tim Henman'. Rarely am I embarrassed to be British, but when you read that kind of rubbish . . .

The British press, especially the tabloids, can be cruel to its sportsmen, and over the years I have found the treatment of our up-and-coming tennis players especially infuriating. It is difficult enough for many of them as it is, trying to make their way in a highly competitive international game of great depth, when they have been cocooned in a domestic infrastructure that at best can only be described as unsatisfactory. Players stack shelves in a supermarket just to pay their way and give themselves a shot at the big time; they battle through the Wimbledon qualifiers, scrape into the second round and then wake up the following morning after a defeat in which they have given their all and read the headline: 'Union Jerks!' Is it worth all the bother, they must wonder.

Leaving aside the jokers who stop me in the street and ask me whether it is going to rain today, by some distance the question I have been asked more frequently than any other over the years, both at home and abroad, is: 'What on earth is wrong with British tennis?' To which I reply: 'How long have you got?' Everybody involved with the sport has their views on the problems and the solutions, and if you have the time and the inclination, make yourself comfortable and I'll give you the benefit of my thoughts on the subject, for what they are worth. Depressingly, more intelligent and powerful people than me, with bags of money at their disposal, have failed to arrest the decline of the sport we, as a nation, invented, codified, presented as a gift to the rest of the world and excelled at for the first 60 or so years of its existence in an organised form.

One of the main challenges facing reformers is that tennis does not exist in a world of its own, but within a far wider social and sporting context, and to some extent the difficulties are beyond the control of the sport's authorities. There are dozens of sports being played by hundreds of thousands of young men and women out there, potential champions, but the vast majority of them barely give tennis a thought. The thrust of my argument is that it is tennis's challenge to grab the youngsters at the earliest age possible.

The LTA have taken a positive step in this direction through the launch of a campaign targeting the inner cities in an effort to attract youngsters and widen the appeal of what is often regarded as an exclusive sport. That, for me, is an eminently sensible policy. For years, it has been my view that the tennis authorities should elbow their way into the nation's comprehensive schools and get to the kids as early as possible. Each school has its quota of outstanding athletes, but most of the boys will have already chosen football, or another sport, by the time they are in their teens. Imagine if tennis had been able to get hold of a Daley Thompson, David Beckham, Steven Gerrard or a Jonny Wilkinson? It's a bit of a chicken-and-egg situation because when, or if, British tennis does manage to capture and nourish talents and personalities of that calibre, they would automatically become charismatic role-models for generations to come, and they in turn would maintain the momentum for the next. At the moment, British tennis has no such momentum. Henman and Rusedski are both household names but, much as I would wish it, they are not going to go on forever, even though Tim is riding higher than ever and Greg is getting back to his best form after his lay-off, and if you were to stop someone on the street and ask them to name three other British tennis players, most would be unable to do so. However, hopefully in the coming years Andrew Murray, Miles Kasiri and perhaps some members of our under-14 squad can change this sad truth. The All England Club is also doing its bit to nurture new talent through the successful running of a junior tennis initiative.

These are hopeful signs for the future, without doubt, but they still don't remedy the biggest problem facing tennis – that schools do not have the facilities and our hard-pressed teachers simply do not have the time for extra-curricular activities as they once did. Moreover, at school level I can see the attraction of team games over individual sports because you can put a couple of dozen kids on a football field all at once. Tennis will never be able to do that, and so the authorities must try to encourage them to join local clubs instead. Grammar schools and public schools have all the facilities and between them, year after year, they produce a crop of excellent young sporting talent, but unfortunately, for sport, most of the pupils go off to university and then embark on careers in one of the more traditional professions. If you managed to collar the best of these athletes and channel them into academies, Britain would have a lot more truly outstanding sportsmen and women.

When Bjorn Borg became the first Swede to win Wimbledon, his country's tennis authorities passed a directive making it compulsory for all clubs to open their doors to juniors, free of charge, for one day a week. The result has been generations of great players such as Edberg and Wilander and also Anders Jarryd, Michael Pernfors, Magnus Norman, Thomas Enqvist, Thomas Johansson, Jonas Bjorkman and others. Success, backed up with some imaginative and tough initiatives, can breed more success. To be fair, the LTA have tried similar initiatives in recent years, such as handing out loans to clubs on the condition that they do more to bring on the juniors, and although the benefits are not immediately obvious, we may just be beginning to see some green shoots appearing on what has been pretty barren earth for such a long time.

The class element is also a major problem for the development of tennis in this country. To many youngsters, tennis is a sport for soft middle-class children in fancy private clubs. That was the view amongst my contemporaries when I started playing, but hopefully the LTA's initiative can help combat this impression. In addition, the most inspirational aspect of the Williams sisters' astonishing story is that they were inner-city kids and their success will certainly encourage more children from that background to take an interest in the sport.

It is fair to say that in recent years Britain has managed to produce a handful of very talented youngsters. Our under-14 boys' team won the European Championships in 1998 and again in 2004, while our under-18 girls' team won the Maureen Connolly Trophy in 2004 by beating the United States. Three of our juniors, Hannah Grady, Clare Peterzan and Katie O'Brien, have recently improved their ranking by 500 places on the WTA list. However, our experience over the past 30 years or so seems to suggest that this young talent will not push through at the senior level. One of the reasons for this, to my mind, is that there are nowhere near enough tournaments of sufficient quality being played here. It is only in the furnace of real competition that good players can be forged. You can go to coaching sessions every day of the week, but until you get the experience of regular contests against top opposition in a meaningful competition, there is no way forward. In Spain, one of the world leaders in tennis these days, they have hundreds of tournaments all year round, which gives their youngsters a great advantage over others. In Britain there are very few such events, and even the National Championships, once a highly popular and successful focus for the British game, have now been discontinued for financial reasons. It is also a dreadful irony that the major international tournaments staged by Britain are so well run that many foreign players come back again and again, thus making it more difficult for our home-grown talent to gain some experience and exposure while picking up some important ranking points along the way. On the plus side, however, the LTA does seem to have realised this and, taking a leaf out of the Spanish book, has begun to organise more events, starting in 2004 and going forward. In addition, the All England Club runs a large junior tournament every year, called the Road to Wimbledon.

These steps are critical if Britain is once again to become a serious contender in world tennis. Without sufficient competitiveness in the domestic structure, you are not going to generate a truly competitive mindset in the players. Not long ago, to give just one example, I was the referee at a Fed Cup match between Russia and Slovenia in Portoroz, and every player's level of commitment on each point was 100 per cent. I do not mean to malign British players, but rarely have I seen that kind of desperate death-or-glory commitment here in recent years.

One of the saddest facts is that British tennis, unlike many of its rival sports, cannot complain about a lack of funding. Far from it. The sport is awash with cash. Each year the All England Club, under an agreement with the LTA, hands over all the profits from the Wimbledon Championships, less tax, for its investment in the grassroots of the game. Since 1996, Wimbledon has been making in excess of £26 million and that figure virtually doubles when you take into account the money raised through lottery funding and other initiatives. To outsiders, in the conspicuous absence of any tangible success, it may seem that the money would be better off being poured straight down the drain. For all the LTA's initiatives and hard work, nothing seems to have worked yet. But as I have said, there are hopeful signs.

What progress that has been made, however, has not been achieved without its fair share of setbacks. One of the most damning and depressing developments recently has been the downgrading of a project to open up a string of eight regional academies around the country. At the announcement of the plan, there was great excitement in tennis circles, because here finally we seemed to have good intentions translated into bricks and mortar – real physical institutions, rather than just another scheme. But not long after the system was set up, the LTA suddenly announced that they were shutting four of them because they had not attracted enough players to fill them. When I heard the news of the closures I felt like screaming: 'Well, why don't you go and find them? Wasn't that part of the enterprise?' At the same time, they also cut the number of coaches across the country, claiming financial constraints, but can that really be so, with all the money dropped into the bucket by Wimbledon year on year? Perhaps I have got my figures wrong, but lack of cash seems a bit of a spurious argument to me.

It should be noted that Britain is not alone in its problems, though for a highly developed, rich country our record is embarrassing when set against the East Europeans and the South Americans. But even the United States has had its problems in recent times, and for a long while Sampras and Agassi carried the sport there in much the same way as Henman and Rusedski have done over here. At least now, though, they have Andy Roddick, James Blake and Mardy Fish to name but a few in the men's and Lindsay Davenport and the phenomenal Williams sisters in the women's to try to inspire a new generation.

Setting Henman's success to one side, the green shoots that I mentioned previously certainly seemed to establish themselves in the past year, during which there was a remarkable improvement in the achievements of the British boys and the girls. I've mentioned already the successes of the under-14 boys, under-18 girls, Andrew Murray's win at the US Open junior event and Miles Kasiri's runner-up position at junior Wimbledon. Add to this the fact that our Federation Cup team was promoted from Division 2 to Division 1 and at Wimbledon we had more victories in the first two days than for a very long time, and we can look back with a degree of satisfaction at the progress made in 2004. Part of the reason for this is that the LTA is now spending in excess of £5 million a year on improving facilities and providing top-class coaches for our most promising players, as well as helping independent squads and academies. It is said that approximately 600 players between 9 and 22 years old receive year-round support. In addition, the official winter training base at La Manga in Spain is available to all. By the end of 2006 the LTA should have their new tennis centre up and running at Roehampton, which will offer 16 outdoor and six indoor courts, as well as a fully equipped gym together with sports science and medical facilities.

What this all means is that there are many more of our boys and girls on the international rankings list which increases the breadth of the 'bottom of the pyramid' and this, in turn, will hopefully generate greater competition which should result in some of them fighting their way to the top.

Chapter Nine

Not Shy, but Retiring

The 2004 Championships proved to be one of my most difficult years — thanks to the weather I need hardly add. Two-and-a-half days were completely rained off and in an attempt to catch up with the programme we had to play on the middle Sunday once again, which was another great success.

Rain as it did, the weather could not dampen the quality of the tennis. Nor the level of excitement. Nor, indeed, the controversy. One of the main talking points of the whole fortnight was the ladies' second-round match between Venus Williams and Karolina Sprem. At 2–1 to Williams in the second set tiebreak, with the American a set down, Sprem served a ball down the centre which was called 'out' by the linesman. Chair umpire Ted Watts missed the call and the rally continued with Venus returning the ball and Sprem hitting it back into an empty court. The umpire called the score 2–2 as Sprem walked back to the side of the court from which she had just served, intending, it would seem, to take her serve again. The score at this point should have been 1–2 with the second serve to come. Strangely, however, neither player queried the 2–2 score, so when Sprem did serve again from the same side, and Williams won the point, the score should have been 1–3 with Sprem to serve one more point from the right-hand court. But it was called 2–3. Sprem had been awarded a point she had not won. Venus went on to lose the tiebreak and the match.

It seems almost unbelievable to me that such a thing could happen. I can understand the umpire not hearing the first call of 'out', but I cannot understand him allowing Sprem to serve twice from the same side of the court. Likewise, I cannot fathom how the players didn't realise that something was wrong, when everyone else watching around the court seemed to be aware of the situation. And I am afraid my incredulity doesn't stop there. It is easy to be wise after the event, I know, but I can't help but wonder why the line umpire who made the original 'out' call did not draw the chair umpire's attention to the error or, for that matter, why none of the other officials around the court didn't. It was the most bizarre of happenings.

I was only made aware of the situation when a television executive came rushing into my office, interrupting a meeting on the next day's order of play, and asked if I would come and see a rerun of the incident. I did, of course, and was astounded at what I saw. I then went on television to explain how the rules should be applied, stating that at that late stage nothing could be done to change anything, as the match was over. I spoke to umpire Watts and he could hardly believe that he had made such a mistake and immediately offered to hand in his badge. He was duly suspended for the rest of the tournament and, as with all umpires and line umpires, his position will be reassessed at the appropriate time. That was the correct procedure to follow.

At the risk of repeating myself, for me perhaps the most amazing aspect of the whole affair was that neither player queried what was happening, as it has always seemed to me that players have an inbuilt awareness of the score at all times. In her post-match interview, Venus was very gracious towards the umpire, saying that he had umpired several previous matches and there had never been a problem. 'I don't think one call makes a match' was her view, proving once again what a worthy past champion she is.

Away from the controversy, 2004 ended up being something of a record-breaking year. The men's doubles event had to be reduced because of the weather, from five to three sets, up until the semi-final. The eventual winners were Todd Woodbridge and Jonas Bjorkman and the victory gave Todd his ninth title, beating the record held by eight-times winners Laurie and Reggie Doherty at the turn of the twentieth century.

Roger Federer continued where he left off in 2003, successfully defending his title. In the first set of the men's singles final Andy Roddick came out like an express train, hitting not only his serves but also his groundstrokes as hard as I have ever seen any player hit the ball. Federer was perhaps a little fortunate in the rain delay that followed this first set because it gave him time to assess the match, regroup and change his tactics to nullify the power game with exquisite artistry. There can be no doubt that he is currently far and away the best player in world.

In the women's competition, Maria Sharapova caused one of the greatest upsets in the history of the tournament when, on an afternoon of rare sunshine during that fortnight, she beat defending champion Serena Williams in straight sets to become the third youngest woman ever and the first Russian to win the Wimbledon crown. Her enthusiasm and sheer delight when Serena mishit a forehand return into the net were truly infectious. In a scene reminiscent of Pat Cash in the 1987 final, she climbed into the stands to embrace her father before doing something that placed her firmly in the twenty-first century and was a first for a Wimbledon champion – she produced a mobile phone on Centre Court and tried to call her mother in the United States to share the emotional occasion. I doubt if anyone will forget that moment.

Martina was back as well to defend her mixed doubles title with Leander Paes. It is testament to her dedicated commitment that the pair lost in the third round to the eventual winners Wayne and Cara Black in the longest match of the tournament, 7–6, 6–7, 13–11. I hope and expect her to be back once again in 2005.

Maria Sharapova's victory typified a magnificent year for Russian women's tennis. In addition to that Wimbledon victory, Anna Myskina won the French Open and Svetlana Kuznetsova the US (both players defeating compatriot Elena Dementieva in the final), and at the end of the season ten Russians occupied places in the world top 50 (the United States had eight). Jokingly, of course, we wondered whether we could claim some credit for these remarkable achievements!

In 1963 we had flown to Moscow, with Mike Hann and Caroline Yates-Bell, to play in the Russian championships. Getting there was quite a nerve-racking experience as we had to travel on one-way tickets and were required to give our passports to the aircrew before we got off the plane. Our hotel was very traditional, with a female concierge on each floor. Poor Caroline tried desperately to enlist her help on the first night to remove a pigeon that had hopped into her room – but as her Russian vocabulary didn't stretch to varieties of bird life it proved an almost impossible task.

In the tournament I won through a couple of rounds before falling to John Newcombe. Part of the deal of the overseas players being invited to enter the competition was that afterwards we would be divided into groups of four and flown to other parts of the country to help promote the game and encourage people to play. As I said, the results of 2004 certainly seem to suggest that we didn't do a bad job – even if it took over 40 years for things to come together!

It was a wonderful time to be in the Soviet Union, with the space race well and truly underway. While we were there a Soviet craft was scheduled to land and there were huge celebrations planned in Red Square to mark the occasion. We tried to get there to join in – against the wishes of our interpreter. As it happened, we didn't get very far as all the roads were blocked off and, being unable to read the traffic signs, we got a bit lost. We ended up watching on an old nine-inch television in our hotel.

After a week in Moscow we flew to Kharkov to play a few matches against a local team. We were really looking forward to the chance to get to know some of the Russian players we were travelling with in more relaxed surroundings away from Moscow, but sadly we had been put in different hotels. We didn't let that deter us, however, and on the first evening we set off, successfully, to find where they were staying and ended up having a wonderful evening in which the lack of a common language was made up for through much gesticulating and waving. On discovering that their Russian opponents were unable to purchase items like nail-varnish and talcum powder, Jill and Caroline happily left all theirs with them.

Back in Moscow, after a brief trip to Sochi on the Black Sea, there was a party arranged for all the players and we were excited to see a pile of white bread and butter. After all our travels, during which we had been sampling a wide variety of food, we found we had missed such simple, recognisable fare. We then discovered that one of Russia's great treats, and something that we had never tried before, was also available at the party and we jumped at the chance to combine the best of both worlds – and rustled up caviar sandwiches all round.

The people we met on the trip were truly wonderful – always hospitable and welcoming. I also discovered when refereeing the big international tournament – the Kremlin Cup – in Moscow some years later that the president of the Russian Tennis Federation and captain of their Federation and Davis Cup teams, Shamil Tarpischev, had been a ball-boy when we were playing there. I have met him a number of times at various tournaments and in 2004, when refereeing the Russia–Thailand Davis Cup match, I was touched when he made a speech, after a few vodkas I remember, during which he thumped his chest and announced I had the heart of a Russian.

The final stop on our tour was Poland, and after collecting our passports and visas we headed off to Katowice via Warsaw. The budget available to the organisers of the tournament we were playing in was clearly very tight because we only had two tennis balls per singles match, and one poor ball-boy was run ragged trying to keep things going. While there we also met a couple of young Romanian players who went on to become household names – Ion Tiriac and Ilie Nastase.

Another country with which we have had very happy relations through tennis is Japan. Jill and I first went there to play at the invitation of the All England Club, travelling via Anchorage to refuel (there were no direct flights at that time). We went with Virginia Wade, John Curry, Jenny and Chris Gorringe and other members of the committee. We were all determined to embrace the culture as much as possible but I'm afraid our first attempts to eat cross-legged and with chop sticks were less than impressive. We visited Kyoto and then went on to Tokyo to play at the Tokyo Lawn Tennis Club. While there we decided to try a bit of sight-seeing on our own, without a guide, and ventured on to the subway where we discovered (and perhaps we shouldn't have been surprised) that there were no signs in English. We did eventually manage to work out where we wanted to go – and much thanks for that must go to Virginia, who took charge of the expedition. We weren't at all surprised by her leadership abilities, but we were surprised at just how many of our fellow travellers recognised her. The whole trip was a huge success and we felt privileged to have been give the opportunity to have a glimpse of this most intriguing of countries.

We returned to Tokyo in 1993 when I refereed the Ladies Pan Pacific Open, the foremost ladies' tournament in Asia and one of the most respected in the world, and I have been lucky enough to continue in that role for the past 12 years. The event is staged the week after the Australian Open and attracts all the top players – Graf, Navratilova, Davenport, Capriati, Seles, Hingis and Sharapova have all taken part, along with Japan's own champions, Date and Sawamatsu, and many others. One year when we were out there we were even invited to accompany Steffi on her farewell tour of the country. It proved to be a memorable two days and neither Jill nor I will ever forget seeing a group of children positioned around the court at one of Steffi's matches, each holding a single flower. At the end of the match Steffi took the time to go to every single boy and girl to collect their flower. It was very moving.

We have always been looked after so very well on our visits and in the last few years we have even been invited to sit with the Akishino Prince and Princess for a match in the Royal Box, which is a great honour. The tournament also arranges events for the players and last year Jill went with them to watch sumo wrestlers train. An incredible experience at the best of times, but made even more so for Jill by the fact that women are not usually allowed. It was all very formal as you might expect – shoes off, no speaking and no flash photography. More unexpectedly was the fact that their Grand Master Asahoryu was there and after the training session he welcomed them all, allowed photographs to be taken and, most surprisingly of all, issued an invitation to a traditional sumo lunch of chanko, which can best be described as a form of soup or chowder, although the exact ingredients remain something of a mystery.

Tennis has afforded us the chance to meet some truly delightful and amazing people, including many of the greats of the game but also countless others from different walks of life. Top of the 'amazing' list has to be Nelson Mandela. I was referee for a tournament in Cape Town in honour of this incredible man and we attended a dinner for him during the event. What an evening! We went by helicopter from our hotel, just before sunset, flying at a height that made it possible to study the landscape, which was breathtaking. At the dinner we were able to meet and have a brief chat with the great man. I asked him if he would like to come to Wimbledon and he said he would. In fact, he continued, he had listened to a Borg–McEnroe final when he had been imprisoned on Robben Island. What could you say to that?

During the trip we had the opportunity to visit Robben Island, and a lot of our party left in tears. What really hit home was that the guides weren't saying 'this or that happened here,' but instead it was 'we did this and we did that here.' They had been inmates themselves. It was a very humbling experience.

All the players involved in the tournament gave their time free of charge, and everyone had the opportunity to go on safari. Andre Agassi and Boris Becker chose to go before the tournament started and their enthusiasm told us we were in for a great treat. We joined up with Mal Washington, Richard Krajicek and Leander Paes for our safari, and it was an unforgettable experience. Getting up early allowed us to see the animals wake. Watching hippos have a morning bath and lions yawn and stretch at such close quarters is truly sensational, as were the elephants – Jill's favourites. Quite simply, memories of the whole trip will stay with us forever.

In recalling many of the high-points in my life so far, 2004 in a way brought two of them together in the form of a family christening for our daughter Penny's children, Holly and Charlie. Our son Barry also attended with his daughter Eliza. Thinking about that day now takes me back a few years to another ceremony, because the christening itself took place in the crypt of St Paul's Cathedral and the only reason we could arrange it there was because I had been awarded the OBE in November 1996.

When the letter arrived at our home, asking whether I would accept the award, both Jill and I thought it must be a practical joke. However, having examined the quality of the paper on which the invitation was written we decided it was either a very expensive prank (and we couldn't think of anyone we knew who would go to such lengths) or it had to be genuine. Now convinced, we had a very hard time keeping the news from Barry and Penny. It was a stipulation in the letter that no one must be told, so when we suggested lunch at Wimbledon to Barry and Penny the day we knew the announcement was to be made, we assumed that they did not know. In fact, they had already put two and two together. Even so, when we told them officially it was a special moment.

The day the four of us went to the Palace was indeed a day to remember. Barry had come over from the United States and Penny was already at home. On the morning there was great relief all round that no one had succumbed to a cold or anything in the night that might jeopardise the appointed arrival at the Buckingham Palace at 10.00 a.m. The security was intense but cheerful when we parked our car in the grounds – to the extent that one of the guards suggested he might have to search under Penny's hat!

I was shown into the room for OBE recipients while Jill, Barry and Penny were shown to their seats. The atmosphere was formal but friendly, and when everyone was seated we were taken in groups of five to await the presentation by Prince Charles. A wonderful day in bright November sunshine was topped off with a dinner at the All England Club with the committee and some good friends, at which several speeches were made about our past, prompting Barry and

Penny to comment that they had learned more in that evening about us then we had ever told them ourselves.

The 2005 Championships will be my last as Wimbledon referee. The All England retirement age is 65 and I feel it is time now for a younger person to take over. (The Club and I have been working together for a while to put this in place.) Accordingly at this significant moment in my career it is perhaps time for a moment's reflection. The tournament has played a large part in my life. The years have flown by far too quickly, but I know I have been very lucky, never dreaming I would have been given the chance to do half the things that I have done. Competing at Wimbledon is every tennis player's dream; being the referee has been a professional privilege; and for Jill and I both to be members of the All England Club in our own right is very special indeed. The club has certainly played a significant role in our social lives. I remember once we were having tea there a few years ago and one of the members of our group looked round the table and commented that we had all known each other for over 30 years. It was not a prearranged celebration or party – we just all happened to be there.

Tennis runs through our whole family. Apart from Jill and me, Barry played in the junior event at Wimbledon, won a scholarship to an American college and is now tennis director at the Dominion Country Club in San Antonio, Texas, which hosts the Tournament of Champions, which benefits the Special Olympians. Rod Laver, Patrick McEnroe and many others are always there to offer their support. Penny also played junior tennis and had a scholarship to Hawaii University before coming back to go to the London School of Economics and then qualify as a lawyer.

As will have been clear from the stories in the book, through the sport we both love Jill and I have been offered, and gratefully accepted, the opportunity to travel extensively and it has been a great bonus to have been able to do so together for so many years. Jill has been a wonderful fellow traveller and companion on my journeys: we have had fun, she can always make me laugh and we once, when about to set out on a 45-hour train ride to Portugal, wisely instigated a non-irritability pact before we embarked.

There will continue to be a tennis life for me after Wimbledon 2005. I will referee other tournaments around the world for a few more years and, as a club member, I will still be attending the Championships as a spectator every year. So in some respects, nothing will change. But Jill and I may be able to spend more time on the golf course, and with the children at either ends of the earth we will be able to travel to see them while we can.

There is no doubt that tennis has been very good to us over the years. We've been involved from juniors, through seniors, veterans and officiating. We've both very much enjoyed our time with the veterans (although sometimes I wonder about that name – nowadays 35 years of age qualifies!) and have been lucky enough to travel a lot with our great friends Shirley and Roger Becker on the tour. We still laugh at many of the things that have happened to us over the years. We've certainly seen the good, the bad and the ugly of the hotel world, and perhaps even the best – the Palace Hotel in St Moritz where we have been fortunate to have organised tournaments and coaching.

Being so involved with all these different aspects of the game has meant for us that it is like being part of a very large family. You don't necessarily see everyone regularly but somehow, as is the case with good friends, whenever you do meet you just pick up immediately from where you left off.

John McEnroe gave me a copy of his autobiography two years ago with an inscription written in it. He has occupied many pages of this book and as I 'can be serious' I think it is only right that he should have the last word:

To Alan. You have always treated me fairly even when I didn't deserve it. You are a good man, even if you are now a referee.

Index